JOSHUA THOMAS

THE AMERICAN BAPTIST HERITAGE IN WALES

PART ONE

THE HISTORIES OF FOUR WELSH BAPTIST CHURCHES
C. 1633 - 1770 SELECTED FROM

THE HISTORY OF THE BAPTIST CHURCHES IN WALES

by

JOSHUA THOMAS

PART TWO

JOSHUA THOMAS

a biography
by

ERIC W. HAYDEN

EDITED BY
CARROLL C. and WILLARD A. RAMSEY

PUBLISHED BY
CHURCH HISTORY RESEARCH and ARCHIVES AFFILIATION
LAFAYETTE, TENNESSEE
1976

In Memory

of

HALQUA DALE CLIBURN

We pause to pay special tribute to the memory of our departed brother and fellow laborer in the kingdom of our Lord - Halqua Dale Cliburn. *Beginning with us in the work of transcribing and typing the manuscripts "Hal" worked with rare dedication. But his work was interrupted by a call to the armed services of his country. On June 26, 1970 Halqua Dale Cliburn was killed in action in Vietnam. He was twenty years of age. He lived only to glorify his Lord and Saviour, and this grand purpose will be vindicated when our Lord Jesus Christ has put all enemies under His feet and "death is swallowed up in victory." This historical work was his love, and a consuming interest to him. In the last letter written from the front lines of the death-dealing battle, his interest and love for this work was gleaming with the light of hope. "Is it well with the progress of our book?" he asked. As his prayers are answered and his labors preserved, we are pleased to answer, "It is well."*

CONTENTS

PREFACE

For forty–three years the Rev. Joshua Thomas was Pastor of Leominster Baptist Church, Herefordshire, England. Previously there had been two other long ministries: one of twenty-nine years and another of thirty-four. Following Joshua Thomas there were two notable pastorates of twenty-one years each. Joshua Thomas exceeded them all!

The Church was founded in 1656 and is one of the earliest Baptist causes in the country, and certainly the earliest in the county of Herefordshire.

At the beginning the Baptists in Leominster met in various houses and cottages in and around the town. In 1696 two dwelling houses were converted into a meeting place and given to the Baptists of Leominster, with a garden and land for a graveyard. In 1771 a wealthy spinster, the daughter of a London jeweller, gave a new church, the Manse, two almshouses, gardens and graveyard. This was during the long ministry of Joshua Thomas.

When in 1754 the Rev. Joshua Thomas was invited to the Baptist church in Leominster the cause had fallen on bad times. The membership had declined and numbered only thirteen. By the time Thomas died in 1797 the membership was well over one hundred.

Up to this present time no one has attempted a full scale biography of this great man. His fellow-countrymen have from time to time written articles and brief biographies, but no full length biography has been available to English readers. Yet he was not only an eloquent preacher and a diligent Pastor, but he kept a day school to supplement his meagre wage. He became a notable author and Welsh historian.

The research student can only wonder at the patience and diligence of Joshua Thomas in seeking out and recording such facts as make up four volumes of history of the Welsh Baptists, a history of his own church in Leominster (and other churches in surrounding counties), and at the same time carry on a regular correspondence with the Rev. Benjamin Francis upon matters spiritual and theological, doctrinal and homiletical. All this time he was not only preaching and visiting in Leominster, but in the surrounding counties and far into North Wales. Calls for help to revive dying Baptist causes were frequently received. One wonders how he managed to write his many manuscripts in such neat and orderly handwriting since he must have done this early in the morning or late at night (probably "burning the candle at both ends"!) between his pastoral duties.

Some of these valuable manuscripts were preserved at Leominster Baptist Church. Others were deposited by his son at Bristol Baptist College. A few found their way to Regent's Park Baptist College, now at Oxford. The Leominster Church, realizing the worth of the original documents in their possession, deposited them with the National Library of Wales and received photostat copies in exchange. The present writer discovered that those at Bristol had never been copied and so arranged for copies to be made and kept at both Leominster and the National Library of Wales. Since these are only available to research students (a very small minority), and since the old-fashioned style of writing and spelling (and abbreviations) is difficult for some to decipher today, we can only be grateful for the reprinting in America. of Joshua Thomas's works, beginning with selections from his *History of the Baptist Churches in Wales*. To them also, I owe a great debt in making my own *Biography* of Joshua Thomas available in one complete volume with the *History*.

In 1969, at the invitation of the Director of Extra-Mural Studies of the University of Wales, I had the privilege of giving a lecture on Joshua Thomas at the Brecnock Society. This was to mark the 250th anniversary of the birth of Joshua Thomas. The Lord Lieutenant of the County was present and presided at the lecture. Previously celebrations to mark the 250th anniversary had been held at Leominster Baptist Church, the Mayor and Corporation of Leominster being present at the service, and also at Caio, the birthplace of Joshua Thomas. On this latter occasion the Member of Parliament for Carmarthenshire was present and spoke in appreciation of Joshua Thomas. This shows something of the mounting interest in this great preacher, pastor and historian, an interest that is sure to be fostered on the other side of the Atlantic by the publication of this volume.

This Preface has been written in the actual study of Joshua Thomas, the room in the Manse in which Thomas prayed, prepared his sermons, carried on his correspondence, and wrote his monumental works. From time to time people come just to look at Joshua Thomas's tomb in Leominster Baptist graveyard, or to stand in this study where he walked round the table praying or sat at it and wrote. The building is preserved as an Ancient Monument. It is holy ground. It is an inspiration to work in the same room. The spirit of the man seems not to have left it. That same spirit must surely come through his writings, so even if you can never visit Leominster and 'sit where he sat' you can catch something of his devotion to his Lord and His cause as you read his own words and as you read about him in the biography.

Eric W. Hayden

Leominster Baptist Church
Herefordshire
England

ACKNOWLEDGEMENTS

The publication of this volume is the result of the joint efforts of many persons whose help the editors wish to acknowledge with genuine gratitude.

We want to express our thanks to Eric W. Hayden, former pastor of the Leominster Baptist Church in Wales, for his kind assistance in the acquisition of copies of the Joshua Thomas manuscripts, and for his consent to permit his valuable biography, *Joshua Thomas,* to be published with this volume.

To those who labored in the meticulous task of transcribing the manuscripts, typing, and proofreading, we express our warmest thanks. The names of those who dedicated themselves in this way are: Paul Cook, who carried perhaps the greatest work load, and his wife, Carolyn; Billy Beasley, Gladys and Arthur Curtis, Myra and Bobby Strode, Wanda and Jerry Lambert, Nina Mahaney, Windy Ragland, Jimmy Stinson, Debbie and Van Mathis, the late Halqua Dale Cliburn and Joyce Lynn, his wife until his death; Donald and Betty Smalling, Judy Cothran, Jean Briggs, Nancy Peifer, Rebecca Morris, Anne Hawkins, and Robyn Ramsey with Dorothy Blalock who prepared the justified copy for the printer. Thanks also to Jerry Peifer for the map.

In addition to the present volume, members of this group have transcribed and typed all three of the Thomas manuscripts, containing approximately five hundred pages each, in anticipation of future publication.

For sharing in a number of special ways in this project as an affiliate of CHRAA, in planning, advising, and in financial aid we are also very grateful to Edmond Bevelheimer. Thanks also to our Welsh brother, James James of Ohio, who furnished the initial contact in Wales, which, through many friendly and helpful people there, led us to the location of the Thomas manuscripts.

Many of these determined workers have spent tired and sleepless hours that other "fellowhelpers to the truth" may find greater assurance as they read the true records of many of their troubled kind who bathed their tired feet in the waters of affliction, rested their weary souls in God's promises, and moved the mountains of martyrdom to make a plain paved road for we who have followed.

178

Of Rhydwilim Carmarthenshire.

By all that appears, this is the only Baptist Church in Wales, that was properly constituted in the persecuting time between 1660 and 1688. The circumstances of that formation are not very common, therefore a few particulars must be here given. Dr Calamy in his Account of Ministers ejected in Carmarthenshire informs, that Mr William Jones was ejected from Llangellbithen: such a name I could never find thro' the county. No character is given to him. But I have been informed that Mr William Jones lived at a place called Castell Castell-garw, in the parish of Llanglydwen and county of Carmarthen. Very probably Llangellbithen, was fabricated undesignedly, by blundring writers, transcribers, readers, or printers, from the name of the parish where the good man lived, and to which probably he preached, and from which he was ejected. Report says, that he officiated at Cilmaen-llwyd, in the same county, all that might be true. Dr Walker saith, that Roger Philips "was dispatched by the Propagators" from Llanfallteg, and it seems from Cil-maenllwyd, by him Wolleman Lloyd. In the margin there he says, "One Will. "Jones had Cilmaenllwyd Living in 1655." By all these hints it is easy to conclude, that Mr W. Jones was ejected out of one, or all these places by the act of uniformity, about 1660, probably but one of the places were named. But Dr C. has neither of them, we ought not to attribute the mistake to him. It matters not who blundered.

By a written Narrative taken from Mr John Jenkins, of whom more below, and some other incidental information the further account of Mr W. Jones is thus,

In the time of the commonwealth, he, like many others, by the authority that then was, preached in the churches and else where as opportunity served, but more statedly at Cilmaenllwyd. He was not then a baptist, but an Independent. But in 1660, or soon after, the ministers who did preach in the churches were compelled either to conform wholly to the establishment, or quit the churches and livings. In consequence Mr Jones chose the latter. It is said, that he was much of a gentleman, but very meek and modest; and rather timid in his natural disposition. For this reason, when he was ejected, he was very cautious how he preached. He was with as much secrecy as he could, in the night perhaps mostly. But notwithstanding all precaution and care, informers and spies were so penetrating, that in a short time he was apprehended, and committed to Carmarthen castle. Mr Crosby. Vol. 2. P. 26. 27. informs that Mr Jenkin Jones and some of his friends were imprisoned for religion at Carmarthen in 1660. That Mr Jones was a noted Baptist Minister, for about or above twenty years then, see P. 49. 50. Probably Mr J. Jones and Mr W. Jones had leisure in prison to converse about many subjects, and among many other things, it seems that they happened to fall upon the subject of Baptism

† Pan. 2. P. 337.

But

A typical page of the manuscript in the handwriting of Joshua Thomas.

INTRODUCTION

The Baptists have for centuries shown a special affinity for historical truth as well as for biblical truth. In the continuing spirit of this affinity, seeing a specialized need for more readily available historical materials pertaining to the common Baptist heritage, the Church History Research and Archives Affiliation (CHRAA) came into being. It exists by an organized agreement between certain concerned individuals to help each other in (1) the collection and research of rare church-related historical works of all denominations with particular emphasis on Baptist history, (2) the selection and publication of certain unpublished or out of print works, and (3) the establishment of a central archives where these records may be used for research by any responsible person.

One of the chief aims of such an undertaking is to make careful studies and comparisons of the many histories and historians, that there may be presented to the people of the household of faith the historical records of the churches of the Lord Jesus Christ in as near their pure form as can be gleaned from the available histories and collections of historical materials. All would agree that only the true, unadulterated facts and happenings of any age become true history. Therefore, every effort is being made to carefully research and compare each historical collection available, taking into account ecclesiastical, civil and geographical developments and to quote or publish only the writers who seem to have endeavored to present only the actual events among the people in each age without prejudice, persuasion, or perversion. The Bible itself is the textbook of first and final authority and the sure and certain guide amid the raging multifarious storms of derision and contempt for the doctrines of truth.

In an age like the present, which so vitally needs pure history, the consciousness of the importance of such a task has been deeply felt. Special attention and consideration has been given to a search for likeminded colleagues, trusted, prepared, and devoted, with a strong undaunted faith which is a prerequisite to the accomplishment of any responsible undertaking. God has graciously provided a number of "fellowhelpers to the truth" who are devoted to this special cause and zealous in response to an open door. Their labors have been productive, and the members of this present working force have sacrificed to perform a service in the collection, research, and presentation of historical materials. We trust this has been done without offense to any and acceptable to all, especially to God who has enabled the work to be accomplished thus far.

Through prayer and hard work, the major works of Joshua Thomas – over a thousand manuscript pages – are in process of arrangement for future publication with the permission of our brethren in Wales and by the providence of God. It was God's providential hand that led and provided opportunity, conveyance, contacts, and finally these valuable manuscripts, which when added to the archives with other rare and valuable works, we hope may be used to give courage, faith and blessing to all who love the blessed heritage of the bride of the Christ of Calvary.

The first part of *The American Baptist Heritage in Wales,* the first publication of CHRAA, contains materials selected from a massive handwritten manuscript, *The History of the Baptist Churches in Wales,* by Joshua Thomas (1719-1797). The selection of this material was made among other reasons, to show the historical background of the Welsh Baptist church which came to America, as a complete organized church body, and settled near Philadelphia, Pennsylvania (1701). The church later moved to Newcastle County (now Delaware) and settled in an area they called Welsh Tract (1703). Some of the members of the Welsh Tract Church then moved to South Carolina and settled along the Peedee River. There they organized a Baptist Church known as the Welsh Neck Church (1738), from which many other churches spread over the South. The Welsh Tract Church was the first, and so far as is known the only, "emigrant" Baptist church in America, i.e., an organized church migrating as a unit (see Morgan Edwards, *Materials Toward a History of the Baptists in Pennsylvania,* Vol. I, p. 19), and it is believed that more of the Baptist churches descended from the Welsh Tract Church than from any other. Future publications planned by CHRAA will show these connections more clearly. Other Baptist churches in America of earlier date were formed by the mutual consent of like-minded individual emigrants.

The purpose of this book, to show the Welsh heritage of many of the Baptists of America, is the reason for the special non-chronological arrangement of the four specific churches whose histories are included in this volume. While the Welsh Tract Church is the latest of the four, it appears first because it was thought desirable that the reader be made aware of the American based church which migrated from Wales. Then we "flash back" to the Welsh based churches and present the historical accounts pertaining to the remaining three churches in chronological order as they lead up to the formation of the Welsh Tract Church.

The histories of the four churches in this volume, *Welsh Tract, Olchon, Swansea,* and *Rhydwilim,* were translated into English by Joshua Thomas himself, as part of *The History of the Baptist Churches in Wales,* but were originally written and published in the Welsh language. The material in this volume is the first English publication of the direct writings from the *History.* Others, however, have quoted extensive excerpts from the works of Joshua Thomas and summarized much of the information. An interesting acknowledgement is appended to one of the Thomas manuscripts by the hand of G. H. Orchard as follows:

> With the kind permission of the Rev. T. Crisp, President of the Baptist College, this Ms. of the Welsh Baptist Churches, has been perused, and such extracts made, as were deemed suitable, for a printed history of these interests (?) to be published with a History of the English Baptists at Nashville, Tennessee, U. S. by Graves & Co.
>
> G. H. Orchard, May 15, 1857

This publication of Orchard's history was made by J. R. Graves in two volumes. These rare volumes are now difficult to obtain, however, one of the volumes has been located and is in the CHRAA collection. Another publication that summarizes some of Thomas' work is a *History of the Welsh Baptists* by J. Davis, 1835.

While some of the works of Thomas have been summarized, yet it is important for the serious student of history to go as near to the original source materials as possible and to take the time to read through the details which may occasionally seem irrelevant. Only in this way can one gain somewhat of a "sense of presence" at the "grass roots" of a people. We have therefore left the words, spelling, and punctuation of this material, as nearly as possible, just as Joshua Thomas wrote them. The work of transcribing the manuscripts has been extremely difficult. Not only does the Welsh and British orientation of the language cause some difficulty for an American, but the handwriting in an older English style with many words and letters illegible has made it especially difficult to avoid errors. It is certain that errors will be discovered especially in the names of places, churches, and persons. But we nevertheless trust that the deserved recognition, respect, and gratitude will accrue to our brother Joshua Thomas, and that his work of faith, patience, and unyielding tenacity to produce such voluminous records will be vindicated. So we submit this volume to the judgement of a very great people, and to God the Judge who will render final approval or disapproval as we all stand before Him some glorious day.

It is also important to know something of the reputation and integrity of the historian. In this connection, the biography *Joshua Thomas,* by Eric Hayden, included in this volume is an important and appropriate compliment to the first English publication from Joshua Thomas' *History.* It gives valuable insight into the life and character of the historian himself, and allows the history student to more objectively evaluate his work.

One of the most valuable aspects of the historical works of Joshua Thomas is that he was not a "professional" historian. He was a recorder of facts. The works of professional historians and some self-appointed historians are too often mere commentaries on historical data that reflect the historian's interpretations or biases much the same way that a Bible commentary reflects the personal interpretations of its author. Such writings of course are valuable. However, just as the student of the Bible needs the raw, unembellished scriptural data that he might interpret it for himself, so the history student needs the raw data of history for his own interpretation.

The writings of Joshua Thomas furnish such data. He says little of himself, but records the names, places, words, and deeds of his subjects without embellishment, "warts and all". The would-be historian who weaves personal opinion into the text of historical material to serve a cause has disqualified himself. History must be allowed to establish and serve the cause of truth - not the cause of the historian. Indeed, the opinions of a historian are valuable, but they should always be identifiable as opinions and never concealed among the historical data.

One of the purposes of this and of the future publication of a series of Baptist historical and doctrinal works is to permit the baptistic people of the past to speak for themselves. Within the record they have written, some mistakes and errors will be discernable. Yet many of the historical works written *about* them have omitted or even distorted a very fine quality which is clearly discernable in their own doctrines and deeds. This quality is seen primarily as a unique attitude which is demonstrated by the consistent adherence to certain principles basic to Christian truth which have distinguished the historic Baptists from the Catholics and Protestants.

We might briefly describe this attitude as a unique regard for the principle of submission to the absolute *authority* of Christ as expressed in the Scriptures only. This position, contrary to popular belief, has not been even academically accepted by Catholic or Protestant leadership, historically. While saying *Sola Scriptura,* it is commonly known that the reformers, as their Catholic forefathers, have appealed to tradition as a valid body of authority for certain doctrines and practices in addition to Scripture. Today, many Baptists are moving more and more in that direction.

Nevertheless, the historic Baptists have exhibited, in the face of great suffering, a unique attitude toward the authority of Scripture. This unique difference is not merely a difference of interpretation of the Scriptures, but a basic difference in the attitude toward its *authority*. Most Christians acknowledge the Scriptures to be the inspired Word of God, but the historic Baptist people have not only acknowledged the truth of Scripture, but have made great personal sacrifice to obey its commandments, approved examples, doctrines, and implications. We do not speak merely of such Biblical questions as inspiration, infallibility, accuracy, truthfulness, or literal vs. historical-critical interpretations, but of simple obedience to Scripture after conceding it to be the inspired Word of God. Historically, this has been the unique principle distinguishing those who have emerged (under the many ancient names imposed upon them) in history as the baptistic peoples. This attitude toward Scripture has shaped the distinctive principles identified historically with the Baptists: a regenerate church membership, believer's baptism, baptism by immersion under the authority of Christ through His churches, liberty of conscience for all men, separation of church and state, the "anabaptist" principle – baptizing those coming from other faiths, the localized autonomous nature of the church body and its perpetual existence in all centuries since Christ established it. These and other doctrines are but the outgrowth of the one great principle of regard for the authority of Scripture. Baptists have held that a church exemplified in Scripture is more than merely a group of saved people. They could never define a church of Jesus Christ apart from the consideration and faithful application of His doctrines, His ordinances, and His commandments. There is no intent to imply by this listing that all Baptists or baptistically oriented people of the past or present hold all these principles, or that no other church movements hold any of them. Historically, however, as a body of distinctive principles, these are pre-eminently Baptist principles.

A further object of these publications is to illustrate that just as God has recognized a faithful people on the other side of the Cross (see Hebrews 11), so there is an historical counterpart on this side of the Cross having had a similar struggle through suffering and persecution through the centuries. It is empirically obvious by the witness of massive historical data that those of the past who have held the distinctive baptistic principles have been subjected to great persecutions by other denominations for their faithfulness to them. Furthermore, those holding these principles have emerged from the dark ages with their principles intact, and those who have espoused those principles for the past four centuries are known as Baptists.

Some are distressed (for reasons hard to understand) when the suffering of this great people is recognized. But it is better that some be distressed than that the example of this noble and patient people be lost to the modern world. We mention it not to generate sympathy (although sympathy is good), but because it is true. To hide it is dishonest.

Baptists should be eager to examine this heritage as it is discernable both in Scripture and in authentic history. The apostles were fully assured of the perpetual nature of the church by its Head and Founder. Its perpetuity as an institution rests on the sovereign authority of the Godhead expressed through Jesus Christ (Matthew 16:18-19; 28:18-20). He purchased it with His own blood and thus called it His own possession (Matthew 16:18; Acts 20:28). He secured the continuation of His church by His promise to be with it always, even to the end of the world (Matthew 28:18-20). When Christ could no longer remain on earth, He sent the Holy Spirit to be the constant companion of the church thus assuring its perpetual existence essentially unchanged in its basic nature, doctrines, and practices to the end of the world. Finally, when its testimony on earth is finished He promised to return to receive to Himself all the redeemed from both sides of the Cross.

Baptists therefore, who have not abrogated their distinctive principles, by the providential power of God have an unbroken heritage, and are compassed about with a great "cloud of witnesses." Surely there should now be a candid re-examination of all the modern denominational superstructure and of all extra-biblical institutions, alliances, and practices. There should be a critical and careful look again at the great Authority, and words of Jesus Christ the "author and finisher of our faith." Baptists must, to please Christ, move from their rather divided positions now to a true Scriptural unity around the truth. The historic attitude toward the authority of Scripture must become the rallying point. The true nature of Christian unity is unity around truth, not around fellowships, conventions, or other corporate bodies, with top-heavy influences, and extra-biblical organizational boundaries. Unity around the truth will melt down the exclusive compartmentalized corporate walls with artificial, extra-biblical boundaries that generate the consciousness of "we" and "they" among Baptists otherwise holding the same basic biblical truth. One could surely expect all who love the principle of the authority of Scripture to be eager to achieve this kind of intrinsic unity. Hence, Baptists have no right to ask one another to pledge themselves to a corporate entity of late extra-biblical origin or to discriminate against one another for lack of such allegiance. Rather, they should ask one another to submit fully in obedience to the commandments, approved examples, doctrines, and implications of Scripture, seeking to vindicate no tradition but rather to win all Christians to the unity and simplicity of the New Testament faith. The bond of unity must be truth. Tradition is not a divine and enduring foundation; the Word of God is (Matthew 5:18,19).

Hopefully, this and future historical and doctrinal publications can help to stimulate a candid, non-defensive, charitable dialogue among all Baptists everywhere who will sincerely search, not to see how far from Scriptural authority we can digress toward a "unity" based on compromises, but to see how close we can come to obedience to Scriptural authority and by this means come close to each other. As we converge toward the center of truth we shall converge toward each other.

True unity is an imperative ingredient for presenting the Gospel convincingly to the world "that the world may know that thou hast sent me" (John 17:23). Baptists who are consciously submitted to the authority of the Scriptures at any cost are close enough together on interpretation and doctrinal principles that there could be a most powerful witness presented if we would give attention to learning more fully that elementary commandment by which all men may "know that ye are my disciples, if ye have love one to another" (John 13:34). The world has not seen very much of this phenomenon in recent times; men just cannot know who the disciples of Christ really are. Christ's real "followers" will be known by the world only when His churches begin to love each other at the local and personal level more than they love the artificial compartmental boundaries of denominational organizations that define "us" and "them". The Bible knows nothing of this structuring of the church, but again the bond of unity is truth: *"Sanctify them through thy truth: thy word is truth. As thou hast sent me into the world, even so have I also sent them into the world. And for their sakes I sanctify myself, that they also might be sanctified through the truth. Neither pray I for these alone, but for them also which shall believe on me through their word; that they all may be one; as thou, Father, art in me, and I in thee, that they also may be one in us: that the world may believe that thou hast sent me" (John 17:17-21).*

FLINT
DENBIGH
CAERNARVON
FLINT
MERIONETH
SHROPSHIRE
MONTGOMERY
ABERYSTWYTH
CARDIGAN
RADNOR
LEOMINSTER
HEREFORD
HAY
PENBROKE
BRECKNOCK
CARMARTHEN
OLCHON
CARMARTHEN
ABERGAVENNY
MILFORD HAVEN
GLAMORGAN
MONMOUTH
SWANSEA
CARDIFF

WALES

PART ONE

HISTORY OF THE WELSH TRACT BAPTIST CHURCH IN PENNSYLVANIA

When the copy was transcribed thus far, I recollected that the next church in seniority was the above. But being formed in Wales, it seems to claim justly this place, rather than where it is above written, as properly by itself and not in the form of a digression as there. Having understood by the *Materials,* so often referred to, that this church kept their records from the beginning and in Welsh to 1732, I sent over for some extracts out of those records more than what was inserted in the *Materials.* It seems the members there now cannot properly write Welsh, but some extracts were very kindly sent to me, turned into English, as well as they could, in 1786. The substance of those extracts is as follows.

Welsh Tract Church Formed in Wales

In the year 1701, there was a number of members of the Baptist churches in the counties of Pembroke, Carmarthen, and Cardigan, inclined to emigrate to Pennsylvania. Having consulted among themselves, they laid the case before the churches, which agreed to grant them leave to go. But the churches considered that as they were sixteen members, and one of them an ordained minister, it would be better for them to be constituted a church in their native land. They agreed, and did so. Being thus formed into a church, they gave them a letter of recommendation for their reception as brethren, should they meet any of the same faith, order, and practice.

They Move to Pennsylvania

They sailed in June that year from Milford Haven in the ship called *James and Mary,* and arrived at Philadelphia the September following. They were cordially received by the Baptist church meeting at Pennepec and Philadelphia, which was then the only church of the denomination in the province of Pennsylvania. They spent about a year and a half in that vicinity. These newcomers kept their meetings, weekly and monthly, among themselves during that time; but held Christian conference with the other church. They wholly agreed with them, excepting the practice of laying on of hands, to which the new-comers strictly adhered: but the majority of the other church opposed. They had several meetings to attempt an accommodation in that matter, yet they could not fully agree. During that year and a half, the sixteen had two and twenty added to them, by letters and baptism, which made them 38. But these and a number of others with them from Wales, at the end of that term, removed and purchased a large tract of land in Newcastle County, on the Delaware: which they called *Rhandir y Cymrn,* in their language, now in English, *Welsh Tract.* This was in the year 1703. They soon after began to divide and cultivate the land. And the same year they built a meeting house. The names of the sixteen constituents were Thomas Griffiths, pastor, Griffith Nicholas, Evan Edmunds, John Edwards, Elisha Thomas, Enoch Morgan, Richard Davis, James Davis, Elizabeth Griffiths, Lucy Edmunds, Mary Jones, Mary Thomas, Elizabeth Griffiths, Jennet Davis, Margaret Mathias, and Judith Morris. Elisha Thomas, in the Records is Eligens Thomas. The names of the two and twenty are also given. Thus were they settled, and were the second Baptist Church in that province. And some did esteem this the most regular church of the two.

The Churches Seek Unity

But the difference about laying on of hands continued which gave some uneasiness on both sides. Yet thus it was till 1706. Then another motion was made for accommodations. The two churches agreed to choose a committee of their respective members, consisting of twenty-five, to consult about this affair. This attempt was made, say the records, for these reasons.

(1) Because brotherly love and unity at the Lord's table are so desirable.
(2) Because scoffers take occasion to reproach religion from the contentions among the professors of it.
(3) Because some members of Welsh-tract Church lived nearer to the other church than their own: and again so some members of the other church.

The names of the committee are in the records. Those deputies, after many prayers and consultations agreed (1) that the members of each church might have transient occasional communion; but the Welsh-tract Church was not to receive any as full members without laying on of hands. (2) That each church might have liberty to preach and practice relative to laying on of hands, without offence to the other. (3) That this matter was not to be mentioned in any yearly meeting or association. Then the writer of the Extracts says, "I am of opinion that the above is the true substance of the records relative to the first settlement of the Welsh-tract Church." Isaiah Lewis.

Then he sent it to Mr. Abel Davis, with this note, "Please to examine the records, and see whether this be rightly translated." Then Mr. Abel Davis signed it, and it was transported to Leominster by Mr. (now Dr.) S. Jones. But there follows, "There were 13 added to them the first year after the settlement at the Tract; two by letters from Wales and eleven by baptism: and in a few years they became numerous, many were added to them from different churches in Wales, and large additions yearly, by personal profession before the church. So that in a few years 112 were added to the first 38. Thus far the Extracts out of the records, which may be considered authentic.

Thomas Griffiths

Now we may carry the history of the church further, as far as materials will admit. It may be proper to begin upon their first worthy pastor.

Mr. Thomas Griffiths, say the *Materials*,[1] was born, 1645, in the parish of Llanfernach, and county of Pembroke. But according to the Register of the members in the Rhydwilim Records, 1689, he lived then in the parish of Myline, in the same county, and was one of the eleven ministers in that church then, coming out of the great persecution. The *Materials* say that he "took on him the care of the church at their constitution in 1701." And that "the instrument of the confederation is still extant, but without a date." That is, it was so in 1770, and probably is still. All this in Wales. Then they sailed as above noted and settled at Welsh-tract.

Mr. Samuel Jones of Pennepec, in a letter to his friends in Wales says, "Mr. Thomas Griffiths, and a few others of the same congregation were honest people. They abode with us some time: and though he was not so able a minister as some others, yet he did much good

[1] In 1770 Mr. Morgan Edwards published the *Materials* for a history of the Baptists in Pennsylvania. Those *Materials* are often referred to here.

among us. But now these several years, he, and those who came over with him, removed fifty miles from us, and are now I think, the largest congregation in Welsh provinces." This was about twelve years after they left Wales.

Mr. Reynold Howell, in a letter to Mr. Miles Harris, so late as Oct. 1752, says that the Rev. Thomas Griffiths and his company came over in a regular manner from Pembroke Shire. He there gives them a respectable character.

The *Materials,* p. 12, mention Mr. Thomas Griffiths assisting at the ordination of Mr. Evan Morgan at Pennepec, 1706. Thus this good man served in the Gospel honorably near twenty-four years in America after all his service and sufferings in Wales. He finished all in July, 1725, aged eighty, and was buried at Pennepec. His posterity are numerous there.

Elisha Thomas

Mr. Elisha Thomas, one of the original sixteen, had been for sometime an assistant in the ministry, and upon this decease he succeeded in the pastoral care. We have no account when he was baptized, but in a marriage cerificate in 1691, Eligens Thomas is a witness. According to his age in the *Materials* he was then about seventeen. Elisha is written in Welsh, Eligens, so it is written in the Welsh-tract Records. He must have been a young man of repute then, to be a witness in that case. Several circumstances incline me to conclude, that he was son of Mr. Thomas David Rees, mentioned so often in Rhydwilim and Pant-Teg, and so many ways useful. Mr. E. Thomas was not long in the pastoral care, but finished in 1730, aged 56. He was buried at Welsh-tract, where a tomb was erected to his memory. He left two daughters, one of them alive in 1770. Both had offspring, several.

Enoch and Abel Morgan

The next successor was Mr. Enoch Morgan. He was a third of the eight men emigrated, consequently one of the first constituents of the church. The *Materials,* p. 22, say, that he was born in 1676, at Allt-goch, Llanwenog parish, and county of Cardigan: and very probably he and his predecessor were of Glandwr Church. Messrs. Thomas Jones and Reynold Howell speak of him respectfully in their letters: the former said that he was a brother to Abel Morgan. He assisted to print his brother's concordance. He continued in the pastoral charge while able, and ended his days and service in 1740, aged 64. His widow was alive in 1770; his descendants numerous.

His son Abel was born in 1713. He turned out a very useful Gospel minister. Mr. Morgan Edwards, in his *Materials* for Jersey, 1792, says, "Abel Morgan was educated at Mr. Thomas Evans' Academy at Pencader, ordained at Welsh-tract in 1734, became pastor at Middletown in 1738." In Mr. Gellie's *Life of Mr. Whitefield,* mention is made of Mr. Abel Morgan as a zealous preacher in the Jerseys about 1740. In the *Materials* just now mentioned, it is further said that Abel Morgan was a man "of some learning and solid judgement, of which he gave evidence both in public disputes and in publications on Baptism. The former were with Samuel Harker, at one time; and another time with Mr. (afterward Dr.) Sam. Finley. But Mr. Finley from public disputing proceeded to writing. He was soon answered. He rejoined; last was soon replied. Mr. Finley wrote a third piece, a copy of which, by some means, came to Mr. Morgan's hands, and he replied to that, it seems; but it does not appear that these last were printed. Mr. Morgan was a man of wit and very genteel irony."

Mr. John Griffiths says in a letter of 1760, that Mr. Abel Morgan was pastor of a numerous wealthy church. He also mentions the dispute with Mr. Finley. Mr. Morgan Edwards, in his printed annual account of the Philadelphia Association informs that Mr. Abel Morgan of Middletown had baptized, in his church, 14 in 1761, 8 in 1762, 16 next year, 14 next to that, and 13 in 1765. His members that year were 167. The largest of the three and thirty churches met then in association, except that of Hopewell in the Jerseys, which had that year the very extraordinary addition of eighty-six baptized. That was the church of the famous Mr. J. Eaton.

Mr. (now Dr.) S. Jones of Lower Dublin, near Philadelphia, in a letter to the writer of this, dated June, 1784, says, that Mr. Abel Morgan was "one of the best and greatest of men;" but then much impaired in his voice, and had his brother's son, Mr. Samuel Morgan for his assistant in the ministry. In a letter from the same hand of November 1785, it is said that Mr. Abel Morgan was in a manner super-annuated. But he wrote a second letter, in about a week after, and sent both together. In the letter, he says, "Yesterday, the affecting tidings of the good and great Mr. Abel Morgan's death reached my ears. The more affecting to me because I have had it in contemplation these two or three years to pay him a visit and spend two or three days with him; in part with a view to know something of his mind about his manuscript; but have neglected it too long. Now may it be said that a great man is fallen in our Israel. Very seldom indeed do the accomplishments and excellencies of body, mind, and grace, meet in so high a degree in one man. As some are said to be below contempt, so he was above envy, for all agreed to give him the preference. As he had no competition, no one felt himself hurt when Mr. Morgan was admired: no one imagining there was any comparison between him and Mr. Morgan. I wish some qualified men may attempt to do some little justice to his character. Mr. Abel Morgan died 24th November, 1785," aged 72 years and 7 months.

Owen Thomas

The next successor at Welsh-tract was Mr. Owen Thomas, born, say the *Materials* of 1770, at a place called Gwrgodllys, Cilmaenllwyd parish, and county of Carmarthen, in 1691; he went to Pennsylvania, 1707: was ordained at Welsh-tract, says Mr. Reynold Howell in the above letter. He was there pastor from 1740 to 1748, then removed to Vincent, near Yellow Spring, where he continued till he died in 1760, aged 69. The *Materials* say that Mr. Owen Thomas left behind him the following remarkable note, "I have been called upon three times to anoint the sick with oil for recovery. The effects were surprising in each case; but in none more so than in that of our Brother Reynold Howell. He was so sore with the bruises of the wagon, when he was anointed, that he could not bear to be turned in bed, otherwise than in the sheet. The next day he was so well that he went to meeting."

David and John Davis

He was succeeded in the ministry at Welsh-tract parish by Mr. David Davis, born, say the *Materials* in 1708, in Whitchurch Parish, and County of Pembroke. He went to America in 1710; took the care of the church at Welsh-tract in 1748, which he continued to his death in 1769, aged 61. Mr. Morgan Edwards was personally acquainted with him, and says that "he was an excellent man, and had in precious memory by all that knew him." He left three sons, and as many daughters. His son Jonathan was minister of the seventh day church at Cohansey in 1770. His son John succeeded his father and was there in 1770, when the *Materials* were printed: yet not as pastor, but as a probationary supply. He left that church before the end of that year; for Mr. Backus in his History, Vol. 2, p. 275, etc. says that John Davis, M.A. was educated at the college in Philadelphia, came to Boston in New England in 1770: was ordained pastor of the second Baptist church there in September following. He there behaved with spirit and judgement in behalf of the Baptist churches, and was scurrilously treated for it by the oppressors; but he confuted their pleas, "without taking any notice of the personal abuse that was offered him." On which account a gentleman present said, "The worth of the man never appeared so great before."

Sept. 10th, 1771. The Warren Association made choice of him as their agent, to use his best endeavors, by the advice of their committee, in concert with their agents in London to obtain the establishment of equal religious liberty in America. But his health soon impaired; in August 1772, he took a voyage to Philadelphia in hope to receive benefit from his native air; and obtaining relief there, he went with a friend who was going to preach to the western Indians, in hope of further relief. But he grew worse and finished his course on the banks of the Ohio, on the 13th of Dec. that very year; in the prime of life, respect and usefulness, the thirty-eighth year of his age. The minister who was with him, informed that some of his last words were these, "In a little time, I expect to be with Christ, to see and know him, as he is now known, and as he is not known. My faith in him as my Savior is unshaken." He was fellow of Rhode Island College, and one of the members of the American Philosophical Society. So far Mr. Backus, but here a little abridged. In a letter from Dr. Samuel Jones it is said, the remains of Mr. J. Davis were laid under a great tree on the banks of the Ohio. The circumstances of the place then, it seems required it to be so. I knew none of these things when the Welsh History was printed: therefore could not relate them.

Griffith Jones

Contemporary with Mr. David Davis at Welsh-tract was Mr. Griffith

Jones. In a letter to Mr. Miles Harris the latter speaking highly of the former.

In 1770 the church had had six ministers, all born in three counties of Pembroke, Carmarthen, and Cardigan, of whom the *Materials* say, "The ministry of this church hath been filled with great and good, who have been as useful and have supported the sacred characters as well as any set of clergy in America." The church is there commended as the first in America who received the London confession of 1689, in zeal for laying on of hands, their strict discipline, and keeping their records, though in Welsh to 1732. By further Extracts out of their records by Mr. Morgan Edwards in manuscript, I have the names of several from Wales added to this church in 1709, four from Cilfowyr Church. In 1710, from Rhydwilim, eight; and from Cilcam, twelve; and from Glandwr, eight; Llangenach, one; from Llanwenarth, two. All these in one year; and some few after that year, not many. The year 1710 seems to have been the chief of all.

This is a tolerable History of this Church till 1770. The principality hath kind of a right in that society to that date at least. But for all that, it is the second Baptist church in Pennsylvania. She is a daughter from Wales, but the head of the family in America. I have no particular account of this church after the last date. What follows seems to belong to it, but I think it rather needless to transcribe any more.

Ministers who have been in Welsh-tract Church, Pennsylvania.

(1) Mr. Thomas Griffiths, the first pastor, ordained in Wales, died 1725.

(2) Elisha Thomas, second pastor, one of the first constituents, finished in 1730.

(3) Mr. Enoch Morgan, 3rd pastor, and one of the first constituents died in 1740.

(4) Mr. Abel Morgan, his son, a very great man in America, died 1785.

(5) Mr. Samuel Morgan his brother's son was his assistant.

(6) Mr. David Davis, the fourth pastor, a very worthy man, died in 1769.

(7) Mr. Jonathan Davis, a minister of the seventh day church at Cohensey.

(8) Mr. John Davis, a very worthy man, died young, 1772.

(9) Mr. Griffith Jones, copastor with Mr. David Davis for some years, died 1754.

HISTORY OF THE BAPTIST CHURCH AT OLCHON

Olchon, or perhaps more properly Golchon, is a small, narrow Valley, in the parish of Clodock, and county of Hereford: nearly on the line between the Hay and Abergavenny, but somewhat nearer to the former, and about 10 miles or more from Hereford. The Western side of it is formed by a long, steep, and lofty hill: part of what is called, the Black Mountain. The situation is rather singular, as in, or near, this valley, the three counties of Hereford, Monmouth, and Brecknock meet; and likewise the three dioceses of Hereford, Landoff, and St. David.

This spot, and parts adjacent have been always inhabited by Cambro-Britons, or properly Cymrn (rather Cymry, W.R.);[1] usually called Welsh or Welch. The writer of this preached there about twice in the month statedly from June, 1746 to November, 1754; always in the British language, except a person happened to be present who did not understand it. But many English gradually intermingling, the language now of course is mixed.

Early Dissenters in Olchon Vicinity

The writer in those years had opportunities now and then to make some observations. The general report then was, that the first Dissenters in the Principality were in and about Olchon. The several great men who originated from the vicinity of the place make the observation very probable; especially these six.

1. Dr. Thomas Bradwardine, who was a very learned and famous divine, in the former part of the 14th century. Fuller, in his *Church History,* B. 3, page 98, saith; that this celebrated man was born at Bradwardine; which is the name of a parish, now well known in the County of Hereford, a few miles from Olchon. Some of the members of the Baptist Church lived in that parish about 1654. The very complexion of the blood seems to plead strongly for the British origin of it. Possibly the parish had the name from the family, or rather the latter from the former. Those things were very common in centuries past. Bishop Godwin, in his catalogue, pp. 137-1615, says that Bradwardine was born at Hatfield, in Sussex. When Fuller wrote his *Worthies of England,* he had seen more authors on the subject. There he names

[1] W.R. are the initials of someone who apparently reviewed Thomas' MS and added occasional notes (Editors).

Camden, Bale, Pitts, and Godwin, all differing in the birth places. But attempts to reconcile them thus, that there was an ancient family of the name, in Herefordshire, which had removed thence for three generations past to Sussex near Chichester and that the Doctor was born there. So he names him among the worthies of both counties. He records a Thomas Bradwardine among the gentry of Hereford in 1433; so it seems that only a branch of the family removed to Sussex.

There is no person well versed in our ecclesiastical history, but hath seen and read the fame of Dr. Bradwardine, as eminent in letters, doctrine, and piety. Godwin says "He was a good mathematician, a great philosopher, and so excellent a Divine, that he is commonly styled, Doctor Profundus." The Reformation from popery had not then taken place. He was a very great man, when we consider the darkness of the time in which he lived. It seems he died about 1348. Very probably the famous Wickliff was the disciple of this worthy man.

It may be still a doubt whether the doctor was a native of Sussex, or of Bradwardine, but being so much abroad it can hardly be supposed that Olchon received much benefit by his personal presence. He might or might not come at times to visit the ancient seat and drop something about religious concerns, he being himself so zealous and faithful, he was chosen to the See of Canterberry, but soon died before he was put in possession of it.

2. Mr. Walter Brute – The first date, Mr. Fox gives of Wickliff is 1371, above three and twenty years after the death of Bradwardine; very probably the former began to shine in the ministry soon after the death of the latter. Wickliff's ministry met with great acceptance and amazing success. One of his zealous disciples was Walter Brute. What follows makes it probable that he was born and lived in or near Olchon.

He was of the Diocese of Hereford, and he gloried in being a Briton by father and mother. It is recorded that he was a graduate of Oxford, a gentleman of rank, learning, and parts; though reputed a layman by the popish clergy. Trevnant (rather Tresnant) Bishop of Hereford chargeth Brute with seducing the people as much as he could, from day to day, teaching openly and privily, as well the nobles as the commons. Messrs. William Twinderby and Stephen Bell, were preachers of note then, intimate friends of Brute, and zealous all for Wickliff's doctrine. By a commission from Richard the II, about 1392, it appears that Twinderby and friends were fled into Wales, out of the diocese of Hereford. Very probably they were gone among the mountains about or beyond Olchon, where so many dioceses and counties met; which was a very favorable circumstance, in persecuting times. They had then, by means and help of Brute an opportunity to inform and instruct the ancient Britons among those lofty hills.

Fox in his martyrology, gave a large account of Brute, his sentiments and zeal taken from the register of the Bishop of Hereford. He refuted many popish errors and reformed much in the article of Baptism. He pleaded that faith should preceed that ordinance; and yet that salvation did not essentially depend upon it. Mr. Thomas Davye, in his *Treatise of Baptism,* 1719, page 96–197, supposes that Brute was more a Baptist than represented by Fox, as the latter was not so himself. Now to me it appears very probable Wickliff received much light in the Gospel from Bradwardine and his writings, and Brute from Wickliff and others; and he began to sow the seed of reformation in and about Olchon, and of Believer's Baptism, among other doctrines; and that long before the beginning of the Reformation began by Luther, King Richard, above named, directed a letter to the nobility and gentlemen of the county of Hereford, and to the Mayor of the city, charging all to prosecute Brute, accused of preaching heresy, in the diocese and places adjacent; and also of keeping conventicles.

It is needless here to enlarge on his excellent character, given by Fox, and many others. It is sufficient for the present purpose, that he was an ancient Briton of rank and capacity, so active and useful among his countrymen on the borders of Herefordshire. He was a reputable writer; though possibly most of his labor that way is lost, except what is preserved by the good martyrologist. He lived about a century before printing began in England. I can find no certainty where or when he died whether a natural death or by violence. He may well be reckoned the first public reformer among the Welsh, after they were wholly over-run with popery. In his *Worthies of Wales,* Fuller names him the first of all. The last date of him by Fox is 1393. He might or might not have lived many years after that.

3. The famous Sir John Oldcastle comes next in course. Oldcastle as Bradwardine is the name of a parish adjoining to Clodock, and situated on the side of the same hill, which forms the western part of Olchon; but is in Monmouthshire. It is natural to conclude that Sir John had part of his instruction in the Gospel from Brute and Bradwardine's writings. His character, suffering and death, are so fully given by Church historians and martyrologists, that it is needless to expatiate on these here. The valiant Henry 5th was born at Monmouth and highly regarding his countrymen, he promoted him to be one of his domestic lords with the title of Earl of Cobham. He was commonly styled Lord Cobham. Yet this Noble Briton, then in the Kings Court, like Daniel, was full of zeal against popery, and the corruption

of those times. He was esteemed the chief in the Kingdom in supporting and encouraging the Lollards as the followers of Wickliff were then called. They were the Protestant dissenters of those days. For these things priests and clergy were full of rage and bitterness against Lord Cobham. They well knew that his influence at court was great. Yet after many consultations, they found ways and means to work so far upon the king, as to have Sir John apprehended, and brought to trial in 1413, about 20 years after the last account I saw of Brute. Lord Cobham was soon condemned to die and under that condemnation was committed to the tower. But he soon found means to liberate himself from that confinement. It is supposed that it was under the influence of and with the approbation of His Majesty that he returned to his native country. The *Memoirs of Monmouthshire* say p. 87, that he lay concealed among his tenants and friends at, or about Oldcastle above four years. Then he was treacherously taken, and barbarously burnt in London. Where Rafim relates this tragical affair, his translator adds this note, "As this was the first noble blood shed in England by popish cruelty, so perhaps never any suffered a more cruel martyrdom." The historian says, "thus died Sir John Oldcastle, Baron of Cobham, with wonderful constancy, perfectly answerable to the firmness by which he had all along maintained the doctrine of Wickliff, which he professed" (*History of England,* Vol. 1, p. 505, 520. 2nd, 3rd, 1732).

This nobleman was another instructor of the good people in and about Olchon, particularly in those four years which he spent among them. It may be concluded that he then did all the services he could, to promote the truth he suffered for. He died 1417, two years after the burning of the celebrated John Huss, abroad, who likewise was a worthy disciple of Wickliff, and a hundred years before Luther began the Reformation in Germany. Now this amounts to a full proof that the inhabitants of Olchon, and the vicinity, had the advantage of hearing the Gospel. In the darkness of superstition and ignorance. This nobleman, it seems was a native of the place, and possibly his predecessor, Brute, was so too, or near it. How the poor people fared after this fiery trial I have no account for a long while.

4. The renouned Mr. William Tyndale must be the next. He bids as fair to be a native of those parts as at any place I can think of. Fox, Wood, and all the authors I can recollect, say that he was born on the border of Wales; but it does not occur to me that ever I saw any information in what country he drew his first breath. Until that can be decided, I may take the liberty to conjecture, that his birth place was not far from Olchon, in one of three counties. His parents, or their son, might have seen and heard Oldcastle and Brute, and he in youth might have reaped benefits as from them. One considerable

motive for my conjecture, that he was a native of those parts is, that Llewelyn Tyndale, and his son Hezekiah, were members of the Baptist Church at Llanwenarth, near Abergavenny at the close of the last century. There are some of the Tyndale stock still about Abergavenny. I know one of the names at Hereford about 1740, 55 years ago. If Mr. W. Tyndale was born in, or near Olchon, as he was young moved to Oxford, then to Cambridge, and after that settled for some years in Glocestershire, it is not to be supposed, that he could much instruct his friends in his native land, unless upon social and temporary visits now and then. Of his translating the scripture into English the first time; of his other writings, his sufferings from the papists, how they persecuted him even beyond the sea, for his zeal to promote truth and the salvation of sinners, and how at last they prevailed against him, had him apprehended, condemned, and burnt in 1536, see Fox, Wood and most of our ecclesiastical historians. Bradwardine, Brute, Oldcastle, and Tyndale will outshine most, if not all, their contemporaries, except Wickliff himself, while church history continues here.

5. John Perry–M.A. according to historians, was born in Wales. Some say "Mountains of Wales and County of Brecknock." This still, is the description of the vicinity of Olchon. Mr. Perry might have been born, near, or further westward. We have sufficient evidence that he was affectionately concerned for the salvation of his countrymen. The very titles of two books published by him in 1588, amount to a full proof of that. The first runs thus, "A View of some parts of such public wants and disorders as are in the service of God, written her Majesty's country of Wales; with an humble petition to the high court of Parliament for their speedy readiness." There in is shown the necessity, and the way to reform in that country. The other title is "An exhortation unto the governor's and people of Her Majesty's Country of Wales to labor earnestly, to have the preaching of the Gospel planted among them." These titles are taken out of *Ath. Oxon.* where an account is given of many other books written by him. Possibly he was the first that preached believers baptism openly and publicly to his countrymen, since that Reformation I am strongly inclined to think, that he was the first that administered that ordinance by immersion, upon a profession of faith in and about Olchon.

Mr. Neale, in his *History of the Puritans* saith, that Mr. Perry was a Welsh divine, and gives him an excellent character for learning, piety, ministeral gifts, diligence, etc., though not a hint that he was a Baptist. However, A. Wood in *Ath. Oxon.* many years before Neale, speaks out plainly saying, that Perry "was a notorious Anabaptist, of which partly he was the Coryphous (or leader). He was educated at Oxford, and went to Cambridge, preached at both places; and was, says Wood himself, esteemed by many a tolerable Scholar, and edifying preacher, and a good man." This was a great character given by those authors to a Baptist in those days. The noted Strype wrote sufficiently acrimonious against Mr. Perry blaming him for saying that popery then was intolerable in Wales. Though even Mr. Strype owns that Mr. Perry expressed a great concern for his native country; yet chargeth him with anabaptistery. So great was the rage and fury against him in those days, that he was apprehended, condemned and put to violent death in 1593 or 1594, aged 34. Dr. Henry Sampson names Mr. Perry among "the several persons that were troubled, deprived, and silenced by Whitgist or agents in the high commissions court, the star chamber, and the courts' ecclesiastical. The Dr. S. Calamy's Abridgement, second edition preface.

6. Sir William Cecil, Earl of Burleigh, though not a minister of the Gospel; yet a very extraordinary minister of state, and a great friend to the Reformation. He sprang from a family of ancient Britons whose name was Lysyllt or Lytsyllt, being of an uncouth pronunciation to the English, the name was turned into Cecil, which is not very different in sound, though so different to the eye. The two names are used in that country to this day. The seat of the family is very near Oldcastle, perhaps in the parish, and is called by the Britons galltyr-ynys; but by the English Alterennis, similar still in sound. I do not find that Lord Burleigh was born there but if not he descended from a branch of the family that removed elsewhere. Part of the family was in that neighborhood lately and possibly is still. He was captain of the Monmouthshire Militia. He wrote his name William Cecil, though called by his Welsh neighbors Sysyllt. Lord Burleigh was the greatest statesman perhaps in Europe, if not the world in his day. He served King Edward VI; yet was too much a protestant to be in Queen Mary's Ministry. But how worthily and ably he served his country, and his Queen through the long and very critical reign of Elizabeth, appears in the historians of those times. His son Sir Robert Cecil was likewise a great man. See *Memoirs of Monmouthshire,* p. 82.

Now though Olchon of itself is a small despicable place, among hills and rocks, yet there are six names, of no small renown. They would do honor to any county in Great Britain. Three, if not four, of them suffered death in the defence of the Gospel. Four were imminent Gospel ministers in dark times. The other two were shining and noble characters. True, it is not proven, that either of them was born within the small valley, properly called Olchon yet reasons are given for the conjecture. Should any of them be disproved on fair ground, the writer is ready to give up such, but not before. I see no cause or reason to doubt, but Brute and Oldcastle did sow the Gospel seed here betimes. No certainty is placed regarding Tyndale; he might or might not have been useful here. It is very probable that Perry began the scriptural way of baptism plainer than those who went before him; yet very possibly he could not form here a regular Gospel church. The time then would hardly bear it, and he was engaged so much in other places. At least, we have no certainty that he formed such a church.

Earliest Known Protestants and Formation of Olchon Church

Upon the whole, it seems more than merely probable that the first protestants among the Ancient Britons were in and about Olchon, and the first society of Baptists also since the reformation, consequently the first Protestant Dissenters. What follows may make it a little plainer. The place is so remote from cities, towns, and high roads; and so retired among hills and rocks, and so situated on the borders of three counties and so many Dioceses; it often afforded shelter to the good people in the storms.

It is noted above, that Mr. Perry died about 1593 or 1594. No account occurs how the good people fared here for about 40 years after his death. Probably a few serious people continued through all that time, yet possibly no particular church connection. It is supposed from circumstances, that they were formed into a church about 1633, that was about 40 years after the death of Mr. Perry. No account is found whether they were formed by mutual agreement guided by the light of the Gospel, or had they any to help in that work. The first Minister among them, that I heard of was Mr. Howell Vaughn, among the Britons Howel Tyden, and sometimes he was called Ychan. His name is in the latter way among those who signed the Breviates of the general meeting at Abergavenny, on the 14th and 15th day of the 5th month 1653, which was 20 years after the above date. This will not amount to a proof that the church at Olchon was not formed 1633, but that Mr. Vaughan was alive at the above general meeting, and able to attend it. It is acknowledged, this is an early date of the church; but I rather wonder it was not formed many years before, when we consider their early privileges; and perhaps it was. But some worthy authors name other places as mother churches in the principality. There are two respectable ones that must not be overlooked here.

One is the author of Mr. Henry Tessey's life, who records that Mr. Tessey, then a worthy independent London Minister, assisted in constituting a congregated church at Llanfaches, in the county of Monmouth, in the year 1639. Then he calls it, the Mother Church in Wales. Probably that author knew nothing then of the small Baptist church at Olchon. No doubt Llanfaches was a respectable society, upon the broad plan of open communion, a mixture of independents and

Baptists. Messrs Wroth, Cradock, etc., were university men so their fame spread, and many reckoned this the real Mother church of dissenters in Wales. Mr. Tessey was not then baptised, but he bore his testimony in that about five or six years after.

The other author is Mr. Backus in his valuable history of New England, 1777 vol. 1. But there he does no more than transcribe what he found in a respectable church book, to which he refers very firmly. That will more naturally come under consideration by and by. But for a moment let us observe what Mr. Vavasor Powell says of this subject. "He was as well acquainted with the state of religion in Wales about 1640, and for 20 years after, as most, if not as any living. He throws some light upon this subject in his brief narrative of the former propagation and the late restriction of the Gospel (and the Godly preachers and professors thereof) in Wales." The 2nd Edition printed in 1662, and prefixed to his *Bird in the Cage Chirping.* There he says that in or about 1641, the professors of religion were exceeding rare and few, unless in some corners of two or three counties, about which time was the first, if not the only gathered church in all the country. This begins in the very first page of the narrative and in p. 8 he says "In the beginning of the wars (which was still about 1641 or 1642) there was but one or two gathered congregations in all Wales." Here it may be noted that Llanfaches church was constituted in 1639. We may be certain he reckoned that for one in 1641. Those in some corners of two or three counties agree exactly with the situation of Olchon, but not at all with Llanfaches, which is near the center of Monmouthshire. But the former being a small and obscure society, having no university person for their pastor, Mr. Powell seemed to look upon it so diminutive that he was rather at a loss whether it were right to style it a gathered church or not; though in the two passages he could not be quite willing to leave it out. In one he says "The first, if not the only gathered church." In the other, "one or two gathered congregations." Now let others judge of these things with freedom. I can give no better account of them. My sentiments are that there had been a few famous people in and about Olchon a long time, yet very probably there had been ebbings and flowings. When they were baptised and formed into a Baptist church I have never been able to learn to satisfaction, though so carefully inquired for near 50 years.

In the last century there was a good man in the society, of considerable note and property, whose name was John Rhys Howell. He was not pastor of the church, but an occasional assistant in the ministry. He sailed to America in the persecuting time, but returned home to finish his days. He died about 1692, very aged. About 1770 the writer of this was told, that this aged man had left a chest full of papers, which was then in a certain house in Olchon. In 1775 he went thither, but it was too late, the valuable papers were demolished. Thus it happened to many papers, which if preserved had been of great services to cast light on others.

From this time, 1641 to 1649, we have no account of Olchon. The times were then very afflictive and distressed by reason of the civil wars that disturbed all the country. The rest of the information regarding religion, in those parts, is by an extract taken out of the Ilston church book, carried by Mr. John Myles to New England, of that see more below in the history of Swansea Church, page 39 etc. It is there noted how the church at Ilston considered themselves as the first Baptist Church in all Wales, that ever they had heard of, since the Reformation from popery. They then looked upon themselves as the Mother Baptist Church in the principality. It is observed above, that Llanfaches Church was reckoned a mother. But that was a mixed church and not properly Baptist, probably there were congregations on the same plan before 1649. But Mr. Myles did not consider them "according to primitive institution. In the Welsh History of the Baptists, Olchon is placed first as the mother church. In this Manuscript, Swansea is set first out of respect to Mr. Myles and the Ilston Church. Above a promise is made to consider and reconcile the priority of the two churches. This seems to be the most proper place to attempt it thus.

There is no certainty now, whether at first Olchon had some independence with the Baptist in communion. If so, they were very probably prior to Llanfaches and on a similar plan, but so insignificant in Mr. Powell's view, that he was in doubt whether it were right to call them a church or not. But if they were at first mixed Mr. Myles was right regarding a proper Baptist Church, very probably. But if Olchon had no Pedobaptists among them at first or about 1641, as they were obscure, Mr. Myles might not know them, or he might suppose some deficiency in their constitution, as not being strictly according to primitive constitution, or he might not reckon them in Wales, Olchon being in Herefordshire, an English county, and indeed Monmouthshire is so accounted likewise. In that respect Mr. Myles was still right. But as above observed, the inhabitants then were Welsh at Olchon, and the Church to this day is among these of the principality and in that connection. Upon the whole I reckon, for the reasons above given, the first reformed in Wales, and the first dissenters, and the first Baptists were in those parts, but as they never exerted themselves and spread abroad, till roused up by Mr. Myles, I think it right for him to have the priority, as he was the first that stood in the principality for unmixed communion. But more of this a little below.

Of Mr. Myles' public spirits and activity see the former part of the history of Swansea below. And it is noted, that being in some settled posture at home, Mr. Myles came in January, (the letter below from Llanigon to Ilston suggests that Mr. Proud was with Mr. Myles then) then called the 11th month, 1649, and preached baptism to a society of professed believers meeting at Llanigon. But he did not baptize any there then, only added further advise to the elders there, Mr. Walter Prossor and Mr. James Hughes. Llanigon is not far from Olchon, but on the other side of a large lofty hill, and in Brecknockshire. It seems all this society were then all Pedobaptist, before Mr. Myles came to them, but his preaching and conversations made considerable impression upon their minds. Those elders promised to send a letter to Ilston to inform what the people would think and say about believers' baptism. According to promise they sent a letter dated 22nd of the 11th month 1649. They made no long delay. A copy of that letter now before me, taken out of the Ilston church book; now in America. That informs, that Mr. Jones had written a discouraging letter to the people, but came soon after to the Hay, and next day to Llanigon himself but was then more moderate than in his letter. Those who were convinced that believers' baptism was right he did not blame if they obeyed, but advised them not to be rash and hasty: without advising with Mr. Vavasor Powell and Mr. Cradock and write to them on the subject.

The letter says that about 11 or 12 of the people were willing to submit, and the others said nothing against it. So it is very natural to conclude, that it was in consequence of this letter Mr. Myles wrote back, and directed the people to appoint a meeting for him at Clifford: a copy of that letter was seen at Abergavenny about 1752. There Mr. Myles promises to defend the truth zealously. The messers Cradock, Powell, and Jones, should be there present. He directed the people to read Gal. 2:7–14 in the Welsh Bible. It seems the people at Llanigon understood the Welsh better than the English, but Clifford is in Herefordshire. The Hay lies between Clifford and Llanigon, those are two parishes.

Besides Mr. Myles' letter, the extracts from America note that the church at Ilston was so affected with the Llanigon letter, that they had a solemn meeting on the occasion and after serious earnest prayer, they agreed to send Br. Myles and Br. Laeison Davis, and a letter to Llanigon without delay: in the letter they encourage them not to be dilatory but proceed to obedience. They there show the several dangers and disadvantages of delays, as 1. that in the very case of baptism it is unwarrantable, Acts 22:16. 2. It lays open too many temptations, Oh saints: said they, believe our experience. While we delayed, we were never free from them, but afterward they vanished like smoke! 3. It gives the advantage to the adverse party, to work their own end, by your delays. 4. The more persons delay, the more dead they become to the practice of any duty, as a coal of fire will soon go out if not kindled. 5. Should you delay it may trouble the spirits of some serious satisfied saints who may think the time long while they dishonor God by their disobedience. 6. While you delay you may lose much of that heavenly comfort, which we can by experience say, saints find in close communion, in the right order of the Gospel, and the true use of ordinances. 7. The present time calls for present obedience, as we cannot say we are sure of the morrow.

That letter further says "whereas you are advised to consult with Mr. Vavasor Powell and Mr. Cradock, though indeed we honor those godly men; yet would we have you to consider, that no man's word in these times are undeniable oracles; and pray, what reason have you to consult with those who hitherto are opposite to this practice? (Is not this a plain proof V. Powell as well as Cradock was as yet against Baptism?) We desire you rather to imitate Paul's example, Gal.1:16,17, and to consult that infallible word of truth, even the words of the apostles and disciples of our Lord Jesus, as Peter, Acts II, Philip, Acts 8, and Ananias, Acts 22.

"Now we desire you dear Brethren, to communicate this our hearty advice to those souls who intend obedience to our King Jesus, lest by a dangerous procrastination they may grow cold and negligent. But we hope and expect to hear better things both of you and them, even that you have actually performed what you now only intend, that then we may once more meet to praise; as we have this day met to pray for you; and then that both you and we according to our talents, by our mutual help and advice may serve one another, and with united strength may be the better enabled to go on with the Lord's work in poor Wales as with one shoulder."

Then they soon conclude their affectionate letters, and close thus, "your Brethren praying for you, the church at Ilston."

This epistle is addressed to Walter Prossor and James Hughes or either of them, then the records add, "Now the Lord went so along with our Brethren whom we had recommended to God by our prayers and to them by our letters, that before they returned there was a considerable number there baptised, and joined together in the order of the Gospel."

Now here is the evident formation of this church; but whether the Olchon Church were at this time, or soon after, incorporated with this people at Llanigon it does not appear by the extracts, nor have we there the date of those transactions; but from the Llanigon letters to Ilston, dated 22nd of the 11th month 1649 we may guess at the time. There they propose to defer five weeks, before Mr. Myles should come again, but the Ilston Church thought such a long delay very dangerous, or at least not right, as they show by the above letters, therefore they sent Mr. Myles and Mr. Leyson Davis and their letters sooner, possibly in about a fortnight or at furthest three weeks. We have no date to their letter. We may conclude that the church was constituted about the middle of the 12th month 1649; according to our present reckoning it was Feb. 1650."

But those things made a considerable clamor in the country. The Extracts proceed thus, "While God was going on there with his work, Satan's Malice and mens envy broke forth against the Instruments, as letters were sent to London, to complain of Bro. Myles, to Major General Harrison, Captain Jones, Mr. Vavasor Powell, etc., which through God's great goodness proved a shock, for the Major was favorable, as more fully appears in a letter sent from Br. Vaughan, who was then his servant, to Br. Myles."

As complaints were made to Mr. Vavasor Powell, of Mr. Myles, some suppose that the former was not a professed Baptist then. (According to Thurloe's (?) State Papers the supposition is well grounded: it seems he did not become a Baptist till at least 1654, or 55.) But the case was thus, Major General Harrison was a friend to the Baptists then, and if we can believe *Ath. Oxon Vol. 2, Fasti. Col. 76, 77 2nd ed.* Wales was appointed to be under his command and Vavasor Powell was his Chaplain, and they had great power in the regulation of the Ministers in the principality, but there it is said that the Major was baptized in 1657. Mr. Baxter, as abridged by Dr. Calamy, *Vol. 1 2nd Edition* p. 67, 68, says "Harrison being authorized thereto, had at once put down all the parish ministers of Wales." But this was not fair representation; for Mr. Vavasor Powell says in the narrative prefixt to his *Bird in the Cage*, 2nd ed. p. 2&3, that the parish ministers were justly ejected for ignorance, scandal, etc., and that upon evident proofs; yet not all (as falsely was reported) for in Montgomeryshire there were 11 or 12 never ejected, so in all other counties, some more, some less."

Captain Jones was Mr. Jenkin Jones, mentioned above, Dr. Calamy, in his *Account* and *Continuations* names him among the ejected ministers in or after 1660 and says, he was ejected from Cadadgston Juxta Neath, in Glamorganshire, had been brought up at Oxford, was a preacher before the war, took great pains in several counties, and was for some time imprisoned. But the doctor calls him a Catabaptist. He was too ready to cast sneers upon the Baptists. But Mr. Jones was a minister of no small repute in his day. It seems he was for some time captain in Cromwell's Army.

Regarding Mr. Vavasor Powell, I suppose he was baptized before this time, (No, he certainly was not: nor till some years after. W.R.) but have no certain information when he submitted to that ordinance. But what is recorded in the Ilston Church Book, and contained in the Extracts is no proof at all that those gentlemen were not professed Baptists at that time. But the quarrel was rather thus, Misters Cradock, Powell, and Jones were great preachers in Wales. The former was an independent Pedobaptist, the other two were Baptists, yet all three were for mixt communion; but Mr. Myles was for strict communion, and would have the Baptists to be by themselves: so he was charged with the crime of rending the churches. This raised the clamor. Mr. Jones in his letter to Llanigon, it seems, was rather sharp but when he came in person was milder and not willing to offend Misters Cradock and Powell. It was quite a new thing then, and when some busy persons wrote to Harrison, Powell and Jones to London, it appears that they did no hurt, though so much power was in their hand, these do not appear to be the opposers to Mr. Myles but some other more private Pedobaptist wished them to exert their power.

Progress of the Baptists in Wales

Mr. Powell, in the place above referred to, says, that the Act for the further propogation of the Gospel in Wales passed in February 1649. So it seems this church was constituted, and that act passed about the same time, at least the same month.

This new church was then not called Llanigon nor Olchon, but the Hay Church, as that was a market town, and probably they soon met there to worship. The church of Llanharan was formed soon after, (see Ms.,p.68). The extracts mention Mr. "Thomas Watkins of the Church of the Hay" as assisting to form that other new society. He was the worthy Pastor at Olchon for many years after, as will appear below. But we have no more account of Mr. James Hughes, the second elder at Llanigon. It's supposed that either he died soon after, or did not continue with the Baptists.

In the Extracts there is a letter sent from the church at Ilston to the church at the Hay in the 6th month 1650. There they mention the opposition they met with from Satan and the world; but their greatest grief was that some of the people of God combined and consulted to stop the truth (unmixed communion) from any further progress in Wales

Then they observe thus: "We hear that their design was to get Mr. Vavasor Powell to come among you to preach against Baptism; (This plainly indicates that Vavasor Powell was not yet a Baptist.) but you and we, find by experience, that the ordering of all men's thoughts, words, actions, and designs, are of the Lord; and we rejoice to hear that he at that time declared so much contrary to their expectations, to the evidencing of the truth oppugned by them."

Abergavenny Papers mention this affair likewise and observe that when Mr. Vavasor Powell came, instead of distressing them, he encouraged peace and purity, so he comforted and confirmed this young church. Of those papers see next page.

The letter from Ilston further says, "Now Brethren, upon these and other serious Considerations we were led to appoint this day to seek the Lord solemnly by humiliation, fasting, and prayer, (1) That God would frustrate the design of the enemy. (2) That he would change the hearts of our dear friends so much opposing us, and that none of the faithful may have a hand in opposing the trûth as people of God. (3) That God would prosper his works now begun in Wales. (4) That he may be pleased to strengthen our brethren and sisters in Wales to undergo the trial, if God shall lay it upon them. (5) That God will be with the ministers sent abroad upon the work and make them faithful and constant. (6) That God would increase the gifts of the Churches, that so they may be the better strengthened against the enemy." Then they proceed in the letters, and define the Hay Church likewise to "seek the Lord solemnly in the same things," and that they might after correspond, for better sympathy and union in their joy and sorrow, etc.

Then the extracts add: "Those three churches (of Ilston, Hay, and Llanharan) met at Ilston the 7th month according to appointment, of the decrees and orders agreed upon there. There we see that the church at the Hay was to send occasional help to Llanharan, see there also what is said of Mr. Prossor, and what is allowed him to encourage his labor in the ministry. The three churches were to contribute 10£ in a year toward the ministry; a brother in each church was appointed to take care of this collection, Br. Leyson Davis at Ilston, Br. Thomas Watkins at the Hay, and Br. Frisson Griffin at Llanharan. It was to be raised quarterly and of the 30£ a year 25£ was allotted to Mr. Prossor: as the Extracts note that he had no maintenance allowed him any other way; it implies that the Brethren Myles, Proud and Davis had other Parochial State allowance.

Above (Ms.,p.7) mentions a letter written from London to the church at the Hay about the close of 1650, the date is not in the Extracts, and for a small part of the letter which runs thus, "Brethren, when we consider that men so eminently good as Mr. Powell, among those who fear the Lord, is thought to be, should so uncharitably vent himself to the dishonor of the Gospel; we often wonder what the Lord is doing: yet let us not think strange of it; Satan is now more busy and subtil than ever, because his time is but short." What Mr. Powell had done to occasion this remark does not appear, very probably it was saying something for mixed communion, (More probably it was saying something against baptism, as he had not then become a Baptist, of which Mr. Thomas was not aware. W.R.) as the famous Bunyan was so much for it afterwards.

Those papers informed, that the Baptist Churches in Wales sent letters by their Messenger, Mr. John Myles, to the Baptist Church in London mentioned before, and afterward, in the year 1651. In those letters they gave a comfortable account of their state, their harmony, peace, additions, etc. That church sent back an epistle to our countrymen, to advise and confirm them in the truth. There they say "Regarding the distance of your habitations, we advise; if you experience that God hath endowed you with gifts whereby ye may edify one another, and keep up proper order and Ministry in the church of Christ; then we may judge you may seperate into more distinct congregations provided it be done with mutual consent, and if there be among you those who may, in some measure, take the oversight of you in the Lord. But if not, we believe it will be more for the honor of Christ for you to continue together." This is signed by Mr. Consett and several of the same names, as in page 46 above.

Of the convention of the four churches at Carmarthen, on the 19th day of the 1st month 1651, and the business and agreement there, see above. Among other things a query was moved there about laying on of hands; of this more below.

In 1652 the church at Abergavenny was constituted. Several of the first constituents were members of the church at the Hay, as they lived nearer to Abergavenny, in the lower parts of Cludock and near Lanvibangel. Of those one was James Landon. Mr. Backus in his history, Vol. 1 page 414, mentions one of the names in that country about 1669, he might possibly fail with Mr. Myles when the trouble came on here.

We had already an account of the first general meeting at Ilston, and a second at Carmarthen, but the extracts gave no account of the next. There is only an accidental hint of one at Llanharan above, very probably they had one at the Hay, though perhaps not mentioned in those records, as it is not in the Extracts, so the letters from Llantrisaint to Ilston, Hay and Carmarthen. Of Llantrisaint see above, and below.

The next account that occurs of general meetings is in the records of Abergavenny. Where one was held the 14th and 15th of the 6th 1653, by the elders and messengers of the churches of Ilston, Hay, Llantrisaint, Carmarthen and Abergavenny. By the minutes of that meeting it appears the Hay Church was very numerous and lay very wide; and they had considerable trouble from several disorderly members, who were supposed to plan a design to set up by themselves, so trouble and rent the church. How that was ordered, and the advice given, see the printed History of the Welsh Association, p.1.

Here it was agreed that the Hay Church should assist the church at Abergavenny to maintain and support Br. William Prichard designed shortly to be sent forth a public minister. This church was now wealthy and numerous, though not very comfortable. We saw already the provision made for Mr. W. Prossor. But as yet we have no account of anything done for the support of Mr. Thomas Watkins, who was a laborious, acceptable preacher, and possibly not an elder yet. It is supposed this assistance to Abergavenny did not continue long, if above one year. Among those who signed the Breviates of this were from the Hay Church, Walter Prossor, Howell Vaughan, Thomas Watkins, Stephen Brace, Charles Garson, Thomas Perry, Howell Watkins; the two last were occasional helpers in the ministry.

The next general meeting was at Aberavon, the eastern branch of the Ilston Church, on the 1st and 2nd days of the first month, that was the beginning of March, 1654. Mr. Walter Prossor was there appointed to assist at Carmarthen in this town. Another article was, a desire that the church at Ilston would spare Mr. Myles often and as long as they may, to be among the churches of the Hay and Abergavenny order to the settling of them, and helping them to judge of the several gifts of the members among them. Here again it was desired that the Hay and Llantrisaint would assist Abergavenny to support their minister. Among the queries proposed at this meeting, one was, "What are the duties of each of the officers and members in the Church?" Here Mr. Walter Prossor and three more were named to answer this query in writing, and bring the answer to the next meeting, Among those who signed at this meeting were from the Hay Church, Walter Prossor, and Stephen Brace.

The ensuing general meeting was at Llantrisaint 30th and 31st 6th month, 1654. There it was proposed and desired that a minister skilled in the English was used in the church at the Hay and that Mr. Walter Prossor and William Prichard would change churches and places of abode. It seems the latter understood English better than the former. It does not appear that this exchange took place; and if it did, the continuance was very short. But English certainly was wanted in the Hay Church, for it was spread to Herefordshire to Ewias Lacy and Bradwardine. These two places are mentioned in the records in my possession. It seems Mr. Prossor was a native of Llanigon, or that way; had he been native of the Hay one might have expected him to be very ready in the English.

At this meeting, the church at Carmarthen proposed, "whether laying on of hands were an ordinance of Christ; and if it were, then upon whom to be ministered." Of this see below. This query was referred to be answered at the next general meeting appointed to be at the Hay. Mr. Walter Prossor and four more appointed to write their sentiments upon the point against that time. This article had been moved before at Carmarthen in 1651. Very probably some from Wales sent to London about this article,laying on of hands, for in the Abergavenny papers mentioned below, there was information there about this time, the exact date was not given. Mr. William Rider came down from London about the subject.

The Narrative there was of a meeting at the Hay upon the occasion. Some of the members declared their thoughts upon Heb. 6:1,2. Then Mr. Rider spoke his sentiments and informed them, where he thought them not quite right. For his assistant he had Mr. Robert Hopkins. When they were satisfied on both sides, hands were layed on fifteen of the members, five men and ten women. The names were all there, but I took only the first man, who was John Rhys Howel, named above. Whether Mr. Rider went to any other place then on the business does not appear. Fifteen was but a small number of the church at the Hay then. There was no minister among the five men. It is supposed that Mr. Robert Hopkins was from Wales. The name is among those who signed at the general meeting at Abergavenny in 1653, and those baptized in 1650, and was of Aberavon.

Neither the extracts from America nor the Abergavenny records give any hint of the general meeting appointed at Llantrisaint to be at the Hay on the last fourth day of the first month 1655, nor the minutes there, what the reason of that silence we cannot now tell. The query at Aberavon regarding the duties of church officers and members, was answered at Llantrisaint, and is inserted in the printed *History of the Association,* page 12.

The next and only general meeting of the churches now heard of in the time of the commonwealth, was at Brecknock on the 29th and 30th of the 5th month 1656. At that meeting they agreed to publish a tract, entitled, *An Antidote against the Infection of the Times, Etc.* Of that see above history page 15. There it is said that the Elders and messengers were from the churches of Ilston, Abergavenny, Tredynog, Hereford, Bradwardine, Clydock and Llangors. There is neither the Hay nor Llantrisaint. The whole is explained in the place just now referred to, but the present concern is with the Hay.

We have had hints before of uneasiness in this church, a wish to change their minister and etc. Probably by this time they were in a shattered condition, it is supposed that Mr. Walter Prossor was gone off, and settled at Tredynog in Monmouthshire, which was probably the reason that name was mentioned at this meeting. Bradwardine and Clydock were branches of the Hay church, and perhaps there were members from those places at Brecknock, as we have only the names of places and not persons, we cannot know now who attended there.

We have no more account of the Hay Church for many years. It is suspected that what follows was applicable to them, as well as other places. Mr. Vavasor Powell was as well acquainted with the state of things in Wales as perhaps anyone living then. He says in his *Bird in the Cage,* pages 109, 110, 2nd ed. 1662, when heavy troubles had come upon the nonconformists in 1660, "The Lord hath, I am persuaded, done more by the afflictions which he hath lately brought upon his people than either was done or like to be done, by any other ways or means. He hath driven his people more together and more one: he hath separated more between them and the world, like winnowing drives the chaff further from the wheat—convinced them more of their miscarriages, both towards him, and toward one another, made them to know persons and things better, they are unloaded and much discharged of the burden of the world, as Sheep by losing their fleece, lose their scabs also, which the heat of their wool increased. This is part of what he saith of them."

On the Restoration in May 1660 the troubles came on, and it fell heavy on this church. Like many more, a few hints here of Mr. Prossor. We found him, as above, an elder at Llanigon in 1649, how long before he had been in that office does not appear. About the close of that year he was baptized, and became the leading minister of a large church there soon, was very useful, laborious, and acceptable in Glamorganshire, and in and about Carmarthen, so much that tradition carried the name of Prossor about Llanelli and Llanon even to our time, and till the extracts from America came, he was thought to be a native of that country. It seems he removed to Tredynog about 1654 or 5. The reason and circumstances of that removal we have not, but there he was found when the general storm came. Dr. Calamy names him there among the ministers, ejected in Monmouthshire in 1660 and 1662, the character given him in the convention at Ilston in 1650 was thus, "We find in him much readiness to serve the Lord Jesus Christ and his saints in that painful and great work of the ministry, wheresoever he is thereunto called." There appears no room to conclude that he was otherwise during life. After the ejection we have no account what his persecution and sufferings, whether imprisoned, or how long or short his trials and life were. All that could be found of him that way was this manuscript hint, "Mr. Walter Prossor was eminent in the ministry, and preached at Llantrisaint, Llangwm and Tredynog. This must refer to the persecuting time.

It was observed about page 16, that Olchon Church was so small and despised about 1640, Mr. Vavasor Powell was at a loss whether it could be deemed a church or not. In about twelve years after it was so spread and enlarged, that it laid aside the old name and was called by the name of a considerable market town, but when they grew numerous and wealthy, it was their unhappiness to become delicate and contentious. By those things they began to weaken themselves; and in 1660 the tempest of persecution came and scattered them grievously. It is supposed that some of the English part of them joined afterward the church that then met partly at Hereford and partly at Leominster. Stephen Brace, and some others are in the church book at the latter place now. In that long storm the church retired again to her old rest, Olchon, and the church at Llanigon bore out through the whole. Mr. Thomas Watkins was then their pastor, and Mr. Thomas Perry the kind assistant. The former lived near Olchon, and the other in Llanigon, and the meeting kept at his house called Wenallt. They had a meeting house fitted up in the Hay town, and occupied it at times till about 1710. The place not known there lately, but it was a dwelling house, as probably it had been before.

Welsh Baptists During the Persecution

There was a meeting at Clifford kept occasionally for a long time. The last there was a very worthy aged member, of very good report, his name was Thomas Tanner. He died about 1740. A meeting was kept there sometime after. The writer of this preached there in 1746 or 7. Now let us attend to Olchon and Llanigon.

Olchon may be styled the Cathedral of their church, though never very pompous, yet there is antiquity to boast of. No doubt the aged people there well remembered the former troubles, before 1640. From 1660 to 1688 they were much persecuted despised, yet a remnant continued through the whole.

They met to worship in various places where they could; sometimes in a friend's house and often out. One day or night they would meet in some retired place of the Black Mountain, but when they understood that informers had heard of the place; then they would change it and fix upon another spot; thus they shifted from place to place. A noted rock, they frequented for the purpose, is called, Y Darren ddn, on the west side of Olchon, and well known still. A little below it, there was then a large wood, there is part of it now; that wood was often their meeting place. That was the estate of Mr. Hugh Lewis, a gentleman of property and influence but no persecutor. His son, Mr. Nathan Lewis, was a strong advocate for the persecuted Baptists. Mr. Thomas Lewis, another son, was a Baptist after and lived at Abergavenny. There was also a daughter, who was a member. So upon the whole they had favor and interest there. This daughter was a very worthy character, was married to Mr. Caleb Evans, eldest son to Mr. Thomas Evans of Pentre of whom see the History of that church, below. She had two sons, Thomas and Hugh, after the names of their grandfathers. On the birth of the latter she died.

He was the late truly reverend Hugh Evans, M.A. Pastor of the Baptist Church at Broadmead, Bristol, and father to the late Dr. Caleb Evans, his successor. Of all whom more in the places just now referred to. Besides the six already named, these are two worthies more, who may be said to have originated from Olchon, on the maternal side. Philip Davis Esq. of Leominster is a grandson, by the mother, of Mr. Nathan Lewis.

Notwithstanding all favors and cautions, the good people were often taken, beaten, abused, fined, and imprisoned. They were hunted like David, through woods, through mountains, and the rocks of wild goats. Of whom the world was not worthy, they wandered in desert, mountains, dens and caves. At times when they met to worship at friends' houses, it was running great risk and hazards. A place called Wern-wen, where Mr. David Watkins and his brother Daniel lived, was often their meeting house. They both were worthy members of this persecuted society. Mr. Thomas John William's house was another place of worship: he was a plain man, but much adored the Gospel in his life and death. Before the persecution was over, it is said that Mr. John Gilbert encouraged them to meet at his house at Baily Back. It was kept there at one of two houses until lately. "The late Caleb Evans D.D. of Bristol was a great grandson to Mr. Hugh Lewis by his daughter Hannah, and P. Davis Evans in the commission of the place a great grandson by his son Nathan."

Now a little of the Llanigon part. Mr. Thomas Perry, was mentioned before. It is supposed that he was a native of this parish. His granddaughter, a very respectable character, gave me a particular account of some peculiar circumstance of his first religious impressions. I wrote it down, and the sum of it follows.

In his youth he was visited with a fit of illness, that rendered life dubious. In that sickness he dreamed that he was dead. He supposed he saw two places before him, very different; one exceeding glorious and delightful, but the other as dreadful and terrible. He was to go into one of the two, but earnestly requested leave to go into the former. He was answered that he should not go then. But he cried, "Lord shall I go sometime? The reply was in the affirmative. But he must first go buy bread. He further asked, "Lord when shall I come?" replied, "after ten days."

Upon that he awoke, and the dream made no small impression upon his mind. He recovered, but was so ignorant he knew not what to do. However, he began to reform, go to church, to be very good, though all on a legal foundation. One day, while going to church it seems, he met a serious person going somewhere else to hear a sermon. They fell into religious talk, which led the young man to go along to hear the sermon, instead of going to church. To his great surprise, the text was, "I am the *bread* of life". Remembering his dream afresh, he was all attention. Being so affected he would go again. The other text was, "Ye shall have tribulation *ten days*." Rev. 2:10. Thus he had his dream interpreted much to his satisfaction. He was informed what the bread of life, and that troubles were to be expected. He then determined to follow Christ and bear the consequence.

The granddaughter said that he was very intimate with Mr. Vavasor Powell, and a fellow sufferer with him at times; and further, that he was the person mentioned in Mr. Powell's *Life,* p.18, thus "When another preacher and myself had lost our way in a very dark night, and had tired ourselves to no purpose; at last calling to mind how God had formerly heard in that case, when I sought unto him; we called upon the Lord, who immediately pointed out our way, and it was as clear to us as if it had been day light." Mr. T. Perry was a very useful man during life, probably he was one of the first constituents of the Baptists at Llanigon.

In those days there was in this parish, a gentlewoman whose name was Watkins. She did live at Pen-yr-Wrglodd, a capital mansion house then. She was a member of the Baptist Church. Of her Mr. Vavasor Powell writes thus, "One Mrs. Watkins of the parish of Llanigon in the county of Brecknock, a gracious gentlewoman having kept her chamber and bed, as was reported, for two years, and not gone from home for the space of four years, hearing that I was come into those parts, sent for me to come and visit her. She having, it seems, some faith that if I prayed for her, she should be healed. The next morning she went to meeting afoot, between two and three miles." This account on the same page of his life as the others, among those remarkable answers he had to prayers. Mrs. Watkins was remarkably useful in the persecuting times, between 40 and 50 years ago (It is now at the time of this writing) aged persons in those parts, speaking of her with great veneration.

One short anecdote more must be here recorded, that happened in the persecuting time. Mr. William Jones is named by Dr. Calamy among the ejected ministers in Carmarthenshire. He was there in Carmarthen Castle for preaching, there he fell into some conversation with certain Baptists. He was convinced by some means that believers' baptism was right. Bur kept his convictions to himself while there. By some means he was set at liberty and he was determined then to answer a good conscience by being baptized according to the New Testament rule. That he might have a proper administrator, the manuscript that recorded it said that he went to the Valley of Olchon to be baptized. Then it may be supposed that the administrator was Mr. Thomas Watkins. Probably this was about 1665 or 6. The manuscript did not below give the date.

In 1668, Mr. Thomas Watkins and Mr. William Prichard of Abergavenny went to form a church of those baptized afterward by Mr. William Jones. So under the great and good shepherd he was the Father, and that young church the mother of all the Baptist Churches now about Fywi River, and west of it. (except Llandysean Cwm–isor(?) and Abergavenny lately formed. It is now 1795.) Of that see more in Rhydwilim.

Baptists Reorganize After the Persecution

After when the Prince of Orange, afterward King William, came in 1688, and put an end to the persecution, the Baptist Ministers in London met and agreed to send an invitation to the ministers in the country to assemble in London September, 1689, to consider the states of the churches after the long persecution, they sent a circular letter to the Baptists in England and Wales to that purpose, many came and a narrative of that assembly was printed. But no body from Olchon appears in the narrative. They there appointed to meet again in the Whitsun week, 1690. Olchon then sent a letter, and the original one fell into my hand, which I still have. It is very short and signed by Thomas Watkins, pastor; Thomas John and James John, Deacons; then Thomas William, Henry Powell, David Watkins, Daniel Watkins, and John Gilbert. The letter gives no account of their number nor state, but the situation of most of the Baptist Churches in Wales was drawn up on one paper and sent to London 1690. That likewise I have. Of Olchon it is there said, that their number was about thirty, that Thomas Watkins was their aged minister, as ordained elder, not able to perform as formerly; that they had help from other congregations to preach and administer ordinances and were particularly helped by Thomas Perry of Brecknockshire. I have two of those papers. One of them mentions a congregation in Radnorshire and Brecknockshire to whom Br. Thomas Perry and Br. Thomas Powell had relations as Elders. Mr. Thomas Powell did live some part of his time in Radnorshire at Maes-yr-Ornen, his own estate. Probably some of the Llanigon members lived in Radnorshire, and some times Llanigon was esteemed a church by itself. Olchon and Llanigon were often assisted by other ministers, as Ministers Lewis Thomas, of Swansea, William Prichard of Llanwenarth, Thomas Evans, of Pentre, Nathaniel Jenkins.

Ministers of the Llanigon Church

The Llanigon part of the church was raised up of very worthy Gospel ministers. Claydock of the house in the Hay province, reports that he was baptized of Thomas Evans of Pentre who died in 1688. If so, the youngster embraced religion in persecuting times, and very probably it was so, for he was about seven and twenty when the persecution ended.[2]

We have no information when Mr. Howell Vaughan, the supposed first pastor here finished his warfare. He and his son Noah, were very honorable and useful here.

The worthy and aged Mr. Thomas Watkins ended his days about 1694 or 5. In the Abergavenny papers there was a letter of thanks from Llanharan to the Hay, dated above 1650, for sparing their Br. Thomas Watkins to them, "who had helped them much in the Lord," they having been there as among wolves and bears. This was a good character, how long before that he had been in the ministry is not now known. At the meeting at Ilston the 9th month, 1650, he and Br. Prossor are named to assist Llanharan, see above.

When Mr. Prossor removed to Tredynog, about 1694 or 5, Mr. Thomas Watkins succeeded in the pastoral care, and continued through all the long tribulation that followed. The most aged men members in Olchon about 1750 told me, that Mr. Thomas Watkins had been the pastor there 40 years. That agrees exactly with the above account. He was the chief pastor that ever this church yet had, on various account, that would be no offence to the present pastor should he ever happen to see this. He was evidently the chief for the duration of time and the sufferings in that time.

He was married twice, by the first wife he had only a daughter, she had two sons and two daughters, who all had children, and spread to several families. Several of whom were useful members of this

[2]Approximately three paragraphs have been omitted here because the MS. was not legible (Editors).

church, and some are so still. The present pastor, Mr. George Watkins is one of the desendants. The second wife likewise had one daughter, who was a worthy member of the church, she had several children, of her more below.

Mr. Howell Watkins some named above as an occasional helper in the ministry. He went to rest soon after. It is supposed he died about 1700, or perhaps sooner, aged informers could not be particular regarding dates.

The church now was become almost destitute regarding the ministry; though Mr. Thomas Perry was alive, yet he was far advanced in years. But the Abergavenny, or rather Llanwenarth and Blaenau Ministers were very hard to assist. Mr. John Gilbert, named before, was also an occasional helper. In 1699 Trosgoed (now Maesyberllan) was formed. But the old and the new church were without pastors. By advice and consultation, it was agreed that Olchon, Llanigon, and Trosgoed should all agree to be under one pastor, and they chose Mr. Richard Williams to be so. He was a member of Rhydwilim Church, and had been for some time in the ministry there. About the same time Mr. Morgan Griffiths came from that church to Hengoed, this scattered church that lay so very wide was well served by Mr. Richard Williams. The three capital meetinghouses were Bay Back, Wenallt, and Trosgoed, but all dwelling houses.

Now to take leave of that good man Mr. Thomas Perry of Wenallt, in Llanigon. His name is to the Breviates at Abergavenny in 1653, and to those at Llanwenarth in 1705. He died 1709. I never could find his age. His son David succeeded at Wenallt, and the grandson Nathaniel followed. Worthy men. The meeting was long kept there, the descendants are very numerous, and many of them church members, in Wales and in England, and probably in America. I do not recollect any ministers that were raised up among them.

Mr. Richard Williams bore an excellent character, his labor was indefatigable. He was much respected in the Association, was beloved at home and abroad, he had many trials, but was a son of peace, though some of the members were not eminent for that, yet during his life they had no great contention. But after death they had trouble plenty. He finished his course with great honor and respect in 1724, having served the church, or rather the two, about 24 years.

When the faithful pastor died, there were three young men in the church, who had begun to exercise in the ministry, Messrs Thomas Price, Rees Williams, and Philip Morgan; the two former of the Olchon part, and the latter of Trosgoed. The late pastor rather favored Mr. Philip Morgan, there were some objections to the other two, particularly at Olchon. The former of the three did not continue to preach many years, the debate was chiefly about the second; some for and others against him. The Olchon part mostly if not all were not for him, but the Trosgoed part were rather on his part. After tedious and afflictive altercations, they divided in 1729; Llanigon there joined Trosgoed, thus the old church was again confined to the former seat, Olchon, and near vicinity.

During those years they were very kindly assisted in the ministry by Mr. John Harris of Blaenan. Mr. Richard Williams went off to Trosgoed on the separation, and Mr. Thomas Price not like to have the pastoral care, the church was under a necessity to look out for a minister. They united in the choice of Mr. William Williams, a young man from Cilfowyr, Pembrokeshire. He was ordained in 1731, but they did not long continue comfortable in that connection. In about seven years Mr. Williams left them and removed his communion to Trosgoed.

He was soon succeeded by Mr. Jacob Rees, from Pen-y-sai, Glamorganshire. Not long after he came, he baptized Mr. John Powell, who soon began to preach, if he had not exercised some that way before. He was a young man from Abergwessyn, in the upper part of Breckknockshire, of a very uncommon talent for popular itinerant preaching. The Methodists had then lately begun in Wales, so he had many hearers of all denominations. But he had not a sufficient degree of prudence in the whole of his conduct. Some applauded him perhaps too much; others were offended, some grieved. But his race was soon run, he died in 1743. Mr. Jacob Rees continued here but about the same time as his predecessor, some uneasiness arose and he went off in or about 1745.

In (Ms.,p.60), it is observed, that Mr. Thomas Watkins had a daughter by his second wife. That daughter had many trials in life, was a widow many years; she had four sons. Her sons William and David were members of this church, and so was the mother. Those three lived together, the two sons were bachelors, and continued so during life. Their name was Prossor. (One of the four sons was Walter, this with some other circumstances, induce the writer of this to say that this Prossor family were related to Mr. Walter Prossor, the former pastor of this church, about 1651, etc.) There were more children, but these only were members of this church, the others were in the establishment.

Mr. William Prossor purchased an estate near a place called Chapel y Ffin. There he and his mother and brother David lived together many years. Though they were not far from Olchon, yet they were members at Trosgoed.

About 1740, or sooner, Mrs. Prossor, the mother, was visited with some kind of affliction, of which she never recovered wholly during life. She was unable to go to meeting, therefore her son got ministers to preach in the house for the mother's sake. They had a large convenient kitchen, and it was fitted up for the purpose. Among those who came to preach, one was Mr. William Herbert, an ordained minister at Trosgoed, his talent was very agreeable, and he came rather often for a little while, but his strength failed, and he finished his course in 1742.

At the separation in 1729, several about Chapel Y Ffin and Llanigon chose to be members at Trosgoed; but in time they found the way far; so they requested dismission from Trosgoed to Olchon, which was granted about 1746, to twelve members. This dismission was observed in the letter to the Association that year. Now the church was in three parts, Olchon, Chapel Y Ffin, and Llanigon, and preaching at the two former about equal, and often in the latter.

The next successor in the ministry was Mr. Joshua Andrews, an ordained minister, assisting at Penygarn, near Pontpool. It was not convenient for him to remove his family, so he only supplied two Lord's Days in a month, and administered ordinances. They were destitute the other two days, except they could get supply. But they were not long in that situation, for in June 1746, the writer of this came to live at the Hay, and supplied here the other two Lord's Days in the month, thus the ministry was carried on till he removed to Leominster in November, 1754.

The cause of bringing the meeting to Mr. Prossor's house was his mother's uncommon weakness, she continued in that feeble state about twelve years, but was very comfortable in her soul. After she died the meeting still continued in it's usual course, commonly in the morning at one place, and in the evening at the other.

Mr. Walter Prossor was remarkably useful, and contrived how to be of service to promote the interest of the Gospel. Advancing in years, he supposed it might not, after his days, be convenient to keep the meeting in the dwelling house. To remedy that, he gave the church about an acre of land, to errect a meeting house upon it, if necessary. He did enclose and fence it for the purpose.

His life continuing he was willing to do more. In his life time the meeting house was built, and he assisted, with a good will to carry on the work under his own eye. This was done in 1762. It is a very convenient place. This is the first and only proper meeting house yet built in this ancient church. There was a place at the Hay, as noted before, but that is supposed to have been a dwelling before, as well as after. As observed above, Mr. John Gilbert fitted up his house in Olchon for preaching. He had a pulpit made there, with the date on it 1703. I preached there in that pulpit in 1776. Probably it is there still. There are two houses, they preached sometimes in the one, at other times in the other. The two brothers lived many years after the house was built, and continued very useful to the close of a long life, very hospitable, and an ornament to their profession. They both finished their course in the same year, 1780. I did not hear their exact age, but suppose Mr. Walter Prossor was about eighty-seven as I think he was born before his grandfather Watkins died.

After 1754, they were considerably straitened for a ministry. Mr. Joshua Andrews came as usual, two sabbaths in the month, but the other two they shifted as well as they could, till about 1762, or perhaps a little sooner, Mr. George Watkins, already named, was encouraged to exercise in the ministry, and was found acceptable; then he filled in the vacancies. In 1773 he was ordained, that he might administer ordinances when Mr. Joshua Andrews happened to be by weakness not able to come. But he continued to assist many years after, yet the dependance gradually fell on Mr. Watkins. At last Mr. Joshua Andrews' strength failed, he was confined at home and gradually to his house, then to his bed, and in June 1793, he finished a long course of many afflictions, aged about 85. He ended well and comfortable. (Of Mr. Joshua Andrews, see more in the Baptist Register, Vol. 2 page 108.) Mr. Noah D. Lymonds should be inserted here, see more of him on next page.

In 1788 Messrs. James Price and James Perrott were baptized. Not long after the two exercised their ministerial talents, the former removed to Glamorganshire, where he continues, and keeps a school, preaching occasionally when wanted. The latter is mostly at home, and assists in the ministry.

They had some members in and about a place called Tfooddog, four or five miles from Chapel-Y-Ffin Southwest. They began to preach that way, and in 1789 they had a house liscensed there to preach. Ever since they administered the Lord's Supper there, once a month. The same also at the meeting house near Chapel-Y-Ffin; and at Olchon, so they break bread in the church three times in the month. The number of members now is about sixty, mostly poor.

In page 33, above it is observed that Llanigon joined Trosgoed, and left Olchon. Excepting a few years then, Olchon and Llanigon were in the same connection about or near a hundred and twenty years. Maes–dorglwyd was the last house in the Parish of Llanigon where the meeting was kept. Mr. William Maddy lived there, he was a kind helper of a weak society for many years. In that house he finished his course. The widow was married to Mr. John Thomas, and they resided at Pen-yr-heal, see below. When Mr. John Thomas settled there and preached at his own house, the few members on that side the hill naturally joined there by degrees, so that branch is extinct now to Olchon, but still alive and strong.

One of the two houses at Baily-back, in Olchon has been a preaching place near, if not quite a hundred years, see above. But of late those two houses are gone into other hands, the meeting is now kept at Mr. Delahay Symmonds house, in the Valley of Olchon still.

It is remarkable, that nonconformity in the Principality began here, and were of the Baptist denomination, yet it does not appear that ever the Association was kept here till this year 1794. It was kept in branches of the church a few times, the *History of the Welsh Association,* page 14 informs that the general meeting was appointed to be on the Hay on the first month 1655, we have no account of any after till it was kept at Maesdorglwyd in Llanigon, 1753, near 100 years after the former, and at Chapel-y-Ffin, 1770. It is supposed they were afraid the congregation that commonly attended the annual meeting could not be accommodated at Olchon. But last year Mr. Delahay Symmonds wished to have it, for once before he died; it was granted, and his life spared to see it, and all was managed comfortably, had there been more people, there were lodgings ready for them. June 1794.

Mr. Noah Delahay Symmonds was not an original member at Olchon, but his father and mother were, and very friendly, hospitable and useful during life. So was his grandfather Symmonds, who was a grandson to the former venerable pastor, Mr. Thomas Watkins, by the eldest daughter. In short the body of this church, so many years, were the descendants of that worthy minister who had labored so hard and suffered so much in the cause of Christ. Some of them besides the pastor are members there now, and some in other churches. Though many of them be degenerated from the paths of their great ancester. At the house of Mr. Noah Delahay Symmonds' father, meetings were often kept, and ministers lodged there. In that house, it is now statedly kept, as noted above in this page.

Soon after Mr. Noah Delahay Symmonds was grown up he went to London, and was there for years. He was baptized while in the city. But sometime after he returned to his father. There he was encouraged to exercise his talent for the ministry. He again left his father's house in 1772, was some time in the Bristol Academy for further improvement. From thence he went to the Baptist Church at Boocy Trace, Devon, where he continued a few years; but removed to the Baptist Church at Brumpton in the same county, in 1776, where he was ordained the following year.

Olchon Ministers

1. Mr. John Penry, supposed to have been the first Baptist minister this was 1593 or 4.

2. Mr. Howel Vaughan, supposed to have been the first pastor of the church here, died after 1653.
3. Mr. Walter Prossor – a contemporary with the former, supposed to have died after 1672.
4. Mr. James Hughes, is not known what became of him and when he died.
5. Thomas Watkins. The most worthy of all the pastors of this church died about 1694.
6. Mr. Thomas Perry; a very useful assistant for a long time. 1709.
7. Mr. John Rys Howel. Very useful in his day, supposed not ordained, 1692.
8. Mr. Howell Watkins; an occasional exhorter of great repute died about 1700.
9. Mr. Thomas Powell. Sometime here, of him see Maes-y-berllan.
10. Mr. Joseph Price, often at Leominster, then pastor at Tewkesbury where he died 1721.
11. Mr. Thomas Price, in the ministry some years, uncertain when he died.
12. Mr. John Gilbert – an useful member, various ways, time of his death unknown.
13. Mr. Rees Williams – an original member here but no credit to his profession, 1759.
14. Mr. William Williams – pastor for sometime, then removed to Trosgoed, 1771.
15. Mr. Jacob Rees – likewise pastor a few years then removed, 1772.
16. Mr. John Powell – a very popular preacher, soon finished his race in 1743.
17. Mr. Joshua Andrews – he served half the time above 40 years, died 1743.
18. Mr. George Watkins – the perfect pastor.
19. Mr. Noah Delahay Symmonds – began here.
20. Mr. James Perrot – an assistant here now, but since ordained at Hengoed.
21. Mr. James Price – an occasional preacher.

Before the close of 1794 Mr. James Perrot assisted at Hengoed. As they so much wanted assistance, he was invited to settle with them. He complied, and in their letter to the Association in 1795, they inform that he was ordained there, to assist the aged pastor.

Mr. James Price went to Bristol, not long after he began to exercise his talent for the ministry. He was at the academy there about half a year. Dr. Evans judged that his talent was not for much improvement there, for that reason he advised him to return home, which he did. Then went to Glamorganshire as noted. After some time he married a woman who kept a shop, and gave up the school, then gradually took to a kind of a pedlery way to sell his shop goods. The account I have is, that his character is good, and that in his travels he preaches occasionally, and rather often. Is still a member at Olchon. May 1797. Signed J.T.

THE HISTORY OF THE BAPTIST CHURCH AT SWANSEA

In the *Welsh History of the Baptists* in the Principality, published in 1778, it was supposed that the church had been formed soon after 1642; there being no certainty then found of the very time when that was done. But since that time authentic account appeared. The church was not formed originally at Swansea, but at Ilston, which is the name of a parish in Gower-Land, a few miles from the town. Dr. Walker, in his *Account of the Sufferings of the Clergy* (Vol. II, p. 278), informs that Mr. W. M. Houghton was sequestered from the Rectory of Ilston, and was succeeded by one John Miles, an Anabaptist. But we are not informed when that sequestration and succession happened. That is immaterial.

The Origin at Ilston

In 1777, the Rev. Isaac Backus, published the first volume of his, *History of New England with Particular Reference to the Baptist Denomination*, printed at Boston, New England. There page 350 says that the first Baptist Church within what is now called the Massachusetts State was constituted in Rehobath in the year 1663. Then in process thus:

For a more clear idea of its original, we must look over into Wales, where at Ilston in Glamorganshire, a Baptist Church was formed, October 1, 1649.[1] The beginning of which their records describe thus— 'We cannot but admire the unsearchable wisdom, power, and love of God, in bringing about his own design, far above and beyond the capacity and understanding of the chiefest of men. Thus to the glory of his own great name, hath he dealt with us; for when there had been no company or society of people, holding forth and professing the doctrine, worship, order and discipline of the Gospel, according to the primitive institution that ever we heard of in all Wales, since the apostasy,[2] it pleased the

[1]Here Mr. Backus happened to mistake a few months; for about the beginning of October they began to baptize that way as will soon appear from the church records.

[2]Since Popery prevailed.

Lord to choose this dark corner to place his name in; and to honor us, undeserving ones, with the happiness of being the first in all these parts, among whom was practiced the glorious ordinance of Baptism, and here to gather the first church of baptized believers.' Then from the records Mr. Backus adds, "From whence they go on to relate how Mr. John Miles and Mr. Thomas Proud went to London, the next preceeding spring, and by the direction of Providence came to the Baptist society, at the Glasshouse in Broad Street under the care of Mr. William Consett and Mr. Edward Draper. This was immediately after that society had kept a day to seek the Lord, praying that he would send laborers into the dark corners of the land.

These travelers were well received and soon, in about a fortnight, went back into their own country again, where they were influential in gathering a Baptist Church, which, by a blessing upon their labor, increased by the close of the next year to fifty-five members. In 1651 forty more were added. In 1652, forty-seven (were) added: and by the twelfth of the 6th month, August 1660, they had added to them two hundred and sixty-three or four according to the records. Several of them were added by recommendation from other churches, so not all (were) baptized at Ilston. The book taken to America contained a distinct account of the means and methods they took to promote vital and practical religion among the several branches of their society, as also letters of correspondence to and from their brethren in various parts of England and Ireland. Most of this paragraph is from Mr. Backus' History, but a little varied in some places.

What is said here of Ilston's being the first Baptist Church in Wales after the Reformation, and of the priority of Olchon above, see that record in the history of the Church last named, page 9. When I saw this account (after the Welsh History was printed some years, for it came not to my hand till late in 1781), I wrote to Mr. Backus to request some extracts out of the Swansea Church records, as the History reported it to be full. The request was soon and readily granted, large extracts were copied out by Mr. Backus' own hand in 1784. Though those were very servicable, they yet gave room to suppose there was more information still to be had in that book, than could be found anywhere else upon earth. Therefore a second application was made. Here it is readily acknowledged that good Mr. Backus with almost immediate readiness, transcribed more, once and again. And all his labors lost once or twice by some unhappy miscarriages in seaports. When he understood that, he very obligingly set about the tedious work of transcribing again, and four large extracts out of the original book. For his remarkable kindness and perseverance the writer of this record here (expresses) his gratitude and repeated obligations. Thanks are due not only from him alone, but every one that wishes well to the History of the Baptists among the ancient Britons. The letter with the last extracts is dated 1792, informing that large extracts had been sent with a long letter in 1787, and he never knew that it had miscarried until 1791. But he set about the work, and at last succeeded. Now the last use is to be made of them.

The extracts give the names of the 263 members above mentioned, and most of the parishes and places where they lived. They lay exceeding wide and scattered indeed. Westward as far as Carmarthen, Llanelli, Llanon, etc. East and North, at Neath, Britain–ferry, Aberavon, Kelligan, and even the Hay. But the book does not always distinguish between those baptized, and those recommended, etc. It only says *added.*

Now to attend more closely to the history of this church. Besides what is cited above out of the printed history, the record says, "It is wonderful to consider how this was brought to pass, as there were manifold oppositions, and the means so weak, by whom the Lord wrought, yet the success with which God blessed those improbable means. Therefore, that God may be admired by all those who shall hear or read this our narrative; we shall begin to declare how He began the work. He chose not the mighty and most eminent, for he needed not the help of men; but he first manifested his will to our brethren, John Miles and Thomas Proud, who, compared with others, were in the eyes of men far inferior to many in these parts, especially in natural abilities, that so the work might more eminently appear to be of God Alone."

Then the journey to London is related as above and their return. It is supposed that Messrs. Miles and Proud were baptized in London. In about a fortnight after their return, they observed some signs of a people to be gathered about Ilston. But it was about the beginning of October, 1649 when the two first were baptized there. When that was done, it appeared a day of small things, for at that time there was no great probability of any more (being) added to them. Yet the Lord went on, and four more were added, as the records observe. These were six women who had the honor to lead the way. The records say, "But afterward the Lord prospered the work, that in a short time we were grown to a considerable number" of men and women as appears there. "And being now in some settled posture, Brother Miles went into Brecknock Shire, about the middle of the 11th month, January,[3] where he had the opportunity to preach baptism to a society of professed believers meeting at Llanigon". But he did not Baptize any there then, only added

[3]The Baptists then began their year on March 1.

further advice to the Elders there, Messrs. Walter Prossor and James Hughs. Soon after, a letter was sent to Ilston, signed by these two Elders, dated the 22nd of the 11th month, 1649, informing how things went on. It may be supposed by that letter, that Mr. Proud was then with Mr. Miles at Llanigon. To that letter a reply was soon sent from the church at Ilston. Of these letters see more in the history of Olchon. Thus they went on prosperously for the first year successful at home and at a distance. They had a particular church meeting on the 16th of the 8th month, October, 1650.

The records give the names of all that had been added from the 1st October, 1649, to that day, and the parishes where most of them lived. That time was one year and a fortnight (Note: English fortnight fourteen nights, two weeks). The number then amounted to forty-three,[4] including Messrs. Miles and Proud, who probably were baptized in London.

On that church meeting (Oct. 1, 1649), they took into serious consideration the great distance of most of the brethren and sisters one from another, with other things that prevented their meeting together at their common place of worship, as often as they willed, during the winter season. Therefore, they then agreed that the church should break bread at Ilston on the first day once in three weeks. And the other first-days, the members in the Western parts of Gower, to meet at Llanddewi; those near Ilston, at Ilston; and those in Carmarthen Shire and those parts, at Jane Jones' house, or where most convenient that way. They appointed meetings in the week also; in the Welsh parts,[5] or Gower Land, on the 3rd day of the week, Ilston on the 4th, and at Llanddewi on the 5th. On these meetings inquiries were to be made regarding the conduct of those in the vicinity of the respective places, and advice, admonition, etc. given as appeared proper. There was a meeting for church discipline to be at Ilston, upon the 4th day morning once in three weeks. The chief ministers as yet, were, Messrs. Miles and Proud. There were others who exercised their gifts as will appear below.

The year 1650 was remarkable in these affairs. The letter from Ilston to Llanigon is mentioned above. That letter is in the Extracts, and also with the letter the church sent their brethren John Miles and Leyson Davis. After the letter, the Extracts says, "Now the Lord went so along with our brethren, whom we had recommended to God by our

---

[4] By the close of the next year, above, when 55 were added, we are to understand to the end of the 12th month, February, 1650.

[5] Gower Land was then and is still mostly English, so the borders of Carmarthen Shire they called the Welsh parts.

prayers, and then by our letters, that before they returned, a considerable number was there baptized, and joined together in the order of the Gospel." Now this is a plain account of the formations of this new church. See more of it in the History of Olchon, as above.

Ministers Added and New Churches Formed

The Extracts note that not long after this, Mr. David Davis, the minister at Kelligan sent to Mr. Miles to desire him to come over there; he went, and Mr. David Davis was baptized. He had been the minister of that parish some years before; he is among those added at Ilston this year. Though he had been so long in the ministry before, yet being a new member at Ilston, they had had his gifts tried there, and being approved, the Extracts say, "Being found very well gifted and able for the great work of the ministry, we thought good (together with the assistance of certain brethren of the church at the Hay)[6] to send him forth to preach to the world, and recommended him by our prayers, to the grace of God." Here we see two churches sending him forth.

The Extracts further say, "Not long after, it pleased God to discover unto us a work in the eastern parts of this country, where first there were some baptized, and joined in fellowship at Kelligare, Bro. Miles and Bro. Davis being present, and afterwards, our Bro. Miles and Bro. Leyson Davis, being sent from this church, together with our Brother David Davis and Brother Thomas Watkins of the church at the Hay, there was another considerable number baptized at another place not far,[7] and added to our said brethren at Kelligare and both parts being thus joined agreed to meet at Llanharan, and so there was another golden candlestick put up in these dark parts." Now here is another church set up, three in all. There is a letter, in the Extracts, sent from Ilston to the Hay in the 6th month, 1650. The Extracts present us with the following citation:

> The decrees and orders of the members of the two churches of the Hay and Llanharan assembled at Ilston, the 6th and 7th of the 9th month, 1650, who were sent thither by the said chur-

---

[6] The Llanigan brethren were called the church at the Hay then present.

[7] I think now that place is Brydes-Mynor in the Abstracts, see below, Brides- Miner is near Penysai.

ches to the brethren at Ilston, to consult with them concerning such affairs as are, through God's assistance, by them now determined and herein expressed.

The brethren seriously weighing the great scarcity of such ministers as will soundly hold forth the word of truth in Carmarthen Shire, and had seasonable opportunity now afforded by the providence of God for the propagation of truth in those parts, do judge that Brother David Davis shall henceforth endeavor to preach two first days of every two months at Carmarthen town, or thereabout; and that Brother Miles shall preach thereabout one first day in every two months; and that Brother Prossor likewise shall preach there one first day in every two months. Our Brethren are desired to consult and agree among themselves when it is most convenient for them respectively to be there . . . . And upon the like serious consideration of the present condition of our brethren at Llanharan, it is by the brethren here judged convenient, that a constant meeting be there kept by the churches until the Lord shall raise up more able men among themselves, and that Brother Davis be desired to be there present as often as he possible can; but when he is necessitated to be at Carmarthen, then our brethren of the Hay are desired to take care to send thither Brother Prossor or Brother Thomas Watkins, or some other whom they shall judge convenient . . . . Further, considering the present condition of such brethren as are to be employed in the work of the ministry, and the duty that lies upon each member to provide for them, it is judged necessary, and therefore it is desired, that the sum of thirty pounds be sent by the churches in equal proportions, ten pounds in each church, toward the maintenance of the ministry . . . . And as our Brother Prossor is not allowed any maintenance by any other way; and as we find in him much readiness to serve the Lord Jesus and his saints, in that painful and great work of the ministry, wheresoever he is there unto called, it is our duty to take special care of him; it is therefore desired, that out of the said thirty pounds a year, he be allowed twenty-five pounds a year.

Then the care of that collection is commited to three brothers there named, one in each church, the collection to be made quarterly. The remaining "five pounds to be disposed of as the churches shall jointly order." Here be it observed that Messrs. Miles, Davis and Proud, had what was then called *State Allowance* for their ministry, very probably.

The First Baptist Association in Wales

Here we may consider this meeting as the very beginning of the Baptist Association in the principality; it does not yet appear whether any were before in the kingdom except the seven churches in London. That this meeting was in consequence of serious consultations appears from the following passage in the Extracts:

> These three churches being thus settled, the Lord's goodness is still extended to us, insomuch that they are very much increased and settled, both with gifts and members, to the praise of his great name, and being so settled in some measure through grace, they be thought themselves how to carry on the work in Wales, and therefore mutually agreed, that upon the 6th and 7th days of the 9th month, 1650, they should have a general meeting at Ilston, of the members of each church.

Now this is a plain evidence that the above meeting was appointed before hand, and with a general view to promote the religious interest of the churches.

The Extracts say that the labors of the ministers above appointed to preach successively at Carmarthen, "were blessed with such success, that upon the 22nd of the 11th month, 1650, there was a considerable number Baptized and joined in church fellowship. The brethren Miles and Griffith being then and there present, so now there is another city of God in that town where Satan's seat was."

Letters From the Church in London

In this year there was a letter sent from the church at the Glass-house in London to the Churches of Christ in Wales as follows:

"Beloved in the Lord in Christ our Head:

We salute you, praying daily for you, that God would be pleased to make known his grace to you, so that you may be made able to walk before him in holiness and without blame all your days. We assure you it is no small joy to us to hear of the goodness of God to youward; that now the scriptures, again are made good, namely, to those who sit in darkness

God hath wonderfully appeared; even to you whose habitations were in dark corners of the earth. The Lord grant that we may acknowledge his goodness in answering prayers, for we dare boldly affirm it to be so, for we have poured out our souls to God, that he would enlighten the dark corners of the land, and that to them who sit in darkness God would arise, and God hath risen indeed. We cannot but say that God sent our Bro. Miles to us; we having prayed that God would give to us some who might give themselves to the work of the Lord, in those places where he had work to do; and we cannot but acknowledge it before the Lord, and pray that it may be more than ordinary provocation to us to call upon our own hearts, and upon each other's hearts to call upon that God who hath styled himself, God hearing prayers. And now brethren, we pray and exhort you to walk worthy of the mercies of God, who hath appeared to you; and that you exhort one another daily to walk with God, with an upright heart, keeping close to him in all your ways, and to go forward, pressing hard after the mark, for the mark, for the prize of the high calling which is in Christ Jesus. The Lord grant that you may be strengthened against the wiles of that evil and subtil enemy of our salvation, knowing that he and his servants turn themselves into glorious shapes, and make great pretences, speaking swelling words of vanity, endeavoring to beguile souls: but blessed be God, we hope you are not ignorant of his devices. Time would fail us to tell you how many ways many have been ensnared and (have) fallen; yet praised be his name, many have escaped his snares, even as a bird from the hand of the cunning fowler. So committing you to God, and the word of his Grace, we take leave, subscribing ourselves:

Your brethren in the faith and fellowship of Christ, according to the Gospel:

William Consett, Edward Cressett, Joseph Stafford
Edward Roberts, John Harmon, Robert Bowes.[8]

This letter happened not to be dated in the records; but the next is dated "At the Glasshouse, London, 12th of the 11th month, 1650," which was written to the young church at Llanharan.

The next letter in the Extracts is addressed to the church at the Hay, and signed by several of the above, and by Ri. Graves, William

[8] Of Thomas Bowes, see Crosby, Vol. 3. p. 137.

Comby, Thomas Carter, Rob Skyner, Pat Row, R. Cherry, Ralph Manwaring, Wm. Haines, and Nathan Allen. Then follows a letter to the Church at Carmarthen.

In a letter to Ilston about that time, they say, "We would know of any, whether those who have not been by water baptized into Christ, have put on Christ in the account of the Scriptures:

(1) Whether Baptism in water be not an ordinance of Christ expressly commanded by him, to be practiced by saints in the day of the Gospel;

(2) Whether it be not the duty of every believer to be obedient to every command of Christ in his word;

(3) Whether it be not sinful and disorderly for any who profess themselves disciples of Christ, to live in the neglect of a plain and positive command;

(4) Whether the Scripture commands a withdrawing from every brother that walketh disorderly;

(5) Whether Christ be not as faithful in his house as Moses was; and whether Christ's Commands, under the Gospel, be not to be observed with as much care.

Here it appears how remarkably friendly the church in London was to the infant cause in Wales, their letters were frequent, very judicious and instructive, as may be learned from what is given of them above. They behaved as a Mother Church indeed.

Administration of Baptism and Receipt of Members in the Different Meeting Places

In the 19th of the 12th month, 1650, the church at Ilston considered that the sister part of the church, about Aberavon was so far away that they could not be at Ilston on every general meeting (ordinance day probably); so it was judged more to the glory of God and the furtherance of the work, that when any would propose for baptism, there should be a meeting in those distant parts on the first day of the week to consider and judge who are proper subjects to be baptized. Then that ordinance was to be administered in those parts. But they were not to be members of the church until they came to Ilston and there be admitted. Members from Ilston might go upon those occasions to those distant parts to assist; and it was ordered that the brethren in the eastern parts would without fail send two or more from them to every general meeting at Ilston to acquaint the church there with the state of all things in the east, that so they might the better watch over them in the Lord, and perform such duties toward them as are required by the Lord our King.

Now we are come to the close of the notable year 1650. What a year that was in many respects! Mr. Miles began to baptize about the beginning of October, 1649, and by the close of 1650 they were about fifty-five members, as observed above, and not only that, but three other new churches formed, and these not very small either, still within the year 1650.

Further Associational Work

On the 19th of the 1st month, 1651, the deputies of the churches of Ilston, Hay, Llanharan, and Carmarthen, assembled at the place last named. This we may call their second Association. Here they considered the state, and consulted how to promote the welfare of the four churches, and observing the great want of an able ministry in and about Carmarthen, they with one consent determined and ordered, that the brethren first sent forth to the ministry be desired to take special care that the four churches be as much supplied as they, and with a constant ministry. To that end they desired Bro. Walter Prossor to be at Carmarthen three days in every eight weeks, and Bro. David Davis two first days, and Bro. Miles one first day, and the other two first days they were to be without any public ministry. Also, that when Bro. Prossor is absent at Carmarthen, Bro. Miles go to the Hay one first day, and Bro. Davis another, so that the place may not be slighted, nor the church hindered by Bro. Prossor's absence; and that while Bro. Davis is at the Hay, some brother from the Church be sent to Kelligare or Llanharan and that the Church at Llanharan may not be hindered by Bro. Davis' absence while at Carmarthen, it is ordered that Bro. Prossor be one first day, and Bro. Miles another at Llanharan or Kelligare, or thereabout, where it shall be judged most convenient; then the ministering brethren were to consult and agree among themselves when they were to be at the respective places. Then they considered and agreed how the expenses of traveling were to be defrayed. At this meeting also questions were proposed to be considered by the churches concerning singing in divine worship, and laying on of hands. Here we see not only the being but the real business of a Baptist Association in Wales.

On the 2nd of the 2nd month, 1651, for the ease and conveniency of the eastern part being far off, it was then agreed further, for the glory of God and edification of the whole church, and that members might not be burdened with long journeys, that the church should break bread at or near Bagland or Aberason, once a quarter when most convenient; and as many from about Ilston as can, may go thither then; that all the members of the eastern parts shall attend at Ilston once a quarter to break bread; and that two or more from those parts should be at Ilston every time of breaking bread. Several things were agreed upon regarding church discipline and government; also collections to be made for necessary uses in the eastern parts. The brethren Morgan Jones and William Thomas were appointed to take care of these things. The same day it was agreed that they should administer the ordinance of baptism in the western parts of the Church, on the borders of Carmarthen Shire, but still they were to come to Ilston to be received into church fellowship if approved.

Selection and Discipline of Ministers

On the 14th of the 3rd month same year, agreed "that Bro. Morgan Jones be approved to prophesy in the church, or any part thereof, before the world." By prophesying they understood to be preaching according to 1st Cor. 14: 3, etc.

On the 4th of the 4th month of the same year, "Bro. Proud was desired to preach publicly at such places as there are church meetings; and the brethren are to take special notice at every sermon, of his gifts, in order to his further approbation for the public ministry of the word." Mr. Proud was before a kind of an inferior preacher in the church.

The 15th of the 4th month, "Bro. William Thomas of Bagland was approved of to prophesy in all church meetings before the world." They exercised a considerable time in private among the members before they were admitted to preach publicly.

On the 16th of the 5th month, 1651, a member recommended to Llanharan. The same day, the abstracts say "Thomas Proud, having grievously sinned against God, by broaching that destructive opinion of maintaining mixed communion of the baptized and unbaptized in visible church fellowship, and having endeavored to draw others to the same judgement, by several ways and means, and so to rend and divide the church; as in preaching publicly contrary to the advice and order of the church; as also in willfully leaving and contemptuously forsaking thereof, upon discontent, when he was called to account for former offences; together with his slighting and contemning of the general meeting of the churches at Llanharan[9] as was certified to us by divers of the churches of the Hay and Llanharan, the church therefore withdrew from him the said Thomas Proud." Here is a proof how much the church was against mixed communion.

We are not to doubt but this church was properly constituted before this time, though no certain account is given in the Abstracts when that was done, and possibly that was omitted in the records; yet they were not properly organized and settled with proper officers, it seems, until the 29th of the 7th month, 1651. On that day they took into consideration their unsettled state for want of proper officers among them. That day they set apart to seek the Lord, by fasting and prayer, for direction in choosing church officers. Then with one consent, Bro. Miles was chosen and declared to be the pastor of the church: Bro. Morgan Jones, was chosen and ordained an elder and assistant in the government thereof to Bro. Miles; Bro. Leyson Davis was chosen and ordained a deacon; and the brethren, William Thomas of Bagland, and David Thomas, of Langenach were desired to exercise the office of deacons upon trial.

At this time it seems, Mr. Proud was out of communion, so he was not chosen to any office; yet the Abstracts observe that on the 29th of the 8th month, 1651, "Bro. Thomas Proud, from whom the church had withdrawn from the offences above mentioned, having often proposed, and been before the church, gave that day such full satisfaction, in all particulars to the church; and the community, with one consent agreed that he should be restored to communion, which was done with joy." He was out, it seems, about fourteen weeks.

Letters of Encouragement and Exhortation Among the Churches

The 13th of the 10th month, one of the members near Briton Ferry was recommended to the church at the Glasshouse, London, Mr. William Consett, pastor.

---

[9] This general meeting at Llanharan must have been in 1651 before the 16th of the 5th month.

There are no particulars of 1652 in the Extracts but a few members recommended to different places where it was convenient. But there is a letter from the church at Llantrisaint, to the churches of Christ at Ilston, Hay and Carmarthen, dated Llantrisaint 17th of the 8th month, 1652. It is not a long letter, but as it is a good one, and Mr. Backus was so kind as to send it, we shall insert it here, thus (See what is said at the close of the following letter, pg.53):

Honored and endeared Brethren:

We bend our knees to the father of our Lord Jesus Christ, that he goes along the countries, enlarging the kingdom of his dear Son, delivering souls that were held captive under Satan, who is called the God of this world, and the prince of the power of the air. Oh, the admirable love of God to us! that he should bring us from darkness to light, from the power of Satan to God; to receive remission of sins, and an inheritance among those who are sanctified, through the faith that is in Jesus! That he should fetch us home when we wandered from him, and manifested himself to us, who were alienated from the life of God through the ignorance that was in us, because of the blindness of our hearts! He hath made us near to himself, to be sons and heirs of God in Christ, who were afar off, even enemies and strangers to the covenants of promise. Our good God give us hearts to consider the wonderful things he hath done for us, and the inestimable things he hath promised to us; that we may be wise and watchful, how to walk worthy of such great mercies . . . . Dear brethren it behoveth you and us, to consider whither the goodness of God leadeth us, and whether we be better thereby, does it lay any ties or engagements on our spirits to keep close to the Lord, and to walk more holy before him; seeing the Holy Ghost hath told us, this is the will of God even your sanctification? Indeed we have great cause to mourn, and to walk humbly with our God in the sight and sense of our manifold failings and frailties; but our corruptions are so strong, and our graces so weak; that our God is so full of mercies to us, and we so empty in thankfulness to him; that he hath done us so many honors above all about us, in upholding, sparing, and protecting us, against all men's imagination that were designed against us, But oh! we have done little honor to God; we have been wanting to God, to ourselves, and to one another, in sundry duties, in our several stations. Let the word of the

Lord be dear and precious to your souls, by which you were called to the knowledge of God the Father, and of his Son Jesus Christ.

In all your actions, let your candle be lighted by the word, as David made it a lantern to his feet, and a light to his path; so shall you be taught how to walk one towards another and towards all men, and how to order the church of Christ. If your knowledge and gifts be increased, let grace humble you, lest jealousy swell you up. Oh! that the Lord would teach you and us to condescend one to another in things indifferent, minding the counsel of the Apostle, none to please himself, but every one to please another. Take heed of judging one another as void of grace upon every failing, lest all fall to judge one another as carnal, and as bite and devour one another, till you be consumed one of another: for it is not one act that makes one gracious, nor one failing that makes one ungodly. Let there not be such a spirit among you that strives to prepossess others against a brother or sister, to work prejudice or hard thoughts one against another, for that may divide the hearts of saints, and if our hearts be divided we shall be found faulty (Hos. 10: 2), and the grace of love will be lost among us. In the word we are advised to love one another, and that all our things be done in love. Saith the Apostle, love envieth not, thinketh no evil, suffereth long, is kind, doth not behave itself unseemly, is not easily provoked(1 Cor. 13: 4). Oh dear brethren! cry to the father that this grace may abide and abound in and among us; so shall we have much joy and delight in the society of each other, and be amiable in the sight of others, do not lie open to Satan's onsets: for it is his design to make breaches, and to enter in at all the breaches he hath made; to hinder the peace of the churches. Beware of watching faults in each other, but watch over one another, in love, to prevent faults. Watch to see corruptions in yourselves. So will you be humble in yourselves, and tender towards others. If some grace appears among many weaknesses in a brother, let the sight of that grace stir your affections to endeavor, in love, to recover the brother from his corruptions; and be not embittered by his weaknesses to deny or disown that grace which is to be seen in him. It is rich mercy that grace is to be seen in a Brother; and we must consider, there is more corruption than grace in the best. Let all the gifts and graces that God hath given you be employed to the edification of the body. Obey them who have the oversight of you, and esteem them for their work's sake.

Let not discipline be slacked or neglected among you. Let not him that hath five talents despise him who hath but two; and let not him that hath two envy him that hath five. Let every member study how to serve the body in his place and calling. Let not the foot "say" because I am not the eye, or the ear, therefore I am not of the body. Take heed of being wanton under mercies received; search the word and your own hearts, to bring them both together, and be not wise above what is written . . . . We the rather take occasion to call these things to mind, to you and to ourselves because of the willingness and watchfulness of the enemy to work upon any distemper that may arise in or among you or us; for Satan is busy here with us, presenting his designs afresh, seeking to delude unstable souls, and if it were possible to deceive the elect, to slight and suspect the ways and word of God, and the ordinances of our Lord Jesus Christ.

Wherefore, dear brethren, Let us cleave close to the Lord, his word and ordinances, and to each other, through whose grace we stand unshaken against the power of antichrist; and the Lord is adding to us such as believe.

Now dear brethren, desiring you to mind us before your and our Father, that he will continue his goodness to us, and pour of his Spirit of grace upon us, that we may stand unmoved, and go on in wisdom and power of his Spirit, to bear witness to his truth; as we shall likewise for you. We commit you to God and to the word of his Grace, to strengthen, settle, and establish you in every good word, work and rest.

Your brethren in the faith of Christ and fellowship of the gospel.

David Davis, Howell Thomas, Thomas Jones, Edward Prichard, Wm. Thomas, and Thomas Evans.

Now it may be just observed how profitably those young churches and the churches in London corresponded. Besides what is noted above, several letters and messengers passed between them, and no doubt were of mutual service. See more in the history of Olchon, page 17 etc. Now it is time to return to Ilston.

On the 24th of the 7th month 1653, a solemn consultation was held about prudent and imprudent marriages, and serious advice given upon that important subject.

That year was a general meeting or Association at Abergavenny, consisting of messengers from the churches of Ilston, Hay, Llantrisaint, Carmarthen, and Abergavenny. Of these general meetings here and elsewhere, see the *History of the Welsh Association,* printed in the *Baptist Register.*

In the Abergavenny records there is a letter thus prefaced, " A copy of the first letter we have received from the church at Ilston, for the church of Christ at Abergavenny." It bears no date, but by the contents it is probable that it was sent this year, 1653, either before or after the Association. It is an epistle of friendly advice, the close of it runs thus, "Endeavor to have peace with all men; speak and deal kindly with the poor blind world, pitying their sad condition as infants cast into the open field to the loathing of their persons. Endeavor in love to turn them to righteousness; for then you shall shine as the stars for evermore. Love and honor all saints, though as to baptism hitherto dissident: yet take heed lest your affections to them make you too much to bear them in their disorder. Go not you to them in their error, but let them come to you, who are in the truth; only be sure that your carriage towards such be very meek and affable. Take all seasonable opportunities to persuade them to their duty. Dear Brethren, we pray you, accept of these few exortations as the fruit and testimony of our dearest and tenderest affections towards you; so desiring to salute everyone of you in the Lord, we recommend you to our Father's Grace, desire your prayers, and rest.

"Your brethren in the faith and fellowship of the Gospel of Christ, John Davis, William Thomas, John Price, Lyson Davis, Hugh Matthew, John Miles, Harry Griffeth, Thomas Proud, John Gwilim, Matthew Davis, William Rees, Owen David, Simon Butler, Thomas Farmer, Evan Lewelyn, Thomas Hopkins, Morgan Jones, Thomas Ab Evan, Lewis Thomas, Evan Thomas, Llewelyn Ab Evan, Edward Hilzey."

This letter, like many more, breathes the love, friendship, and fellowship of those early days.

General Meetings of the Churches

On the 25th of the 10th month, 1653, a stated meeting was appointed to be at Swansea. It seems they had no stated meetings in the town before.

Though the Abstracts say nothing of it, yet the Abergavenny records say, that a general meeting of "the elders and other messengers" of the five churches was held at Aberavon the first and second days of the 1st month, 1654. This place was the eastern branch of Ilston Church. In all these general meetings, Mr. John Miles was the leading minister. The next general meeting of "the elders and messengers of the five churches was at Llantrisaint, on the 30th and 31st of the 6th month the same year. They had agreed at Aberavon to keep those public meetings half yearly, except any remarkable occurance caused it to be otherwise. At Llantrisaint meeting, the elders and messengers of the respective churches did sign separately, not mixed. Those from Ilston were John Miles, Morgan Jones, William Thomas, Morgan Jones, Harry Griffeth, John Davies, and Hugh Matthews.

The churches then put several of their members upon trial for the ministry, and when tried, several of them were not approved. In 1654, the community at Ilston agreed upon and wrote down a particular order regarding those brethren upon trial, and the time of their exercise, to prevent confusions.

There was a general meeting of the elders and messengers of these churches at Brecknock, on the 29th and 30th of the 5th month, 1656. The names of the elders, etc. are not in the printed account of that meeting, but Ilston is the first church named there. Of that see *The History of the Welsh Association.*

Letter From the Church at Dublin, Ireland

About this time of year there was a friendly epistle from the church of Christ, at Dublin in Ireland, addressed "To the churches of Christ at Ilston and Llantrisaint, in Glamorganshire." As it is not long this also must be inserted here:

Dublin,, 12th, 4th month, 1656

Dear Brethren:

We wish you a more deep rooting and stablishing in the faith. That no storms of persecution on the one hand, nor error and heresy on the other hand, may shake your faith. We thankfully acknowledge the good hand of God toward you in the multiplication of your members. The Lord multiply also your graces, that your faith may grow exceedingly; and the charity of every one of you all toward one another may abound. Ye are now in prosperous times, it will be your wisdom to prepare for a storm; for brethren, when ever did you know the people of God long without persecution? (Note: Four years after this letter a long persecution came, begun in March 1660.) Yea, and that from the powers of the world. Mariners in a calm, strengthen their tacklings against a storm to come. Besides ministerial teaching, we would commend unto you the use of good books, and take advice of some godly preacher, what books are fit to buy. Especially read the Scriptures, and study them: if you also study your own heart you shall do well.

Be careful to preserve entire unity, not only in keeping your communion together, but also in keeping your hearts together; sweetened in affection, one to another without grudgings and murmurings. Let those who are among you strive to be largehearted to the poor among you; and so much the more because of the present distress, and because of the great hatred of the world, which saints of our judgement endure. Be very wary against scandals, because where the Gospel comes in power the devil is wont to rage by scandals to swallow up, if it were possible, the church of God. We shall desire you to follow after enlargement of heart both in contributions toward the poor, and other churches, and in the maintenance of them who dispense the word to you, that such dispensers may give themselves wholly to the work, remembering that he who soweth sparingly shall reap sparingly; in which duty some of us have observed on your side of the water, sundry persons, yea we fear churches have come short. Individuals and churches in England since have been very generous and liberal. We desire you to press on for a stablished ministry and eldership in your churches, and herein be careful to buy the truth and sell it not.

Take heed of the sin of earthly mindedness, which sometimes lies hid under a large profession. Be careful of your weak members, lest wolves in sheeps' clothing, through pretended sanctity and seeming mortification, get in among them. Labor to keep in one another's hearts an honorable esteem of the Holy word of God; in opposition to the present delusions of the times. Engage not yourselves in heartless and speculative disputes; but rather be much in practical edifying truths; knowing that the principles which necessarily conduce to salvation are but few. Be careful that upon the pretence of church meetings, you neglect not closet prayer in which be careful to mourn under straits and rejoice in enlargements.

Labor after a just, blameless, and shining life, that the world by your harmless and holy lives may be instructed.

Treasure up large assurances against an evil day to come. Take heed of hardness of heart and declining affections toward the Lord. Let your conscience witness your blameless conversations for time past since your effecrual calling and your holy purposes for God in the future. We remain your affectionate brethren in the Gospel of Christ.

Thomas Patient, Christopher Blackwood, Edward Roberts, Richard Lawem, Thomas Seward. Henry Jones, P.Gudmore, William Hopkins, Arnold Thomas.

Regulations Drawn up by Ilston Church

On the 8th of the 5th month, 1657, the Church at Ilston framed nineteen new regulations, regarding the several branches of churches. Mr. Backus was so obliging as to write them at large in the Extracts, but the following are the most material of them, some given at large, some abridged, and others omitted nearly:

(1) The meeting at Ilston to begin every Lord's day at 8:00 in the morning; and to be every 4th day there, and that to begin at nine.

(2) To break bread at Ilston every month and on that day, Brother Proud or Brother Jones to exercise the first hour; then an approved Brother to exercise in Welsh the next hour; after that a sermon to the World, then proceed to break bread, etc.

(3) On other days, the first hour to be exercised in private by gifted brethren not yet sufficiently tried and approved, if business of discipline hinder not: the next hour to be exercised by approved prophets, or gifted brethren.

(4) That Brother Miles, or some other public minister, exercise on each of the said days, after the said brethren. If no other public minister be present, then Brother Evan Lewelyn to exercise instead of such.

(5) That for the present the Brethren John Davis, John Kneyth (probably Knight), Leyson Davis, and Jenkins Franklen,are to exercise successivly, so that one of them be sure to perform the said first hour at every meeting, and Brother Proud or Brother Jones the second hour. Should either of these be absent in his turn, he must get one to supply.

(6) The further Exercises on the Lord's Days when they do not break bread.

(7) The first 4th day of every month to be kept a solemn day of humiliation according to our agreement with the churches of Ireland, etc., to begin at 7:00 in the summer, and at 8:00 in the winter; to be ended as the church shall think fit. Very probably this day was observed by the five churches in Wales. (See the *Baptist Register,* par.1.p.14,etc).
(8) A meeting to be at Aberavon every Lord's Day and every fifth day about the same order as at Ilston; but dealing with offenders, and receiving into church fellowship to be always at the place last named: or upon their breaking bread days at Aberavon or Neath once in every 8 weeks.
(9) A meeting to be at Neath every Lord's Day and every 6th day: the Brethren David Davis, William Thomas, Lewis Thomas, John Thomas, Evan Lewelyn, to see that the meetings at Aberavon and Neath be properly supplied always by one of them at least to teach publicly at each of the said meetings. And a few things more under this head.
(10) A meeting of the Church officers to be at Ilston on the 6th day preceding every breaking bread day there; for Discipline and other church affairs. They wished all that were under trial for ministry to attend those meetings.
(11) A meeting to be at Swansea on the 2nd day preceding every breaking bread day at Aberavon and Neath, similar to that at Ilston, last article.
(12) A meeting to be at Swansea every Lord's Day that they do not break bread in any part of the church. The Brethren E. Lewelyn, Lewis Thomas, and John Thomas, to keep them in succession. Another meeting to be there every 3rd day of the week, to be kept in succession by brethren John Miles, T. Proud, M. Jones, D.Davis, and William Thomas. Another meeting to be at Langenach every Lord's Day and E. Lewelyn, Lewis Thomas, and John Thomas, to take care of them, any others upon trial to exercise there. A meeting for discipline there too, breaking bread and baptizing to be there also.
(13) This was about the collection in several parts of the church, and who was to care for it.
(14) That no Brother be admitted to hold forth any doctrines before the world at any appointed meetings, except such as are approved prophets or put upon the trial of their gifts for prophesying before the church.
(15) Regarding the important subject, marriage, nearly as above noted.
(16) The members of the several parts of the church give their names and the places of their abode to the deacons, that they may know who is absent, etc. and the deacons send the names to the pastor, so also all persons deceased, disorderly, or cast out.

(17) John Davis, John Pryce, and William Rees appointed to record in a book all church affairs, at the respective meetings; one of them to take care to be present then.
(18) Neither the church or private members to pass any censure, receive any members, or pass any acts, without the advice and consent of those who are over them in the Lord.
(19) That any brother or sister, being dissatisfied, may object against receiving any member "into fellowship that is baptized; and they should endeavor to satisfy them before they proceed to receive him" or them.
After these things the kind writer of the Extracts adds thus; "These are the last acts that I find recorded, except of Baptisms which are before given."

The records of Baptism after the above date are in the Extracts thus, "14th of the 6th month, 1657, two baptized;23rd of same month, two; 20th of the 7th month, four; 20th of the 8th month, one; and 13th of the 10th month, one. Ten in all that year."

The 7th of the first month, 1658, two; 23rd of the 4th month, two; Only four this year.

The 18th of the 7th month, 1659, five; 13th of the 9th month, one; 5th of the 12th month, two. Eight this year. The 24th of the 4th month, 1660, five; 23rd of the 5th month, two. The 12th of the 6th month, one. All this year eight; and these are last recorded in that book. The names of the three last ones, as in the Extracts, Jo. Weliteyeard of Lanridian, Thomas Morgan of Llamon, and Margaret Philip of Swansea. Here endeth the Abstracts.

Persecution and Scattering of the Churches

Now a few remarks:
1. The Restoration of Charles II, was on the 29th of May, 1660. About that time the persecution amounted to imprisonment, even in Wales, as appears near the beginning of Crosby's second Volume. The day last mentioned was the 29th of the third month, according to the year with the Baptist then. But by the above it appears that they baptized in Ilston Church in June, July, and August that year, before the pastor set off for America.
2. Mr. Backus in the History above referred to, page 351, says, "By the end of 1660, 263 persons had joined to that Church," at Ilston.

That appears to be true by the names in the records, and even in the Abstracts; yet they were not all baptized there, for several of them were recommended from other places. Nor does it appear how many members the church consisted of in 1660, as we have no account of those deceased, nor those excluded, etc.

3. The Abergavenny Records give an account of three general meetings in 1653 and 1654, and narratives there are much fuller than in the Ilston Records, it seems. The Extracts mention but one of those three, and say nothing of that at the Hay nor of that at Brecknock. Yet there is little more in the Abergavenny Records than those three meetings, nothing at all of any other general meetings. The Ilston Records are very full, but they cannot contain all things. We are highly obliged to the transcriber of the Abstracts. Had it not been for his kindness and repeated labor, in all probability Baptists in the Principality of Wales would have been in the dark regarding their origin in the country since the Reformation, as churches separate from the pedobaptists. By the last Extracts that is probably cleared up.

It does not appear when Mr. Miles sailed for America, when he landed in that country, nor what family, friends, or neighbors accompanied him. The first account we have of him west of the Atlantic is in Mr. Backus' History above referred to, Vol. 1, Page 353, naming Mr. Miles among the ejected ministers, it is added, "upon which, he and some of his friends came over to our country, and brought their church Records with them. And at Mr. Butterworth's in Rehobath, in 1663, John Miles, elder, James Brown, Nicholas Tanner, Joseph Carpenter, John Butterworth, Eldad Kingsley, and Benjamin Alby, joined in a solemn covenant together."

This was the first Baptist church in that part of America as noted above. It seems the men members of it were only seven. What number of women members there were we know not. It does not appear that any of the men members went with Miles to America, but Mr. Nicholas Tanner, said in the records to have been baptized on the 11th of the 11th month, 1651. This young church was then in Plymouth Colony; where they had quiet about four years: but at a court holden at Plymouth, 2nd July 1667, the society was fined in a considerable sum of money, and ordered to remove from that place. On the 30th of October ensuing, that court made them an ample grant in another place, which Mr. Miles and his friends called Swanzay. It seems they so spelled Swansea in Wales then. "There they made a regular settlement which has continued to this day . . . . Their first meeting house was built a little west of Kelly's Ferry, against Warren; but Mr. Miles settled the west side of the great bridge which still bears his name," Page 354.

In an Indian war, which broke out in 1675, Mr. Miles house was made the headquarters (Page 419). And in page 460 it is said, "The Baptist Churches in Wales gathered by our Mr. Miles and others, published a confession of their faith." There is no account of this in the Extracts; and perhaps not in the original records; but Mr. Backus found it somewhere. Speaking of the Baptist fathers at Boston in New England. Mr. Backus says;

> "The liberty they had enjoyed, with a blessing upon the ministry of Mr. Miles and others, had caused such an increase of members that in Feb. 7, 1677, they agreed to divide into two churches. But in January, 1678, they revoked that act, and concluded to build them a meeting house in Boston, and to defer the affair of dividing till they could obtain the settlement of an able sufficient ministry there. They first nominated Mr. Russell for this end, and then talked of his going to Swanzay in Mr. Miles' room. But in conclusion Mr. Miles returned to his old flock. (page 480)."

Page 506 etc. says, "The learned and pious Mr. Miles having returned to his flock in Swanzay fell asleep in Jesus on Feb. 3rd, 1683. And his memory is still precious among us. We are told that being once brought before the magistrates, he requested a Bible: and upon obtaining it he turned to these words: Ye should say, why persecute we him? Seeing the root of the matter is found in Me (Job 19:28). Which having read he sat down, and the word had a good effect upon their minds, and moved them to treat him with moderation if not kindness. His son went back to England, and his grandson, Mr. Samuel Miles, was an Episcopal minister at our Boston, in 1724."

This honorable character is given by Mr. Backus to our venerable country man during the space of about, or above, twenty years which he spent so laborious and useful in that country. It may be but right to add what a famous American writer, no less than the celebrated Dr. Cotton Mather, says of him; mentioning some godly Anabaptists, as he thought proper to style them, he names Mr. Hanford Knollys, then says: "And Mr. Miles of Swanzay who afterwards came to Boston, and is now gone to his rest. Both of these have a respectable character in the churches of this wilderness" (Crosby, Vol. 1, 120).

Dr. Calamy, in his *Account of the Ejected Ministers,* 2nd edition, said no more of this worthy minister than, "Ilston, Mr. John Miles, an Anabaptist." The name is wholly omitted in the index. But in his *Continuation*, it is added, "This was the sequestered living of Mr. William Houghton, Walker, (page 278, par. 2). Mr. Miles, after his ejection went to New England. Mr. Palmer only says, "A Baptist, he afterward went to New England." Probably the latter happened not to recollect what Crosby had cited from Mather; otherwise, I believe he was candid enough to have added that.

Swanzay in America is now a considerable town. The first Baptist Church there founded by Mr. Miles, is in a thriving state. There was a second church formed in the town in 1693. Mr. Backus in his letter of the 26th of October, 1792, says, "There is a large number of excellent Christians in both churches." A few hints of two more who *sailed* with Mr. Miles.

1. Mr. Nicholas Tanner, above named. It seems he was the only member of the church who accompanied the pastor to New England. He was one of the first constituents of the church there, as observed before. Of him Mr. Backus says, in the letter just referred to, that "He was a useful man in the town and in the church for many years. Having no child, he sent for his nephew, John Thomas, who was chosen a deacon in the first church in Swanzay, May 22, 1718, and was a worthy officer there for many years as his son Nicholas Thomas also was until his death a few years ago. John Thomas had a brother, Lewis Thomas, who was a zealous Episcopalian, as appears by his letters to his brother from Oxford, London.
2. Mr. Backus in the same letter says, "Obadiah Bowen came from Wales with Mr. Miles and hath a numerous, and respectable posterity in our land to this day."

Now let us take leave of New England and return to the persecuted church at Ilston, whose worthy pastor had left in afflictive circumstances. Several assisting ministers are named already. It does not appear that any of them went to America, either with or after the pastor. Some of them are named by Dr. Calamy, among the ejected ministers, but he gives little account of them, how they fared, what they suffered, where or when they died. The few hints found of them follow:

1. Mr. Thomas Proud. He went to London with Mr. Miles in spring, 1647, as before observed. In the letter from Llanigan to Ilston that year, he is represented as a very humble man. He is often named above as laborious and useful. It appears that he once embraced for a time, the opinion of mixed communion. For that his communion was suspended. He was again reconciled to the church and joyfully received into former fellowship (see page 50). For the first impression of Dr. Calamy's account he is called Thomas Proud. In the second edition it is Mr. Thomas Froude, an Anabaptist ejected from Cheryton Glamorganshire. This very probably was a slip at the press, but Messrs. Crosby and Palmer followed the error of the 2nd edition. The latter says nothing of him, but "A Baptist" and the former says: "I can find nothing of him." It seems he preached statedly as occasionally at Cheryton, as Mr. Miles did at Ilston. His being in Dr. Crosby's *Account* shows that he did not conform. So we need not doubt but he shared in the troubles of that time, though we cannot now learn how many, how great, or how long his sufferings were.
2. Mr. William Thomas was an assistant here, but of him see below.
3. Mr. Morgan Jones, there are two of these names in the list of members added. The first of Britain Ferry, added in the year 1650. The other of Lanmadock added, the 30th, of the 8th month, 1653. Two of the names signed as messengers from Ilston to the general meeting at Llantrisaint (see page 17 above) Dr. Calamy mentions but one of the names among the ejected Ministers. He says, he was ejected from Llanmadock, so probably he was the latter of the two above. But the character he gives to him is "An honest plowman," then adds, "had he been cast out for insufficiency, there had been no room for complaint."

Dr. Walker says that "George Perry, A.M. Rector of Llanmadock, was succeeded by an ignorant fellow, "one Jones." Here the two Drs. agree pretty well in the character of a Baptist and in their view of the matter. Dr. Calamy says not a word to vindicate him in his continuation had he not been a Baptist probably something had been said for him. When Dr. Walker said of two of Dr. Calamy's friends in Brecknockshire that one was a ploughmen, and other a weaver; the two are mentioned in the continuation of the ploughman. It is there said, "Still he might have got a living as well as others, if he would have but conformed." Of the weaver he says, "If we were to judge by others, he would not upon that account have been refused, if he would have come into the established church." But no such hint given in favor of poor Jones, though an honest man which is not said of the other ploughman, even of the weaver. But there was somewhat besides honesty that qualified him for the ministry, it seems in the judgement of the Baptist church at Ilston and of the Commissioners who then were appointed to put proper ministers in the proper churches instead of insufficient ones. The church and the commissioners knew the man better than either of the two Doctors did. What his sufferings were for his nonconformity we know not, nor where he died. But many worthy ministers in the principality, pedobaptists as well as others held the plow at times, as an agreeable exercise for relaxation.

4. Mr. Morgan Jones of Britain Ferry. Dr. Calamy takes no notice of him, but the extracts mention him very respectably, informing that he was added to the church in 1650, and probably was one of the first constituents of the church: that on the 14th of the 3rd month, 1651 he was approved to prophesy or preach in any part of the church before the world. See above that on the 29th, 7th month, same year, he was chosen and ordained elder and assistant to the pastor in the government of the church. And in several other places above he is named as a respectable, useful and reputable minister of the Gospel. Though Dr. Calamy said nothing of him, yet Dr. Walker (par. 2 page 338) mentions one whom he styled Morgan John, who very probably was this person, for he bestows on him the title of an Anabaptist. And says that he succeeded Mr. Theodore Price at Laleston, Tithegston, New Castle and Bettens in Glamorganshire. Of him see more in the history of Llenelli.

5. Mr. Evan Lewelyn. He is said in the Extracts to have been added the 23rd, 2nd month, 1651, but of the church at Llanharan, therefore probably he might be an original inhabitant of the bounds of the counties of Glamorgan and Llanmonth. In the regulations above (No. 4) it appears that when Brother Miles or some other minister was appointed to preach if none of those happened to be present then brother Evan Lewelyn was to exercise instead of such, this shows that he was then an approved minister to preach publicly. And in no. 12 above, Mr. E.L. was appointed and named the first of the three to take care of the meeting at Swansea, on certain days. And in the same number he is named the first of the same three named to take care in their courses at Langenach on certain days. Those hints amount to a proof that Mr. E. Lewelyn was a regular approved preacher in this church. We have no further account of this man. Therefore can give no information whether he died before the persecution began in 1660, or if he lived longer. What his sufferings were when he died see below.

6. Mr. David Davis. Of his see the history of Llantrisaint. ed in
7. Mr. John Thomas. The extracts name John Thomas of Margamas added to the church, on the 27th 9th month, 1650. And another of the same name and place added 13th, 3rd month, 1655. It is not quite certain which of those were the minister. But very probably the former. Be that as it may, he and Mr. E. Lewelyn are two of the three mentioned above, to take care of the meetings at Swansea and Langenach. As we have no further information of him, we can add no more concerning him but what is said above of Mr. E. Lewelyn his fellow laborer.
8. Mr. Lewis Thomas. The extracts inform, that he was of Margam and added to the church the same time as Mr. John Thomas, 27th, 9th month, 1650. For he was a public approved preacher in 1657 (see above regulations, no. 9 and no. 12).

Among all the sons this church brought forth and brought up for the ministry, this is the chief if not the only one left to guide her through the long tribulation from 1660 to 1688. A faithful guide and friend he was through all the storms: so is very probably the successor of Mr. Miles in history; though very probably Messrs. Proud and Jones, as them, were useful perhaps for a considerable time. But as we have neither printed nor written account of them as a church during that period, there is little to be now recorded of them, but that the society weathered through that long storm as others did generally.

Mr. Lewis Thomas was an indefatigable minister through all the tribulation. And by what is now known, his chief assistant in the meetting then was Mr. Robert Morgan. He does not appear in the abstracts as original member of this church. In the general meetings of 1653 and 1654 as recorded in the Abergavenny book, Robert Morgan is among those who signed the Breviates of those meetings, as a messenger from the church at Carmarthen. We hear of no pastor that ever that society had. Mr. Robert Morgan might, be a gifted brother then upon trial for the ministry. He must have been a member of some note then, as his name is fourtimes in those three general meetings at Abergavenny, Aberavon, and Llantrisaint. At the last they signed twice. It seems that when the persecution came on, they dissolved their church state at Carmarthen gradually, and that the members who stood their ground joined with the western branch of Ilston Church in Carmarthenshire and the borders of that way. Among the rest Mr. Robert Morgan united and by degrees took part of the Ministry. He resided in the western part of the church and Mr. Lewis Thomas in the eastern.

It does not appear that our denomination in Wales wrote any, or very few, records during the persecuting time. It was rather dangerous to write lest they should fall into the hands of persecuting enemies who then so frequently rifled the houses and the papers of the Nonconformists. In a manuscript, "Elegy composed on the Death of Mr. Lewis Thomas," it is said "that he shone as a star of great magnitude upward of forty years." Very probably he was fifty years or upward in the ministry. Messrs. Lewis Thomas, William Prichard, Dr. Christopher Price, and others in Wales bore their testimony honorably and cheerfully through all the hardships of those times. They were public spirited and like apostolic men. Besides there were Messrs. Thomas Quarrel, Thomas Watkins, Thomas Evans, Henry Gregory, Thomas Perry, William Jones, etc. These all weathered through the tempestuous times, and most of them afterward enjoyed years of peace and quietness.

Mr. Lewis Thomas lived at the Moor in the Parish of Newton Nottage, not far from Margam. His church lay very wide and scattered; they met to worship in a number of places. In a course of time the branches formed seperate churches for conveniency. They are now six or seven churches. The pastor was very laborious indeed, not only among his own wide flock but among other churches in Monmouthshire, etc. as appears in several places below. The Elegy observes that he preached and exerted himself indefatigably in Wales and England.

The Ilston Church Eventually Became Concentrated at Swansea

No more particulars can be found of this mother church during the persecuting time, and no record of those tribulations appear. No doubt their trials and hardships were many. In the printed narrative of the General Assembly in London, 1689, Mr. Lewis Thomas is named as pastor of the Church at Swansea. Ilston was then forsaken as the town was found more convenient. It cannot be found now how the original place had been left. Now that name must be dismissed as of further use in this History; yet be it done with respect for the sake of former times. I have now in my possession the original letter sent from this church to the General Assembly in London, dated the 4th of the 3rd month, 1690, at the house of John Morgan in the parish of

Llanon, Carmarthenshire (of this place see the history of Llanelli; there the two ministers above named are mentioned respectfully). I have also the state of churches in Wales, sent or taken to the same assembly. There likewise the two are named.

The number of members in this church is set down to be above seventy or eighty living mostly in Glamorganshire. This was a great reduction in the space of thirty years, yet we have no information how many members were there in 1660. Though 263 be recorded, and in the Extracts as added from the beginning to that time, yet they might be not many more than half that number in actual communion in the close of that year, as it had been trying, winnowing, times. The pastor and one or more members with him had gone to America, some frightened by the persecutions, some gone to distant places, others to their long home.

In a letter from Mr. Robert Morgan, to Mr. Benjamin Keach, London as supposed, dated 30th-10th month-1687, it is said that many of the wealthy did not keep well their places in the persecution, and could not be recovered by all the means the church could use. Some of them had conformed, and others in a halting situation. These things reduced the churches in Wales, and other places, in those long continued troubles.

In the Narrative of the General Assembly in London, 1692, Swansea is mentioned and Mr. Lewis Thomas, pastor as before. After that year the General Assembly divided into two, for the conveniency of shortening the journey, and lessening the expense: one held in London the other at Bristol. Wales attended the latter, being nearer. The account and narratives of Bristol and Western Assemblies from 1693 to 1700 cannot be sufficiently found now. In the Blaenau records, there is a list of churches met by their Messengers at Bristol in 1694. The Welsh churches were there. But Llanon is named and not Swansea. That was the meeting place of the Western branch, and in Carmarthenshire, but still it was Swansea church.

The churches of the principality of Wales attended at Bristol, and in the west, annually till 1699. By that time our countrymen wished to have an association themselves, without crossing the waters, and they did not all understand English well. For various reasons they agreed to have it, the first of that kind after the Revolution was held at Llanwenarth near Abergavenny, 1700. There a commodious meeting house had been lately built. The association was held there next year in the same place; but at Swansea in 1702. By that time they had a convenient meeting house there likewise. After that the annual meeting was held alternately at those two places until 1708. Then it succeeded in a kind of rotation after that.

The association then, and ever since sent a circular letter to the respective churches, and the ministers and messengers generally signed it, till they agreed to print the letter. While Mr. Thomas lived, his name was first in signing, being the leading minister in those conventions. He signed the letter at Llanwenarth in 1703, though then aged, and the way so far, yet he attended. Next year the association was at Swansea: but Mr. Thomas had gone to a better Assembly the preceeding March, 1704. He had been strong, vigorous, and active through many tribulations, but his vigor and strength were much worn out and exhausted at last. The Elegy informs that when he could not stand, he like Jacob prayed leaning upon his staff. It observes further that he had been instrumental in the conversion of many souls. Suffered himself to be plundered and imprisoned rather than to forsake his profession and sin against God. In the letter from the church to the association in 1704, they lament the loss of their most able, and noted pastor, who had been long a faithful shepherd.

Thus this great and able minister finished his course, having long fought a good fight, and kept the faith. His memory was precious and edifying to most, if not all, that knew him while they lived and many who never saw him were much affected by the great things they heard of him.

On the death of the pastor the church had two or three among them who exercised in the ministry: Mr. Robert Morgan was far advanced in years, and had long borne the burden and heat of the day; Mr. Morgan Jones who began his ministry about the end of the persecution, 1688, or possibly before; and Mr. John Davis who is supposed to have begun his ministry not long before the pastor died. As Mr. Morgan Jones was of a very acceptable talent, and they had the trial of him so long he was naturally fixed upon; the others being one very aged, and the other young; so he accepted the pastoral care.

In the persecuting time, and years after, this mother church had no proper meeting house, they met to worship in friend's houses, for near fifty years. And long after the branches so met. They had several houses where they assembled as most convenient, in and near Llanon and Llanelli and Carmarthenshire, also in Llangyfelach and several other places in Glamorganshire. It appears above that they kept meetings in Swansea before 1660, but it is not now known where they were kept. The first place that the late Mr. Griffith Davis heard of as a meeting place in the skirts of the town was the house of Rees ab Evan called by the English, the Washing Lake. According to the Extracts, Rees ab Evan of Swansea was added to the church on the 1st day of the 12th month, 1656. It seems he lived long and bore the troubles of the times with honor and dignity, they met here until 1698. The house was since taken down and rebuilt.

When the dissenters enjoyed the blessing of liberty, the Presbyterians in town fitted up a place of worship. But in 1698 they erected a more commodious house for the purpose. Then the Baptists took the old place at an annual rent, and from that time forward they had open public worship in the town. The Washing Lake was rather in the skirts. Probably this was the reason why they did not date letters at Swansea in 1689 and 1690, but the printed narratives of the assemblies in London in 1689, etc. call the church Swansea, as they met near the town, and lived in and about it. And even after they began thus to worship in town, they did not transact their church affairs in that meeting house, and for some reasons they quitted the old place, the Washing Lake, then met at a friends house called Llodraubrith about a mile or more out of town. That was the dwelling house of Mr. William Morgan, a very worthy member, living in good repute upon his own estate. The Extracts mention William Morgan of Bishopston as the third man that was added to the church, about the last of 1649, so this was one of the first constituents of the church. There is another William Morgan of Swansea, added the 30th of the 8th month, 1653, probably one of these lived at Llodraubrith. Be that as it may, he that lived there about 1700 was no small honor and credit to his profession.

At his house they kept church meetings. There they baptized at a place fitted for the purpose; this continued for many years. But the son of the same name, did not follow the steps of the father, nor did he much adorn the Gospel. He being reduced in the world, the paternal estate was sold before he died. He also lost a son of the same name, who was a very worthy young man, similar to his grandfather. It is supposed that he was baptized at Llodraubrith when a very young man, in 1739. Soon after he was dismissed to Blaenau in Monmouthshire, as he then resided with an uncle there.

In that church he was regularly called to the Ministry about 1744. His talents were acceptable and promising. He was very ready in both languages, which is not common in the principality. In 1748 he accepted an invitation to the destitute church at Shrewsberry. There he was during life, which was not long. In the summer 1753 he set out with the design to attend the association at Halifax, Yorkshire; but falling ill on the road he returned as far as Chester, where he finished all his work and soon gave up the ghost. He was interred in the burying ground belonging to the Dissenters at Wrexham. He was an acceptable Gospel minister. At death he left a mournful widow and three children. The mother died lately, now about 1795, though next summer it will be forty years since that event, and one of the children if not more is now dead.

The church used the old meeting house in Swansea for sixty years then took a fresh lease on the land for ninety years and erected a new meeting house upon it in 1758. Mr. Griffeth Davis, their pastor then exerted himself much to bring about the new place and finish it. Not many years back they kept their church meetings and baptized in the town.

These things about meeting houses and places are here put together as the information was given by Mr. Griffeth Davis just now named, who was born near the town in 1699, and his parents were very active, hospitable, and useful members. Besides his own memory, which was very good in these things, he had a small book containing some church records in the beginning of this century. There it is noted, that about 1708, meetings were kept in several distant places in the country. Besides the places already named, they met to worship at Bryngwyn in the parish of Castle Llwchwr, by the English Longhor. The letter to the Association in 1704, says that the church met in Llanon, Bryngwyn and Swansea. But for many years back, the second of these three places hath not been occupied for public worship.

It is observed above, that Mr. Lewis Thomas was succeeded in the pastoral care by Mr. Morgan Jones. Of his ancestors, see Llanelli. They lived at Alltfawr (vulgarly called Allimawr), in the parish of Llanon. There the meeting was chiefly kept in that branch. Mr. Jones married a daughter of Mr. Griffeth Griffiths, a gentleman of reputation and family in Carmarthenshire. The daughter was a godly, serious, young woman, and a member of the Baptist Church: but the parents were no friends to that denomination. They were so displeased with the daughter, that they deprived her of what was her right and equity of her own. Their plea for such a conduct, was that she had left the established church, and turned to be a phanatic.

By these things, with the repeated plunders and oppressions of former persecutions, that were but lately over, Mr. Jones was sometimes reduced to considerable straits. Mrs. Jones bore an excellent character every way, but she died young and left children; yet her parents absolutely refused to the last to give or leave her rights, either to her or to her children, though on her death bed she solemnly charged them as they were to answer before God not to deprive her husband and her motherless children of what was their just due.

Account of Dr. Philip James

As another affair similar to this happened in this same country it seems to demand a place here. The case was thus. There was another country gentleman in these parts who had a son; the report of present descendants is that he was an only child. He was designed for the church in the establishment, and educated with that view. Information says that the father lived in the parish of Landilo-tal-y-bont in Glamorganshire, but adjoining to Carmarthenshire. That was the very panish where Mr. Robert Morgan lived, who was co–pastor of Swansea Church. The young man's name was Philip James. He contracted intimacy with the Baptists and probably was baptized in these parts, that is only supposed. However he was not free to proceed, as the parents intended, and to embrace all the terms of conformity. Therefore he showed some reluctance to proceed.

When his parents perceived it, they were highly displeased, and even exasperated. Not being able by any means to prevail with him and persuade him to go on as it was designed by them, they determined to discard him wholly and own him no longer, but turn him adrift to live or die. According to information they did so; probably this was in the persecuting times, when he was about 21, which was about 1685 or possibly sooner. Being thus turned out, he was directed by some providence to Liverpool. There he engaged for some time with one, Mr. Fabus, a Baptist who followed some branch in the physical line. Here Mr. James made no small improvement, and attained to a very considerable degree of knowledge and skill in physics. He engaged in the ministry among the Baptists, and practiced in public occasionally. Whether he began to preach at Liverpool or no is not certain, though he probably did. Whether he was honored with a diploma or no, his common title was Dr. James. By some providence he became intimately acquainted with Mr. Lawrence Spooner and family at Curborow, a village near Lichfield. In that worthy family, Dr. James found an agreeable partner in life.

How long the Dr. lived with his father-in-law at Curborow cannot now be ascertained. But about 1704 or soon after, Dr. James was invited to the pastoral care of the Baptist Church at Warwick, which he accepted. He continued in that charge until he removed to Hempstead, Herts, not far from London. That removal was about 1718, according to my information; some suppose it was two or three years later. That is not now very material. He finished his course at Hempstead in 1748, aged 84. Mr. Thompson of London, in his account of that church, recorded, that "the church invited the Rev. Philip James, M.D. to the pastoral office among them which he accepted." Then adds, "Dr. James was a gentleman of learning and piety."

Account of Samuel James

Dr. James had four sons, Philip, Caleb, Timothy and Samuel, who are now all dead, and one daughter alive lately, perhaps now 1793. His son Samuel was a very worthy Baptist minister at Hitchin, Herts. In 1760 he published: "An Abstract of the Gracious Dealing of God with Several Eminant Christians in their Conversion and Sufferings." The first account there is of his grandfather Spooner, who was a useful minister, and a considerable sufferer for religion. Prefixed to the abstract, there is a savory serious letter, in which it appears that the editor was settled at Hitchin in 1743. The publication was so acceptable that it went through the third edition in 1766. Mr. Samuel James finished at that place in 1773, aged 57. The Swansea Church has a right to these short hints: and the followings ones.

It has already been observed that Dr. James's father lived in the parish of Landilo-tal-y-bont, and that Mr. Robert Morgan, one of the pastors of this church lived likewise in that parish. He was a school master there many years, and possibly Dr. James might have had part of his education under his tuition. But be that as it may, Mr. Robert Morgan had a son whose name was John, a very promising young man, a good scholar and of an agreeable talent for the ministry. By some means the Baptist Church at Warwick had some intelligence of him and invited him to them, though but young. After some time he agreed to go. He preached a farewell sermon to his friends, and set out for Warwick intending to settle there; but either he fell ill on the road or soon after his arrival so that in about a week he finished his short race. He was buried in the meeting house, and this inscription upon his grave stone, now hardly legible, yet there still:

"To the memory of Mr. John Morgan of Landileo,in Glamorganshire, minister of the Gospel. He parted this life the 12th of May, 1703 in the 24th year of his age. *Sist Advena Mors Tibi etiam progimqua est."* (Translation: He has arrived at the still River of Death).

I am strongly of the opinion that this was composed by Dr. James who was of the same parish as Mr. Morgan, so intimate with the father and the successor of the son. It seems Dr. James was at the association at Swansea in 1704. As the circular letter of that year names him as appointed to preach the associational sermon at Llanwenarth in 1705. These two articles I can hardly call a digression, but part of the real history of this church. Though the strictures on the successor are given first, yet we should remember that the successor was really the senior, and perhaps a senior member of this church.

Account of Morgan Jones

We left Mr. Morgan Jones in a sorrowful state, bereaved of his worthy wife, and his children. He was born about the entrance of that grievous persecution which began in, and before 1662. He had seen much, and had heard more about those troubles from his father, grandfather and others. His heart was much weaned from this world by a blessing among his troubles. His meekness and patience were more than common, he was eminent in prayer, and had some peculiar answers to his petitions. His successor Mr. John Davis knew him well from his infancy, and heard much about him.

In 1776 I happened to have an opportunity to converse with him about his predecessor. He then related this anecdote as certain fact. Mr. Jones at a certain time in a strait, borrowed a sum of money, not large. But the creditor demanded it sooner than it suited the borrower to return it. He threatened that if he did not return it on or before a certain day named, he should have trouble. The good man was much distressed, being so circumstanced that he could not devise where to have it, the time being so short. The day appointed arrived, and the money he didn't have. There was in a certain house in Swansea, a back chamber where Mr. Jones used to retire at times. Thither he came on that day full of trouble in mind. To his chamber he went and earnestly prayed, that deliverance might be granted, by some means, and the gospel not reproached on his account, etc.

The people of the house supposed that he was gone to his chamber to pray, while he was there a person called at the door, and inquired whether Mr. Jones were there. He was answered that he was expected soon. The man said that Mr. Beavan wanted to see him immediately. There seemed to be uncommon haste. Mr. Beavan was one of those called Quakers. Mr. Jones soon came out, and was told that Mr. Sylvanus Beavan had sent for him to come to him with speed. He went and was thus immediately addressed. "Art come, Mr. Jones? I am ordered by friend Pycard of Barnstable to pay thee and Lewis Thomas, so much money. I will pay thee the two sums if thou please, only then take care to it to Lewis Thomas." So he had the money. His own sum was not enough to pay the creditor that day. But the two was enough and plenty over. Thus the whole money was punctually, cheerfully, and honorably paid. When Mr. Jones saw Mr. Lewis Thomas he related the whole story. They both rejoiced and were thankful. Mr. Griffeth Davis said he knew the place where Mr. Jones was praying.

Though Mr. Jones was so humble, meek, and passive, yet he was very quick at replying upon occasion, it was to him a natural talent. This instance may be given here. He happened to call at a house in Swansea, where two neighbors were engaged in a warm debate about religion, one had lately turned to be a Roman Catholic, the other a Churchman. Mr. Jones upon entering the place accidently, entered into this dialoque.

Churchman: Oh neighbor! I was never more glad to see you.

Mr. Jones: Why? What is the matter now?

Churchman: My neighbor here is lately turned to be papist, and he has the face to say, that the church of Rome is the true mother church, and that the church of England is but a bastard of the church of Rome.

Mr. Jones: Ho! Ho! Betwixt you be it, I am neither of the one or the other, so I need not say anything in your debate, plead it out.

Catholic: Good reason why, because you have nothing to say.

Mr. Jones: May be so; but what have you to say?

Catholic: What to say? I say, that the church of Rome is the true Catholic Apostolic Church, and that the Church of England and all you phanatics, are but bastards of that church.

Mr. Jones: Softly neighbor; boast not too much, for if the children be all bastards, then the mother must needs be a whore, you know.

Upon this word, the spirit of the Catholic sunk, and the other began to crow. Here very probably the debate ending. Mr. Jones cut it very short.

Recommending Members By Letter to Like Churches in Distant Places

In the time of Mr. Jones' pastoral care, as well as before, many of the Baptists went from this and other churches to America. The following letter appears in their short records, which shows their orderly way and methods on such occasions. The copy of the original is in the book thus:

South Wales in Great Britain

"The church of Jesus Christ meeting at Swansea, in Glamorganshire, teaching believers baptism, laying on of hands, the doctrine of personal election, and final perseverance. To any church of Christ Jesus in the province of Pennsylvania, in America, of the same faith and order to whom this may concern. Send Christian Salutation: Grace, mercy, and peace be multiplied unto you from God the Father through our Lord Jesus Christ.

Dearly beloved, Brethren in our Lord Jesus Christ:

Where as our dearly beloved brethren and sisters by name, Hugh David, an ordained minister, and his wife Margaret, Anthony Matthew, Simon Matthew, Morgan Thomas, Samuel Hugh, Simon Butler, Arthur Melchior, and Hannah his wife, design by God's permission to come with Mr. Sereney to the fore said province of Pennsylvania: This is to testify unto you, that all the above names are in full communion with us, and we commit them, all of them to your Christian care, beseeching you therefore to receive them in the Lord, watch over them, and perform all Christian duties toward them as becometh Christians to their fellow members. So we commit you and them to the Lord, and to the word of his grace, which is able to build you and them up in the most holy faith. May the God of peace ever sanctify you wholly, and that your, and their spirits, souls, and bodies, may be preserved blameless unto the coming of our Lord Jesus Christ shall be the earnest prayers of your brethren in the faith and fellowship of the Gospel.

Dated the 30th of the 7th month 1710: signed at our meeting by a part for the whole:

"Morgan Jones, John David, William Matthew, Jacob Morgan, Owen Dowle, Morgan Nichols, John Howell, Hugh Matthew, Robert Edwards, John Hughs, Philip Matthew, Thomas Morgan, William Morgan," (and another name not legible).

Mr. Morgan Edwards in his, "History of the Baptists," in Pennsylvania, 1770, gives an account of a church formed by the Baptists there at a place called Great Valley; and noted Mr. James Davis as one of those who came from Wales to that country about 1700. He was an original member at Rhydwilim, on the border of Pembrokeshire. There was another from Radnorshire whose name was Richard Miles. These two and families consorted together, and invited ministers from other parts to preach at their houses. In time several were baptized there. Before the end of 1710, Rev. Hugh Davis and others settled in the same neighborhood, which increased the number to sixteen; they incorporated and formed a church April 22, 1711, and chose Mr. Hugh Davis to be their minister.

Of Mr. Hugh Davis, Mr. Edwards says that he was born in Cardiganshire, 1665, was baptized and ordained at Rhydwilim; was a man of parts with a natural turn for satyr; which he managed to advantage in his sermons. Some years before his death he had severe pain in his arm, which gradually worsened and made life a burden. After trying many remedies he sent for the elders of the church to anoint him with oil according to James 5:14. The effect was a perfect cure, so far that the pain never returned. He died in October 1753. So he lived to a good old age.

In the letter from Swansea he is named Hugh David, but in the history, Hugh Davis. That is a very common case in our country. The letter says he was in full communion at Swansea. The history, that he was baptized and ordained at Rhydwilim. That might all be very true, and be yet in full communion at Swansea in 1710 by some providence occurring.

Account of Robert Morgan

Mr. Robert Morgan was mentioned above. This is the proper place to give a few hints more of him. It is there obvious that he signed at the general meetings in 1653 and 4. His wife died young and left him with six small children, which reduced him to considerable straits. For the support of his family he kept school many years, and preached at home, and abroad, see in the "History of Hengoed", how useful he had been there. Those things are full in the letters giving an account of the churches in Wales above 1690.

By a letter in my possession it appears that Mr. R. Morgan attended the general Assembly in London, 1689, and that in the printed narrative his name should have been inserted at Swansea, and not Francis Giles, who belongs to Llanwenarth. His son John is mentioned above page 66. Hannah Melchior, named among those who went to America in page 75 was his daughter. The father lived with the daughter and her husband the latter part of life. It is supposed that he died either a little before, or soon after they sailed, age about ninety, very weak and worn out. I saw an aged member who knew, and heard him and his son. His son David kept a meeting in his house at Llynlloughor, not far from the place where his father lived. He was very useful in the church.

David had two sons, Robert and Isaac, who also were members at Llanelli; of which see below. Robert was a deacon and died, 1776. I have been of the opinion, for many years that Mr. Robert Morgan's eldest son, was called, after the father's name, Robert, and that he was a school master in London. My opinion is made up by these considerations. Mr. R. Morgan was himself a school master. It was natural for him to educate and qualify his eldest son to be his assistant, and to supply his place as he was often out, especially when he served Hengoed; so far off.

About 1689 the father contacted intimacy with the then famous Benjamin Keach and other ministers of note then in London, as appears by his original letters in my possession being brought here from London among Mr. Isaac Marlow's papers. This might naturally make way for the son to settle in the capitol.

William Crosby (Vol. 4, page 114) gives an account of the origin of the dissenting community school set upon Horsly-down, Southwarls, London, 1715, and that the first school master there was Mr. Robert Morgan a member and an assistant teacher of the Baptist Church under the care of Mr. Benjamin Hinton, successor to Mr. Keach, and successor of the late Dr. Gill, and the present Dr. Rippon in which place he behaved himself to the satisfaction of the society to the time of his death (Ms.,p.123).

Several close inquiries have been made into this affair in Wales, and in London; yet it could never be cleared up to satisfaction; the inquiry was too late.

A late letter from London informs that Mr. Robert Morgan died in 1723, but could give no account of his native place. He left a widow (but it seems no issue) that letter says that the present records of the school notes Mr. Morgan to have begun the school in 1714. This is all I have been able to find out.

Account of Morgan Jones

Mr. Neal, author of the *History of the Puritans,* by some means obtained an account of the Baptist Ministers in Wales in 1715. This in Manuscript which is yet in London probably in the library of Dr. Drew Williams, but this information is often inaccurate. Here it says Carmarthenshire, Melin-Voel, Morgan John, John David Glamorganshire, Swansea, Morgan John. A stranger in reading might naturally conclude them to be two churches, having two ministers of the same name. But the truth was, Melin-Voel, mostly called Llanelli and formerly Llanon, was then a branch of Swansea. Mr. Morgan John was pastor and Mr. John David his assistant. The modern way of John and David is Jones and Davis when surnames.

Although Mr. Jones really succeeded Mr. Lewis Thomas in 1704, yet according to the said little Book of Record, there was a hint of a church confirmation of his choice and call to the pastoral charge, and his acceptance of it, as late as 1717. This certainly should have been sooner.

Mr. Jones was a very discreet, prudent man, and of a very peaceful disposition. When a disagreeable contention happened to break out at Rhydwilim, which grieved many worthy persons, the association was to be at Llanelli still a branch of Swansea in 1725. I have now the letter from Swansea to the assembly, and am confident it is a very affecting, persuasive, work upon church peace. It seems to have had a very good effect: a reconciliation was made at that very meeting.

A word in season, oh how good it is!

Mr. Griffith Jones the pastor's son had begun to preach about 1714. Being then about 19 years of age. He assisted the father, and preached in other churches till 1726. That year Pen-y Sai Church was formed in love for the sake of conveniency. It had been about 76 years a distant eastern branch of Ilston and Swansea. The young church chose Mr. Griffith Jones to be their pastor. More of this in the history of that church.

Not long after this, the father's health and strength gradually, but visibly decayed: yet he continued a few years to serve his people as strength permitted. On a breaking bread day at Swansea, another preached for him, but it seems he administered the ordinance. Upon parting he went to prayer with them all, communicants and spectators. He was carried out in his addresses to God, and was in such a loving, heavenly melting frame that it is said, there were few if any,dry eyes in the place. Then he talked, advised, comforted, the people till his small strength was spent almost wholly. He took a very affectionate leave of them, gave his Bible to a poor member: and desired two friends to support and help him, having not strength to walk himself. On the road home in the town, he turned to a kinsman's house to rest a little. In a few minutes he there expired and entered into eternal rest. Thus the life of this worthy Gospel minister, much resembled that of the famous Mr. George Tross of Exeter, of whom a particular affecting account is given by Mr. J. Palmer in his *Nonconformists Memorial* (Vol. 1, page 427).

This relation of Mr. Jones was given in a letter by his grandson, and rectified by Mr. Griffith Davis the successor, who probably was present at the time. Mr. Jones died on the 29th of November, 1730, aged 68, and was buried at the Presbyterian meeting house, and a stone was upon his grave. After this decease the church was some years without a settled pastor. They had some very worthy men who preached among them. The senior was Mr. John Davis mentioned above more than once. He was a godly acceptable preacher, but so extremely modest that he would not accept the pastoral care of any people. Nor would he be ordained; as Mr. John Davis told me himself.

The next senior was Mr. Griffith Jones son to the late pastor. He was then chiefly at Pen-y Sai and the minister of that young church as observed above: but he administered ordinances at Swansea after his father's death. Part of the church was inclined to choose him to succeed the father; yet all could not agree in that. The other two were Mess'rs. Griffith Davis, named before, and David Owen. These were younger in the ministry, though not very young in years, and worthy men, very acceptable in their talents. Thus they continued for five years. All preached in rotation. Mr. Griffith Jones administered ordinances chiefly and preached often.

In 1735, the Carmarthenshire branch in Llanon, Llanelli, etc., formed into a separate church for conveniency as Pen-y Sai had done nine years before. This young church chose Mr. David Owen to be their pastor. He lived among them.

Account of Griffith and John Davis

Mr. Griffith Davis had many religious privileges and advantages from his infancy. His parents being so hospitable, and ministers often calling as they passed. He had heard much of former troubles, and he remembered well many occurrences and anecdotes he had heard in conversation. He was baptized in 1721, and began to preach about 1726. When Mr. Jones died it seems the major part of the church had their eye upon him to succeed. But for further improvement in the English, and other articles useful in the ministry, he went for some time to Bristol, under the care and tuition of the worthy and learned Mr. Foskett then assisted a little, and much more after, by the late celebrated Mr. Hugh Evans. After he returned to Swansea, he improved much by the kind assistance of Mr. Palmer the Presbyterian Minister there. He blessed God to the last for the great benefits he had received every way by his kindness. With emotions full of affections he used to style him, "the pious Mr. Palmer".

The pastoral care fell upon him gradually. He was ordained about 1736, in a kind of a probationary way, and the whole confirmed and settled in 1739. Mr. John Davis named above, was by this time advanced in years. He had seen and heard much of the former and latter troubles on account of religion; had been very useful and acceptable in this church and in others. It is probable, though not certain, that he began to preach about 1703, if not before.

About 1736, there was a very severe press for soldiers. The association was appointed to be at Swansea that year. The ministers and messengers assembled; the public meeting was appointed to be on the morrow. They heard there was a press going in town, and supposed the contrivance was to come to the meeting to press the young men.

and take them off at once. It was judged prudent to drop the appointed meeting, and all to return quietly homeward to disappoint the hostile plan.

This is recorded in the Blaenau Church book. In those days several young men were pressed at meeting and taken off. I had the following anecdote of Mr. John Davis without any date; but probably it happened about this time. The fact was this: when young, he was a very personable man, tall and genteel. Upon a time he was preaching near Llanelli in that branch of the church. Mr. H.J. a gentleman in that neighborhood was resolved to take the preacher, and said, he would see him fast enough within a week. The air of his menaces was even tremendous. But behold, before the week had expired the gentleman was arrested by death, the King of terrors; thus was himself put fast enough, so that he could not disturb other preachers or hearers. It is supposed he designed Mr. Davis for a soldier.

In his latter days Mr. Davis grew corpulent and heavy, yet was active and useful much respected at home and abroad. In the account of the ministers in the principality, sent to London in 1734 of Mr. Davis is said that he was an aged, affectionate, diligent, useful, and acceptable preacher; and that the church designed to choose him to the pastoral care. But as noted above he wholly declined that.

In 1742 the association was at Llangloffan, Pembrokeshire. It seems he was there: for soon after going from those parts toward Cilfowyr in the same country, he was suddenly, on the road, seized with a pain so acute that it obliged him to turn in to a public house: though there was a friend's house near, where he would have been heartily welcomed and proper care taken of him and his house: yet he could not bear to ride on. There the good man finished his race, and ended his warfare soon, aged seventy-three: he was buried at Cilfowyr. Mr. Griffith Davis had been at the ordination of Mr. Griffith Thomas at Newcastle. So being in the neighborhood he preached at the funeral of his former friend, fellowlaborer, and assistant in the ministry. To his dying day Mr. Griffith Davis gave John Davis a verygood character, as a godly, honorable, sincere man.

After that the care of the church fell more entirely on the pastor. He had not much assistance for years, but what happened occasionally. He served in the ministry with great fidelity, and integrity, and very kindly assisted other churches after the way of a peaceable temper and disposition. He would speak his mind freely, but friendly, and not dissemble. He was invited by other churches to baptize. He having so convincing, persuasive, yet agreeable and inoffensive way of treating the subjects, he often attended and assisted at ordinations, and seldom failed to be at the annual association.

Mr. Benjamin Francis the worthy pastor now at Horsley, Glacestershire, was baptized by Griffith Davis about 1749, and there he joined the church, being about 15 years of age. Mr. Davis happened to reside in a different part of the country when he began to preach: yet as the prospect in him was promising, Mr. Griffith Davis readily used his interest and influence to place him under the tuition of Mess'rs. Foskett and Evans at Bristol. He was dismissed from Swansea to Broadmead in 1753, where he was regularly called to the ministry in 1755, Dec. 11. There he continued to 1756, then for some time he served the church at Sodlcwy; but removed to Horsley in 1757, and was there ordained in 1758. His name, character, and usefulness are so well known that now it suffices to add that, by the goodness and mercy of God he continued there to this day February 2, 1793. He loves his people and is beloved by them in return. May they long continue to do so.

Mr. Rees Thomas was baptized and received a member at Swansea. Mr. Griffith Davis attended the last association in his time, though it was so far as Pantleg, Carmarthenshire, and he so aged. At parting he concluded that solemnity in prayer. He often preached at that convention. He was never married. He finished all here comfortably, 3rd Oct. 1776, aged 77. He served in the ministry 50 years, and in the pastoral care 40 years, and left a very agreeable character at home and abroad. He was faithful and loving to the last.

Soon after the death of Mr. John Davis, Mr. Griffith Davis had some help in the ministry by Mr. John Hopkins a gifted member who preached occasionally, when needed. He was a good man and exemplary in his conduct. He continued to assist till 1779. Then ended his days either late in that year or early in the next.

In the latter part of Mr. Griffith Davis' time, he had some help in the work by Mr. Samuel Davis who was a member of Llanelli; of him see more there.

Though the church was of 127 years standing when Mr. Griffith Davis died yet it was never before destitute of ministers raised up among themselves, and the eastern and western branches, which formed the new churches of Pen-y Sai and Llanelli, and their first pastors from the mother church. But upon his decease there was none of the sons brought up there, to take the bereaved mother by the hand in the pastoral way. Before when one left there was another qualified to supply and succeed. But after his death they were some time unsettled, but were assisted by one and another till 1777, when by agreement they chose Mr. Thomas Philips, then of Caerleon to the pastoral charge. He was the first minister this church ever called from abroad to the pastoral care.

The Swansea Church for a long while kept up their connection with the western nation in England, by a messenger or letter, and often both. The branches of this church have been formerly very wide and their meeting places of worship the names of which were found in like letters. But it is needless to insert them here. When the church was thus wide and numerous, they had several ministers and most of them able men; but they seldom, if ever had co-pastors as several churches in Wales had and still have.

We have no certainty how often the association was there from 1650 to 1660. The beginning of the association was at Ilston on the 6th and 7th of the 7th month 1650 (See above). There was a general meeting at Aberavon, the eastern branch of the church, on the 2nd day, 1st month, 1654. (See above). Very probably those general meetings were held often in one branch or other of this church during those ten years before 1660. There is certain accounts that the association was kept at Swansea in 1702, 1704, and 1706. The ministers came (see above) 1714, 1727, 1746, and 1763, and at Llanelli before they formed a church there, in 1718, 1725, and 1735, while it was a branch of Swansea.

After Mr. Philips came to Swansea, they went on successfully for a few years. At the time Mr. J.D. died, the number of members was about 80. The minutes of the association in 1779 say there were nine baptized: in 1780, baptized 18; in 1781, 15; and 1782, 13. But in that year, if not before, there sprung up gradually uneasiness and unhappiness for them. They were never quite comfortable since, Mr. P. was not like to be useful or comfortable, so went off to Bristol, about the date of 1783. Dr. Evans sent him to the church at Malmsbury, Wilts, that was destitute. He was not there long but removed to Bristol, where he kept a charity school for some time. He declined in health; after Dr. Evans death he left Bristol and came to see friends, and took Leominster in his way where he finished his race in Jan. 7, 1792. aged about 55.

Mr. Peter Rees went from Swansea to Bristol, became a member at Broadmead, and there was called to the ministry. For the advantage of further education he was admitted into the academy in 1778. He was chosen to the pastoral care of the church at Warwick, and was there ordained in 1783, where he had been in a probationary way ever since 1780. It was observed above that Dr. James and Mr. J. Morgan were natives of the same parish. Mr. Peter Rees told me himself that he likewise was born there. Remarkable that three natives of the same parish, should be successively, ministers of the church at such a distance!

Ministers who have been at liston and Swansea from 1749 to 1790. (1) Mr. John Miles, first pastor ejected on or before 1662, died in New England 1683. (2) Mr. Thomas Proud, ejected in 1660, or soon after, unknown when he died. (3) Mr. Morgan Jones of Britain Ferry, supposed to have been ejected, unknown also when he died. (4) Mr. Morgan Jones, of Lammadick, ejected, unknown when he died. (5) Mr. Evan Lewelyn, it is not known what he suffered when he died. (6) Mr. John Thomas, the same as the last. (7) Mr. Lewis Thomas probably the second pastor, lived through the persecution, died 1703 or 1704. (8) Mr. Robert Morgan colleaque with the last through the trouble of the times, died about 1710. (9) Dr. Philip James, probably an original member here 1748. (10) Mr. John Morgan, who died very young in the ministry and in years, 1703. (11) Mr. Robert Morgan, supposed to be a brother to J.M. and a son to the above 1723. (12) Mr. Morgan Jones, third pastor as supposed 1730. (13) Mr. Hugh Davis recommended and dismissed to America, died there 1753. (14) Mr. John Davis a very worthy assistant for many years, 1742. (15) Mr. Griffith Jones, the first pastor at Penysai went to America, died 1754. (16) Mr. David Owen, the first pastor at Llanelli, 1765. (17) Mr. Griffith Davis, the fourth pastor at Swansea, as supposed 1776. (18) Mr. William Morgan, an original member, here, though called elsewhere to preach 1753. (19) Mr. John Hopkins, an honest assistant for years, he died in or about 1779. (20) Mr. Rees Thomas, he did not turn out well. (21) Mr. Benjamin Francis, now pastor at Horsley. (22) Mr. Thomas Phillips, he died 1772. (23) Mr. Benjamin Morgan, who went to Bridgewaters. (24) Mr. John Williams, the present pastor. (25) Mr. John Rees, assistant. Several more were upon trial here for the ministry in the time of the Commonwealth. Mess'rs David Davis, William Thomas, assistant there too then. He there assisted occasionally, as Leyson Davis, John Knight, John Franklin.

Feb. 1793, Joshua Thomas: when I wrote thus far I designed to carry the history no further than 1790, but have since resolved to carry it to 1794. I can now be a little more correct regarding the division.

Mr. Benjamin Morgan succeeded in September 1784. After some months probation he was settled in the pastoral care, but the church continued uncomfortable. September 1785 a party went off, and next month, they formed themselves into a church. But at the association 1786, the seperation was disapproved of, and seven ministers were named by the Convention to meet at Swansea, with a view to reconcile them. But there was no prospect of a proper union. So the party that went off continued seperate. Their number was 45. Mr. B.M. continued with those in the old place, but he was not comfortable, nor were they all satisfied. Thus it continued till August 1791, then he removed to Bridgewater, Summerset, where he now is. The church was not long destitute. Mr. John Williams who had settled at Aberystwyth, removed to Swansea in the same year, or early in 1792. Mr. John Rees, who was a member in the New Church and exercised his ministerial talent, removed to the old Church with a regular dismission at his own will and desire. Their members in July about 60. (Aug. 1774, J.T.)

Mr. Peter Rees is said to have gone from Swansea to Bristol, so he was really a native of the principality, was called to the ministry in England. The particulars of him, are given in the above page 83. But it should be here added, that as he served the church at Warwick for 15 years, it does not appear, that any ministers served that church so long as he did, for a 105 years back, however it was before. Mr. Rees left by will 100£ to the Bristol society.

Mr. David Rees, his brother, was likewise a native of the same country, though called to the ministry at Bristol. It seems they both joined the church at Broadmead before they were there called to ministerial exercise. Mr. D. Rees was admitted to the academy in 1789, was there near 4 years, and died in June 1793, at Warwick, on a visit to his brother.

HISTORY OF THE BAPTIST CHURCH AT RHYDWILIM CARMARTHENSHIRE

By all that appears, this is the only Baptist Church in Wales that was properly constituted in the persecuting time between 1660 and 1688. The circumstances of that formation are not very common, therefore a few particulars must here be given.

Ejection of William Jones by the State

Dr. Calamy in his Account of Ministers ejected in Carmarthen Shire informs that Mr. William Jones was ejected from Llangellbithen: such a name I could never find through the country. No character is given to him. But I have been informed that Mr. William Jones lived at a place called Castell-Garw in the parish of Llanglydwen and county of Carmarthen. Very probably Llangellbithen was fabricated undesignedly, by blundering writers, transcribers, readers or printers, from the name of the parish where the good man lived and to which probably he preached, and from which he was ejected. Reports say that he officiated at Cilmaenllwyd, in the same county; all that might be true. Dr. Walker saith, that "Roger Philips was dispatched by the propagaters from Llanfalldeg" and it seems from Cilmaenllwyd, by him Keeleman Llwyd. In the margin there he says, "one Will Jones had Cilmaenllwyd living in 1655". (par. 2 p. 337). By all these hints it is easy to conclude that Mr. William Jones was ejected out of one, or all these places by the act of uniformity, about 1660, probably but one of the places were named. But Dr. Calamy has neither of them, we are not to attribute the mistakes to him. It matters not who blundered.

Baptism of William Jones

By a written narrative taken from Mr. John Jenkins, of whom more below, and some other incidental information the further account of Mr. William Jones is thus. In the time of the Commonwealth he, like many others, by the authority that then was, preached in the churches and elsewhere, as opportunity served, but more statedly at Cilmaenllwyd. He was not then a Baptist but an Independent. But in 1660, or soon after, the ministers who did preach in the churches were compelled either to conform wholly to the establishment, or quit the churches and livings. In conscience Mr. Jones chose the latter.

It is said, that he was much of a gentleman, but very meek and modest, and rather timid in his natural disposition. For that reason, when he was ejected he was very cautious how he preached. It was with as much secrecy as he could, in the night perhaps mostly. But notwithstanding all precaution and care, informers and spies were so penetrating, that in a short time he was apprehended, and committed to Carmarthen Castle. Mr. Crosby, Vol. 2, p. 26 and 27, informs that Mr. Jenkin Jones and some of his friends were imprisoned for religion at Carmarthen in 1660.

That Mr. Jones was a noted Baptist Minister, for about or above twenty years then, see p. 20. Probably Mr. Jenkin Jones and Mr. William Jones had leisure in prison to converse about many subjects, and among many other things it seems that they happened to fall upon the subject of Baptism. But the information is, that while Mr. William Jones was there in prison he was fully convinced in his own mind, that believer's Baptism was the only scriptural one, and yet that while there he kept his convictions very close to himself. He was then confined about three years, says the information, was much respected for his affability and inoffensive behaviour. At length he was by some favorable providence set at liberty.

After his enlargement, he was determined to be baptized according to the word of God and have the ordinance administered by a proper administrator. Perhaps he chose to go a considerable distance from home, for particular reasons in his own mind. Here it is to be observed, that besides Mr. John Jenkins' manuscript, another larger written by Mr. John Richards, the late aged pastor at Ebenezer, has been penned. Mr. John Richards was judicious and intelligent. He took much pains to collect hints in these parts. His manuscript will be referred to in several places as we proceed. But there is one considerable defect in his collection, he gives no dates. He says that Mr. William Jones went to the valley of Olchon to be Baptized. Probably the administrator was Mr. Thomas Watkins or Mr. William Prichard, probably the former as he was the senior and the proper pastor at Olchon.

We have no information what year that was, but by circumstances it may be supposed to have been about 1665 or 1666. But however, Mr. Jones being thus baptized returned home, began to converse with his religious friends about Cilmaenllwyd, etc., and gradually told them what he had done, giving the reasons which induced him to take such a step. Upon weighing what he and the scriptures said, some judged, that he had done but what was right. After proper time, some others were baptized by him. This church hath now an old Book of Records, but is very concise. It begins with a confession of their faith, which is nearly the same as that of Mr. Vavasor Powell, which is now in the account of his life. After the confession, the date is 1667, then a register or list of those church members who held the principles expressed in the preceeding confession. Probably they had a copy of that confession of Mr. Thomas Watkins or Mr. William Prichard, as we are informed that Mr. Myles and the churches in his connection had a confession.

Others Baptized and a Church Constituted

However that was, the records inform that those church members were in the parish of Narberth, Pembrokeshire, then they proceed thus:

"On the 4th day of the 6th month, 1667, Griffith Howells was baptized and chosen an Elder the same day. At the same time were baptized: Abel Bishop of the parish of Ilebach, and David Richard of the parish of Llanpeter. These three in Pembrokeshire. Jenkin Beavan of the parish of Cilmaenllwyd; Mary Jones of Llanllwm, and Elinor Griffeths of Llanfihangel, these three of Carmarthenshire." The next date is the 25th of the same month, just three weeks after the former. Five were baptized then. Those also are named, with the parishes and counties where they resided. These eleven baptized in three weeks lay very wide in the two counties. It may now look rather odd that Mr. Griffith Howells should be chosen Elder on the day he was baptized. Probably he was the first baptized by Mr. William Jones. The number to choose him an elder could be but six, and no proper church. But perhaps it might be somewhat thus. Mr. Howells was a gentleman of estate, property, and education; and it is supposed, was in the ministry then. Very possibly the choice and eldership of that day amounted to no more than the agreement among those few friends, that he should preach occasionally in his own house, and possibly in some other places, as before perhaps he might.

The next date in the book is the 15th of the 7th month, which was three weeks and still eight are named as baptized then. But the parishes not named, only the county of Cardigan. Possibly they were baptized in that county, and the writer of the book might not know the names of the parishes. By this time they were twenty, including the minister. This was no despicable success in so short a time after they began to baptize; as the persecution then was fierce enough. Possible some, if not most of those people, were convinced before of the nullity of infant baptism and that baptism upon profession was the only valid one; but it seems they could not tell how to proceed before, till Mr. William Jones opened the way.

The date after is the 5th of the 2nd month, 1668, seven were then baptized; and one soon after; and three in the fifth month. This was thirty without the minister, all baptized in less than a year, the names are all in the Register, and all in the Welsh History; it does not appear necessary to insert them here. As yet they were not formed into a regular church. But they consulted and agreed to be constituted according to Gospel order. They recorded a memorandum thus. That on the 12th day of the 5th month, 1668, the church of Christ being assembled together from the three counties of Pembroke, Carmarthen, and Cardigan, received the Lord's Supper the first time, by the ministration of the two brethren, William Prichard and Thomas Watkins, an Elder and a Deacon, sent by the church of Christ at Abergavenny, Olchon, and the Hay. This was the first day of the week; and upon the same day, we gave up ourselves to the Lord, and to each other, having before submitted to Baptism, and laying on of hands. On the same day Letice Morgan of Cilfowyr, and another, both baptized before, came under laying on of hands, and joined in church fellowship.

On the day following being the 13th, our brethren William Jones, and Griffith Howells were chosen elders; and Morgan Rhydderck (or Roderick) and Llewelyn John were set apart upon trial to serve the office of deacons. This is the sum of the record though not exactly verbatim, a few remarks should be made upon those transactions, thus:

Probably Mr. William Jones was ordained before he was ejected about 1660, so before he was baptized. Some think that Mr. Griffith Howells preached in the church by authority before the Restoration. But in this new formed church, they were both chosen as joint elders; though the former was always the leader in the church, yet the latter very respectable and useful. In the above article, Messrs. William Prichard and Thomas Watkins are styled an Elder and Deacon, and the church of Abergavenny, Olchon, and Hay, as one church. This was some inaccuracy in the writing of the Records, except the two churches were united as one for some conveniency in the troublesome times, which is not very probable, as they were two churches before and after the persecution, and these ministers were their respective pastors. It seems Mr. William Jones held laying on of hands from the beginning, and very possibly misters William Prichard and Thomas Watkins practiced it by this time.

Constituency and Growth of the Church

Here it appears that the constituents of this church were thirty three, of whom thirty at least had been baptized in less than a year. We are not informed where this meeting was when the church was constituted. But probably it was at the house of Mr. Griffith Howells. called Rushaere and the chief meeting place of this church through the persecution and long after. Now we see this young church had two elders and two deacons but they lay uncommonly wide and scattered through three counties.

Regarding the book of Records belonging to this church: the former part of it was written by a judicious and prudent hand, probably by Mr. Griffith Howells or by Mr. William Jones or Mr. John Evans; worthy characters all three. But it is supposed the beginning was transcribed from a former book or papers, about 1689. After what hath been already observed, it gives very little account besides the names of the persons baptized and admitted members, of what parish and county, when, and sometimes where, and by whom baptized. But no account at all of discipline, debates, ordinations, deaths, etc. In that manner it continued to the time I saw it about 1776, however it is since. It had been well had other churches done so much; yet it had been better had this and other churches recorded a little more, particularly deaths, ordinations, dismissions, exclusions, and some other occurrances in discipline, when new churches were formed out of branches, etc.

At that time all nonconformists, and particularly Baptists were much persecuted in those parts, yet this young society increased through all the contempts and reproaches of the day. According to the Book the first person baptized after the church was constituted, was Mr. Thomas David Rees, of the parish of Llanarth, Cardiganshire. He was a person of property, estate, and repute. By some circumstances it is supposed that he had preached for sometime among the nonconformists before he was baptized. About a month after him, seven more were baptized; and after that about as many more before the year was out, so in the close of 1668 they were about forty-eight communicants. In 1669, they had nine baptized at six several times, the Records note that on the 27th of the 9th month that year, Brother Thomas David Rees was ordained an elder: and Brother Morgan Roderick and Brother Llewelyn John ordained deacons. These two were put upon trial before, but now approved and confirmed in office.

In the years 1670 and 1671, there is but one in each year recorded as baptized: but ten next year and six the year following, one of whom was the noted Mr. John Evans, named above, of whom more below. The account in the Book seems to be tolerably regular till 1677, and some addition every year. But it appears, that they did not always record the names of those added from Cardiganshire: whereas those added near Rushaere are named with the parishes and counties; which inclines one to conclude, that the writer of Records lived that way. Among those baptized in 1677 Mr. John Jenkins was one, who is supposed to have been the minister of that name, of whom more below. He was then about twenty-one, as appears by comparing his age when he died. The Records note, that one was baptized that year in the River Teivy. Some old papers of Mr. John Richards mention more as baptized in 1677, of whom one was Mr. Thomas Griffiths, of him more below. It is evident from the Book itself, that it does not record all that were baptized. That is not to be wondered at, the times being so troublesome. It is more to be wondered that so many were recorded, as the times were. Many seemed then afraid to write anything at all relating to church affairs, lest their writings should be found out and produced to witness against them. For ten years after, the Book is nct so regular as before or since. But it notes that several were added. We may well wonder how they were supported under the troubles, persecutions, fines, imprisonments, etc., of those times. The Records mention the backsliders of those days; and it is worthy of notice, that of the sixty-nine first baptized, only two are noted as having backslidden. That is truly remarkable.

The Marriage Ceremony

In those days several of the Baptists in the principality married before the church, they did not approve of the common ceremony in the established way. That method continued in Wales, with some, till the late marriage act. Then as far as I know, it was wholly given up, and they conformed in that article. I knew several who were married that way in their own congregation, open and very public, and have been present at some of those meetings. A sermon was preached on the occasion, a certificate given to the new married women, etc. There are several copies of them in those Records. One of them runs thus: We whose names are hereto subscribed do certify whom it may concern, that L.P. and E.J. of the parish of Ll. did, in the presence of God, and of us this people, enter into the honorable state of matrimony, to live together according to his holy ordinance, until death shall them both separate. July 1st, 1682. Griffith Howells, James James, Thomas John, George John, Henry Griffith.

Liberty of Worship Resumes Under William of Orange

The Book does not name the administrator of Baptism before

1687, probably that was omitted on purpose, lest the book should be found by informers, and some danger follow. But in that year Mr. William Jones is named as administering that ordinance. It might be that he w,ould not name himself though probably the former was the true case of that silence. Probably Mr. T.D. Rees baptized mostly in Cardiganshire.

In November 1688, the celebrated William, Prince of Orange, landed; and in 1689, liberty was really and legally granted and established by an act of Parliament.

The General Assembly at London

The General Assembly (of churches) met in London, September that year. Upon that friendly and public invitation, this remote church sent messengers, the very first time, without delay. In the printed narrative of that Assembly, Messrs. Griffith Howells and William Jones are named the messengers of this church, and the latter is styled the pastor thereof. The church is there called Neare which is one of the several errors of that narrative, regarding names of persons and places. Possibly the name aimed at was Narberth, as Mr. Griffith Howells' house was in that parish, not far from the town of that name. His house was the chief place of worship in the church. At that meeting in London there was a confession of faith set forth, and approved of by the whole Assembly, among whom the messengers of this church were.

But that in the beginning of this church Records is not exactly the same as that in London, though in sense they agree in the general. Probably this church had adopted that in their records before the meeting in London, and transcribed, that, with other things from a former book into their present one. There the title runs thus, "A confession of faith of the church of Christ, that meets sometimes in the three several counties of Carmarthen, Pembroke and Cardigan, which are commonly, though unjustly, called Anabaptists, 1689." We cannot tell whether this was before or after the meeting in London, though the date in the Records is the same year, yet the month is not given, so it might be before the meeting in London.

After the confession, the book gives the names of the members as already noted. In that year the names amount to a hundred and thirteen in the book. Of whom 59 lived in Pembrokeshire, 35 in Carmarthenshire, 19 in Cardiganshire; they resided in thirty-eight Welsh parishes, which are not very small in common with this only exception, that one or two of the parishes are named in two counties, being part in one and part in another. The names of the parishes and persons are inserted in the Welsh History, but omitted here. Those 113 were not the names of those added, but the names of those then members in 1689. So there must have been many more added when we consider the dead and excluded, etc. So the increase was wonderful when we consider how difficult those persecuting times.

And what is remarkable of those 113, there were eleven in the ministry. Their names shall be given here, thus, Messrs. William Jones, Griffith Howells, Thomas David Rees, George Jones, James Jones, Evan David, John Jenkins, Richard William, Thomas Griffeth, Samuel Jones, and John David. Those were not occasional exhorters, but most of them very able ministers of the New Testament, sound in doctrine and exemplary in morals. The three first had long born the burden and heat of the day, and the two next had their share of the troubles of those times. They all had tasted of the bitter water. Of each of them in their proper places. As wide as even the church was, they were supplied having so many able hands. Their love and harmony were such, they chose rather to travel long journeys to break bread together, as many as anyway could, than divide into small societies to shorten their journeys.

Mr. John Richards says, that in those times they broke bread once a month; at Rushaere, in Pembrokeshire, one month, and at Glandwr, Cardiganshire, the other month and so on alternately. But as those two places were dwelling houses, they could not well manage church discipline in them, as servants and occurrances interrupted; therefore they transacted church affairs, at a place called Ynys-Sach, in Carmarthenshire, and there they generally baptized.

In the printed narrative of the London Assembly in 1690, we have not the names of the messengers of the churches as such, like the preceeding year; nor have I the letters sent from this church that year, though the Letters from the churches in the South East happened to fall into my hand. That is no sufficient reason that this church sent no letters or messengers, that year to London, but it does not appear whether they were the same messengers as the year before, or others; in that narrative we have the names of the churches. This congregation is there called by three different names. But they were no other than the three places above named, in the three counties, where they chiefly met to worship. It is said, that in those days they also met to worship at a place called Penlan in the Parish of Eglwys Fair Chyrig near Aberlwyn, Carmarthenshire. No doubt they met in many places occasionally, but the three chief places were those above. In the state of the churches sent to London this year, see above. One of the papers has not a hint of this church; the other mentions it, and says that Messrs. William Jones and Griffith Howells were Elders but says nothing of Mr. Thomas David Rees, nor the number of members but that they were in three counties. It seems the writer of that knew little of this church.

It is recorded, that in 1690 Mr. James James administered the ordinance of Baptism. In the list of names in 1689 he is called an Elder, but living in Cardiganshire, Mr. George Jones was his Senior. It is supposed they both had been ordained assistants for some years before, and also Mr. Evan David. Mr. John Richards' manuscript says, that Mr. James James was a Carmarthenshire man (probably a native of that county) and that his elder brother, Mr. John James was in the ministry among the Presbyterians.

Mr. George Jones (or John as he is written some times) was one of the first constituents of the church, and was baptized about three months before it was constituted. The Records give not the least hint when he was called to the ministry, or ordained; nor does Mr. John Richards give any account of that, but saith, that he was the first minister God was pleased to raise up in this church; the other three being in the ministry it seems before the church was incorporated. He says that Mr. George Jones was of a reputable family, and that he began while young to think of soul concerns, and joined the Baptists, when they were a sect much spoken against in those parts. Mr. John Richards further says, that Mr. George Jones was called to the ministry, and James James soon after. It is supposed they both preached a considerable part of the persecution and had their share of the suffering of the times.

In the printed narrative of the London Assembly in 1691, we have no more of this church than was given the preceeding year. In that of 1692, we have the names of persons and places copied out of 1689, and the blunders along, not corrected. Those were the printers faults probably in part.

About this time the Baptists spread considerably in Wales; but were warmly opposed by pedobaptist dissenters. There was an affair that happened here in 1692, which added heat to the debate. Mr. John Philips of Cilcam left the Independents and joined the Baptists, of the particulars of that affair see below. The book records that he and some others were baptized the 18th of the 4th month, 1692. It may be supposed that the debate began early that year, or before. But there is not a word of it in the Records of this church. The noted and aged Mr. Samuel Jones of Brynllwary in Glamorganshire, to whom Dr. Calamy gives a great character and no doubt he was worthy of it, (is cited) in the *Accounts* of the ejected ministers. He was desired to write a defence of Infant Baptism; but he wisely declined the work, as the Baptists had not, in Wales, published anything upon the subject. Then one of his former pupils, the famous Mr. James Owen, then of Oswestry took the matter in hand. He wrote in the ancient British language, that the country people in general might understand it. The title of his book was, *Infant Baptism from Heaven.* He dedicated it to his former tutor Mr. J. Jones, and there observes how earnestly he wished that the latter had undertaken the work. This treatise came out in 1693. The famous Mr. Benjamin Keach undertook the task readily. The title of his answer was, *Light Broke Forth in Wales.* It was printed in both languages, that in Welsh came out in 1694. This was quick work, for that book was large and full, and probably printed in English before it was translated. Mr. Norcott upon Baptism was translated and printed the same year; they were very active indeed. It is not known now that anyone had written before in Welsh upon infant baptism, so this was an introduction of the debate in our country, though believers baptism had been practised in the country so long before. In 1701, Mr. Owen published a brief *Rejoinder* in the same language. There it rested then.

The General Assembly at Bristol

In the printed narrative of the first general annual Assembly at Bristol, 1693, Messrs. George Jones (Johns it is there) and James James are among those who signed the circular letters there. They were the messengers from this church that year. They might be messengers to London before, though there appears now no certainty of it. In the Blaenau Records there is a list of the churches who met at Bristol, by their messengers, in 1694. There this church reckoned as two, that is Ynys–Sach and Glandwr. Rushacre is omitted, though but one church yet.

There was a query sent from Wales to the general assembly at Bristol in 1696, to this purpose, "whether it be lawful for an orderly gospel church to divide, by general consent, into two or more churches, for the sake of edification; because the members live far assunder, and are perhaps numerous?" The answer was in the affirmative, and these reasons assigned for it, 1. There is no command transgressed by so doing, Rom. IV:15. 2. That which promotes the glory of God, and the good of souls should be done, Phil. IV:8, and it is evident, that things are so; as they may thereby better answer the end of communion, and keep the order of the discipline of Christ, more to his praise and to their mutual edification, and the spreading of the gospel. But care should be taken to have ministers in each part, and that each be sufficient to keep up church order.

In that case the assembly gave these directions. 1. To write down the names of the members, and the part to which each chose to join, and that of the whole church. 2. To keep a day of public fasting in each part, where there shall be a minister, or where ministers, and people were called, and gathered together. Then their consent all made public, with supplication to God for his presence and blessing. Then to give instruction and exhortation suitable on the occasion, that they may behave as the church of Christ. This should be done in one part, by the elder of another part; or rather of one belonging to another church. Readers are left to understand these directions and benefit by them as occasion may require.

Probably the query was from this church or Llanwenarth, and might respect this church chiefly, or this and that.

It is certain that Blaenan was formed in 1696, and it is confidently supposed that Glandwr was constituted this year, and both in consequence of the advice from the Assembly at Bristol. But it is amazing that the Records of this church do not give one hint of it. Such important affairs in history are wholly omitted there. It is a wonder they put down the names of those baptized, few other churches did that. It was rather odd that Glandwr Church had not incorporated before, being so far. But by the query to Bristol it may be supposed that they were not all of one mind upon the subject. Now we will consider Glandwr as a new church, and at present follow the mother church.

Early Pastors of the Mother Church

It is to be wished that a more particular account could be given of Mr. Jones towards the latter part of life, as he had been so useful and successful in these parts, laid the foundation of this Prolific Mother Church, and assisted so long to carry on the superstructure.

It seems that he like many of his brethren was reduced by the persecution, to straits and difficulties. In Dr. Price's papers, about 1690. Mr. W. Jones is named among the indigent ministers in Wales. There are in all form papers, of Dr. Price's about that time, each of which gives some light. W. Jones is named in three of them, but as indigent. His name is in the London narratives of 1689 and 1692, as pastor of this church. I do not recollect to have seen his name anywhere after the last date. It had been well, if they had recorded the time when ministers died, but they did not. It has been already observed, that Mr. Jones was naturally of a meek and rather timid disposition, before the persecution: but information says that when he was persecuted, imprisoned, etc. his fortitude and courage were remarkable. He was meek, yet bold as a lion; his conduct winning and inoffensive. He was much respected by the gentlemen in the country. They would fain persuade him to conform, with fair promises of promotion; but he knew how to give grateful obliging answers; and yet suffer straits and difficulties for the sake of truth and peace of conscience. Mr. John Richards' ms. notes, that some reported that Mr. J.W. chose to keep a clear conscience regarding the purity of divine worship, rather than to receive a hundred and forty pounds a year for reading the common prayer in the Establishment. That was no small sum in those parts then. Nor was the temptation despicable, when the alternative was, not only common poverty, but to be stripped of what he had, go to jail, etc. His imprisonment at Carmarthen was mentioned before, it is unknown how many times he was there. Being on the borders of the two counties if taken and committed in Pembrokeshire, then he was to go to Haverford west.

This anecdote is given of him, when at a certain time he was committed to that prison. When he was there brought to town a prisoner, he was known by so many of the gentlemen; and so respected, being invited to their houses; that the officers who had the charge of him were despised, they were ashamed of themselves. But he was detained there some time. He had appointed to preach at a certain place before he was apprehended, and wished to have leave to go and keep that meeting without disappointing the hearers, promising to return punctually to jail again. Leave was soon granted and a gentleman lent him his horse, coat, boots, spurs, etc. to go and preach where he had appointed. He went and returned according to promise, all well his reputation still increased.

In the Welsh History, it is supposed, from Mr. Moses Williams' catalogue, that our friend, now under notice, had translated into Welsh two English books mentioned in that catalogue. But by consulting Dr. Calamy's *Account* it looks more like that it was Mr. William Jones, who was ejected from Denbigh in North Wales, did that kind service for his country. It is not right for one to do the service and another have the praise. There was not the least intention of that in the Welsh History.

It is supposed that our Mr. William Jones finished his warfare before the year 1700. He must have been advanced in years, as he was ejected in 1662, or before. It was wrong, not to record the time of his death, and where he was buried. But very probably his remains were deposited in the burying ground near Rushacre.

His excellent collegue, Mr. Griffith Howells; who is supposed to have been the first baptized by Mr. William Jones, was of much service in his day. He was active in the cause of Christ, and a sufferer, like many others. But gentlemen of property and influence often came off more favorable than others did. He lived on his own estate, as noted already, and Mr. Richards' ms. says that he did preach to the English that way.

The *History of Wales,* 1702, p. 128 informs, that a colony of Flemings from Flanders, emigrated to this island about the year 1105, and planted themselves in the country of Rhos in Pembrokeshire. Those strangers spoke then a kind of English it seems and so they continue to this day, it may be supposed that their language is now considerably improved. Mr. Griffith Howells lived about the border between the two languages. He was then the chief English preacher the Baptists had that way. Some of those English, as they are now called did join the church.

Rushacre was for many years the chief meeting house in this extensive church, it was like the Cathedral of the whole. Being the dwelling house of Mr. Griffith Howells and he himself preached, he must have been exposed to many frowns, fines, etc. But his influence in the country sheltered him more than many. He adorned his profession to the end.

Of the hardships they had to bury their dead in those times, see above. This good man determined to remedy that in his neighborhood. He walled in a piece of land, near the high road to Haverford West, on the west side, in the parish of Llanddewi. His son who was also a member, was very solicitous to have the place properly fitted up, and finished for the purpose designed. It so fell out, that he died soon after and happened to be the first person buried in the place.

A few hints more of other persons and articles before the death of Mr. Griffith Howells is mentioned. Messrs. Thomas D. Rees, James James, and Evan David are to be considered as members of the new church, Glandwr.

Of Mr. George Jones there is no account in the book when he died, nor does any memorandum of that appear. Mr. John Richards' ms. gives no account of those things, the good people in those days, had no notion of recording deaths. The manuscript says that when the church divided Mr. George Jones presided over the one part, and Mr. James James over the other. Information says, that Mr. George Jones did not live to old age. It is supposed that he died rather before 1700. In that year it was two and thirty years since he had been baptized.

Mr. John David above named among the eleven ministers, was son to a rich man of considerable property, but far from being a friend to the Baptists. He was highly displeased with the son for entering into any connection with them. But the son was a very humble patient man. He married one of the members of the church, who had no great affluence of the world, that again displeased the old gentleman. The son was sometimes brought to straits, but he was much regarded by his friends, particularly Mr. John Evans of whom more soon. Mr. John Richards' ms. gives Mr. John David a high and excellent character, for humility, faith, sincerity, etc. He soon ripened for a better life and did not live here to old age. It is supposed he died about 1700. It does not appear that he was ever ordained. He left a widow and some children. His son Daniel was a deacon in this church. Mr. Evan Davis a worthy member of Dr. Stennetts Church in London, is a son to that deacon, another son Mr. Joshua Davis lately was, and perhaps is now, a member of one of the Baptist Churches in Bristol. Mr. Evan Davis I have known for many years, but did not know that he was grandson to Mr. John David when the Welsh History was printed. It seems there are some of the family still members here.

Mr. Richard Williams is named above, as having undertaken the care of the young church at Trosgoed and the old church at Olchon about 1700. He was one of the eleven who came out of the great tribulation in 1689. Of him there is no account in the records, when he was baptized, when called to the ministry, or ordained, but he is in the register of names in 1689. The first account of him after, found in the records, was of his baptizing some at Ynys-Sach in 1696. And it is recorded that he baptized in the same place near the close of 1698. After that he is named as baptizing in one place or another in the church eleven times before the end of 1700. About that time he was called to Trosgoed and had the pastoral care as above committed to him. As far as it appears now, he was the first minister called abroad out of this church to serve elsewhere, but many followed after.

About this time 1700, or soon after, Mr. Morgan Griffiths, another besides the eleven removed from this church to the pastoral care of the church at Hengoed, which had been so long destitute. There it is said that he died in June 1738, and had been pastor of that church for 37 years, then he must have come there in 1700, or soon after. But the records mention him baptizing Henry Morgan in 1701. There is in the book a copy of a letter supposed to be the dismission to Hengoed. There it is testified, that the church had a long trial of his agreeable conduct, his grace and gifts, and that he had been ordained by fasting, prayers and laying on of hands, by the elders of the church. This was dated at Cwm–Cerwyn not far from Rhydwilim the 18th of the 12th month, 1702; if this was the former way of reckoning then it was February, 1702-3, but if the late way then it was December, 1702. It's but two months added. This looks as if he had been ordained sometime before, and as such dismissed.

Mr. John Evans hath been mentioned before. He deserves a place here among the ministers, before we quite close the last century. The following account was given chiefly by his own daughter to the writer of this. Mr. John Evans was the younger of three sons. The father was a gentleman of considerable property. The two had estates left them, but John was to be taken care of by the provident industrious mother. She determined that he should have liberal education to qualify him for promotion in the church by law established. With that view, he was put to a grammar school in the country, to qualify him for the university. But while the mother was meditating promotion and wealth for her son, it happened that John fell under very serious concern about the state of his soul and eternity. He contracted acquaintance and intimacy with the poor people there by way of scorn and contempt called Anabaptists. When the mother talked to the son about Oxford, he did not seem inclined to go. She wondered at that, and now and then would sound him upon the subject and gradually began to reason with him and ask why he was so indifferent. He still waved it, and did not choose to give the true reason. Then said the mother, "How unwise you are! You know everyone bows to the parson". But when Mrs. Evans observed that all fair means failed, she began to frown, and try what rough means would do: and said to this effect, "What! have I been at so much expence upon you to qualify you for repute and honor, and you refuse to proceed after all, but cast away all the expence? If you will not go to the university, you shall quit my house, and then shift as well as you can." The young man gave some mild answer, that he must submit to all consequence, but he could not be a parson.

While in this situation, and not yet turned out, but threatened, it so happened at a certain time, that as the mother was passing by a chamber door, she heard a voice; she hearkened and soon found it was her son praying, she could discern his words, so she listened. He prayed for himself, very earnestly in his precarious situation; then prayed as fervently for his mother. The prayers so affected and melted the mother that she resolved not to turn him out. From that time forward her affections to her youngest son were warm enough. Now it went so far, that she encouraged him to look out for a proper estate for himself and she would pay for it. That was done; he purchased Llwyndwr, near Ynys-Sach. There he lived, and was very hospitable and useful through the persecuting time, and long after. According to the records he was baptized in 1673, as noted in p.43. His daughter said that Mr. Griffith Howells was then in prison for religion. But he chose to suffer affliction with those he esteemed the people of God, rather than all the pleasures emoluments of Oxford and clerical promotion. The two elder brothers did not live long, and it seems all the estate came to the youngest. He lived in affluence and honor, and was a great shelter to the poor persecuted Baptists in those hard times. Godliness is profitable to all things. He was a gentleman of letters and property.

As yet through all the persecution and afterward there was no meeting house in this church, they met to worship in dwelling houses, as noted before. But the liberal deviseth liberal things. So Mr. John Evans erected a decent meeting house upon his own estate, all at his own expence for the use of the church. In the wall of that house, the inside, there is a stone with this inscription, in Welsh; "This house was erected at the charge of John Evans of Llwyndwr, in the year 1701; for the use of the people who hold the six principles in Heb. VI 1-2." At the opening of the house a sermon was preached on the occasion by Mr. Lewis Thomas the aged pastor at Swansea. As far as it appears, this was the second meeting house built by the Baptists in the principality. Besides all that, this generous benefactor settled so much land for the support of the ministry as amounts to five or six pounds a year, or more. This rent is to be divided between the pastor and his assistants in the ministry. Mr. Evans died about a year before Mr. Griffith Howells, and the former in his will, made the latter a guardian over his children. But death soon removed him also, therefore he did not long guard the orphans. Mr. John Evans was by office a ruling elder in the church. It was rather extraordinary that such worthy and wealthy men as these two, had no stones and inscriptions on their graves: but in those days they did shun any thing that appeared ostentatious then. Mrs. Griffith of Glanrhyd was the daughter above referred to. She gave most of this narrative regarding her father in 1776. Her memory and faculties appeared then so good, that she might have been expected to live many years. But pleased God to remove her before the end of that year. Her son E. Griffith Esq. lives at Glanrhyd, is in the commission of the peace, a gentleman of reputation, an active judicious magistrate. He attends at meeting, is ready to assist, very friendly and hospitable, in his mother's time and since.

It should have been observed before the last paragraph, that the meeting house was built in the parish of Llandisilis and county of Carmarthen, on the bank of a small river called Cledden, which divides the county in that place from Pembrokeshire. It seems that from a ford there in that river, the house is called Rhydwilim, which signifies William's Ford. Now the church shall here go by that name. Here see how a new church was formed here in 1701.

A New Church Sent to America

Mr. Thomas Griffith is another of the eleven ministers mentioned. The records give no hint when he was baptized, called to the ministry or ordained. But by Mr. John Richards' papers, it seems he was baptized in 1677. In 1701, he and fifteen of the members went over to Pennsylvania, probably these members were part of Rhydwilim, and part from Glandwr. They went all over in the same ship. In 1770, Mr.

Morgan Edwards published his *Materials Towards a History of the Baptists in Pennsylvania;* there will be often reference to it. The sixteen are named there eight men and eight women. These with their families and others made a considerable company; they lived some time about Pennepec. But they removed and purchased some land, then called it Welsh Tract, they being Welsh. They had formed themselves into a church in Wales and Mr. Thomas Griffith their pastor. The first ordination Mr. Edwards mentions in his *Materials* p.12, is that of Mr. Evan Morgan, there, Mr. Edwards names Rev. Thomas Griffith as the first concerned in that ordination.

Of Mr. Samuel Jones of Pennepec, see Ms.,p.131,134. In a letter from him to his friends in Wales he says, "Mr. Thomas Griffiths and a few others of the same congregation, were poor honest people. They abode with us some time: and though he was not so able a preacher as some others, yet he did much good among us. But now these several years, he and those who came over with him removed fifty miles from us, and are now I think, the largest congregation in these provinces." This about twelve years after they left Wales.

Mr. Reynald Howell, of whom see Ms.,p.81, in a letter to Mr. Miles Harris, dated in October, 1752, saith that the Rev. Thomas Griffiths and his company came over in a regular manner from Pembrokeshire. He gives them a respectable character. Thus Mr. Thomas Griffith bore his testimony and a share of the persecution in Wales. The *Materials* say that he was born in 1645, in Llanfarnach parish, and county of Pembroke. Then he went to America aged about fifty six, and went to rest in 1725 aged eighty, after he had laid there the foundation of a reputable Baptist Church there, and the second in the province.

Pastors of the Church in America

Mr Elisha Thomas had been an assistant in this ministry for some time, and now succeeded in the pastoral care. He was also one of the eight men who went over, so one of the first constituents of the church. The records give no account of him when baptized, but in a marriage certificate in 1691, Elizeus Thomas is a witness. According to the *Materials,* he was then about seventeen. Elisha in Welsh is written Elizeus, as more properly Eliseus. He must have been then a young man of repute, to be a witness in that case. Several circumstances incline me to conclude that he was. Also Mr. Thomas David Rees who had been so worthy and so long a member of this church and in the ministry. I have no certainty of that, but strongly suppose it. He was not long in pastoral care but finished in 1730, aged 56.

The next successor was Mr. Enoch Morgan, he likewise was a

third of the eight men who emigrated, and another of the first constituents. The *Materials* say that he was born in 1676, at Atltgech, Llanwenog parish and county of Cardigan; and very probably he was of Glandwr church. Messrs. J. Jones and R. Howell, speak of him respectfully. The former said he was a brother to Mr. Abel Morgan, of whom see below. He continued in pastoral charge while able; he died in 1740, aged 64. His widow was alive 1770. His descendants numerous. His son Abel was born in 1713. He turned out a very able and useful gospel minister. In Dr. Gellies' *Life of Mr. Whitfield,* mention is made of Mr. Abel Morgan as a zealous preacher, in the Jerseys about 1740. Mr. M. Edwards in his annual account of the association met at Philadelphia, informs that Mr. Abel Morgan of Middletown baptized, in his church 14 in 1761, 8 in 1762, 16 next year, 14 next to that, and 13 in 1765. His members in that year 167.

The largest of the three and thirty churches met in Association that year, except that of Hopewell in the Jerseys, which had that year the very extraordinary addition of eighty-six baptized. That was the church of the famous Mr. Isaac Eaton.

Mr. John Griffith says in a letter of 1760, that Mr. Abel Morgan was pastor of a numerous wealthy church. Mr. Morgan in his *Materials for Jersey,* 1792, says "Abel Morgan was educated at Mr. Thomas Evan's Academy at Pencader, ordained at Welshtract in 1734, became pastor at Middletown in 1738; was never married: of sound learning and solid judgement, of which he gave specimens both in public disputes and publications on Baptism. The former with Mr. Samuel Harker, at one time: and another time, with Mr. (afterward Dr.) Samuel Finley. But Mr. Finley from public disputing proceeded to writing: he was soon answered; he rejoined, but was replied. Mr. Finley wrote a third piece; a copy of which, by some means, came to Mr. Morgan's hand and he replied to that, it seems. But it does not appear that these last were printed. Mr. Morgan was a man of wit and very genteel irony. Thus say the *Materials.*

Mr. (now Dr.) Samuel Jones, of Lower Dublin, near Philadelphia, in a letter to me dated June, 1784, says, that Mr. Abel Morgan was "one of the best and greatest of men!" But then much impaired in his voice, had his brother's son Mr. Samuel Morgan for his assistant in the ministry. In a letter from him dated Nov. 1785, he says that Mr. Abel Morgan was, in a manner, superannuated, but he wrote a second letter, in about a week after, and sent both together; in the letters he says "yesterday, the affecting tidings of the good and great Mr. Abel Morgan's death reached my ears. The more affecting to me because I have had it in contemplation these two or three years to pay him a visit, and spend two or three days with him, in parts with a view to know something of his mind about his manuscript, but have neglected it too long. Now may it be said, that a great man is fallen in our Israel, very seldom indeed do the accomplishments and excellencies of body, mind, and grace, meet in so high a degree in one man. As some once said to be below contempt, so he was above envy; for all agreed to give him the preference. As he had no competition, no one felt hurt when Mr. Morgan was admired; no one imagining there was any comparison between him and Mr. Morgan. I wish some qualified person may attempt to do some little justice to his character. Mr. Abel Morgan died 24th Nov. 1785," aged 72 years and 7 months.

Mr. Enoch Morgan was succeeded by Mr. Owen Thomas, born, say the *Materials* of 1770, at a place called Gwrgodllys in the parish of Cilmaenllwyd, Carmarthenshire, in 1691, went to Pennsylvania, in 1707. Was ordained at Welshtract, says Mr. Reynald Howell in the above letter. He was pastor there from 1740 to 1748, then removed to Vincent near Yellow Spring, where he continued till he died in 1760, aged sixty-nine. The *Materials* say that "Mr. Owen Morgan left behind him the following remarkable" note, "I have been called upon three times to anoint the sick with oil for recovery. The affects were surprising in each case; but in none more so than in that of our brother Reynald Howell. He was sore with the bruises of the wagon when he was anointed that he could not bear to be turned in bed, otherwise than in the sheet: the next day he was so well that he went to meeting."

The next successor in the ministry was Mr. David Davis, say the *Materials*, born in 1708 in the parish of Whitchurch and county of Pembroke, went to America in 1710, took the care of the church at Welshtract in 1748, and continued it to his death in 1769, aged 61. Mr. Edwards was acquainted with him personally and says that he was an excellent man, and had in precious memory by all that knew him. "He left three sons and as many daughters. His son Jonathan was in 1770 minister of the seventh day church at Cohensey.

His son John succeeded his father and was there in 1770, when the *Materials* were printed: but not then as pastor, but as supply and probationer. But he left that church before the end of that year: for Mr. Backus in his History Vol. 2, p. 275, says that John Davis, M.A. was educated at the college in Philadelphia, came to Boston in New England in May 1770, was ordained pastor of the second Baptist church there in Sept. following. He there behaved with spirit and judgement in behalf of the Baptist churches, and was furiously treated for it, by the oppressors, but he confuted their pleas without taking any notice of the personal abuse that was offered him." On which account a gentleman present said, "The worth of the man never appeared so great before." September 10, 1774. "The Warren Association made choice of him as their agent, to use his best endeavors, by the advice of their committee, in concert with his agents in London, to obtain the establishment of equal religious liberty in America." But his health soon impaired, in August 1772, took a voyage to Philadelphia, hoping to receive benefit from his native air and obtaining some relief to preach to the western Indians, in hopes of further relief; but he grew worse and finished his cause on the banks of the Ohio the 13th of December. That very year in the prime of life, respect and usefulness, the thirty-sixth year of his age. The minister who was with him informed that some of his last words were these. "In a little time I expect to be with Christ; to see and know him, as he is now known, and as he is not known. My faith in my Saviour is unshaken." He was fellow of Rhode Island College, and one of the members of the American Philosophical Society. So far Mr. Backus but here a little abridged. In a letter from Dr. Jones, Lower Dublin, it is said, "the remains of Mr. J. Davis were laid under a great tree, on the banks of the Ohio." The circumstances of the place then, it seems required it to be so. I knew none of these things when the Welsh History was printed, therefore he is there only mentioned as succeeding his father, as the *Materials* say he was a probationer there then, which was at that time true, but he soon left the place, as above.

Contemporary with Mr. D. Davis at Welshtract was Mr. Griffith Jones of whom see above. In a letter to Mr. Miles Harris the latter speaks highly and respectfully of the former.

Of the church at Welshtract the *Materials* inform, that in 1770 he was of sixty-nine years standing, it was so long however since that church emigrant had sailed from Wales they had then six ministers, all born in the three counties of Pembroke, Carmarthen, and Cardigan, of whom the *Materials* p. 21 says "The ministry of this church hath been filled with great and good men, who have been as useful, and have supported the sacred character as well as any set of Clergy in America. The church is to be commended also as the first who received the confession of faith of 1689, for their zeal for laying on of hands, their strict discipline, and their keeping exact records, but in Welsh till 1732.

The Beginnings of Welshtract

I sent over for some extracts out of those Welsh records, it seems they cannot now write Welsh there, but they were so kind as to translate some of them into English as well as they could, and the following, the sum of which follows.

"In the year 1701, there was a number of the members of the Baptist churches in the counties of Pembroke, Carmarthen, and Cardigan inclined to emigrate to Pennsylvania. Having consulted among themselves, they laid the case before the churches, who agreed to grant them leave to go. But the churches considered that as they were sixteen members and one of them a minister, it would be better for them to be constituted a church in their native land; they agreed and did so. Being thus formed into a church, they gave them a letter of recommendation for their reception as brethren, should they meet any Christians of the same faith and practice. They sailed from Milford-Haven in June that year, and arrived in Philadelphia in September.

They met with kind reception from the church meeting at Pennepec and Philadelphia. They spent about a year and a half in that vicinity, in a dispersed way. These new comers kept their meetings weekly and monthly among themselves: but held Christian conference with the other church, with which they wholly agreed but in the article of Laying on of hands, to which the newcomers strictly adhered: but the majority of the other church opposed it. In the year and a half that way they had two and twenty added to them, which probably made 38. But at the end of this term, these with others from Wales, purchased a large tract of land in Newcastle county on Delaware, which in their own language, they called Rhandiry cymrn,but being turned into English, Welshtract. This was in the year 1703, and in the same year they built their meeting house. In the extract the names of the sixteen are given, there Thomas Griffiths is called pastor; and Elisha Thomas is called Elijeus Thomas. There also they give the names of the two and twenty added, as above. The extract mentions several attempts made between the two churches to agree about laying on of hands, but that matter could not be finally settled till 1706, when it was agreed by the two churches to choose twenty-five of their members, as deputies to meet and consult about this affair, their names were recorded. These were the reasons of that meeting. 1. Brotherly love at the Lord's table is so desirable. 2. Scoffers take occasion to reproach religion; because of contentions between Christians and churches. 3. Some members of Welshtract church were nearer Pennepec than their own place; and some of them nearer Welshtract.

Those deputies, after many prayers and consultations agreed, 1. That the members of each church might have transient occasional communion but the Welshtract church was not to receive any as full members without laying on of hands. 2. That each church might have liberty to preach and practice relative to laying on of hands without offence to the other. 3. That this matter was not to be publicly mentioned in any yearly meeting, or Association.

Then the transcriber says, "I am of opinion that the above is the true substance of the records, relative to the first settlement of the Welshtract church, Isaiah Lewis." After they sent it to Abel Davis, with this note, "Please to examine the records to see whether this is rightly translated." Then Abel Davis signed it. Then it was transported to Leominster by Mr. (now Dr.) Jones. But there follows:

"There were thirteen added to them the first after their abode at the Tract, two by letters from Wales, and eleven by Baptism, and in a few years they became numerous, many were added to them from different churches in Wales, and large additions yearly by personal profession before the church; so that in a few years a hundred and twelve were added to the first thirty-eight, and many of these were gifted brethren, in all 150." But probably some had died.

New Churches formed from Welshtract

Pages 1–8 above should be considered as part of Rhydwilim History and it does them honor too. It may be looked upon as no contemptible part thereof. But that is not all, a little more must be added here. Mr. Morgan Edwards, author of the *Materials*, in a letter to the writer of this dated 5th Nov. 1784, says "Mr. Joshua Edwards was born in Pembrokeshire Feb. 11th 1703, landed (in America) about 1721, was ordained July 15th 1751, was alive in 1772, had eleven children, but had not the particular care of any church." Then in the same letter he informs, that about the year 1737, about thirty members from Welshtract removed to Peedee, in South Carolina, and there formed a church in 1738, which church is now (said he then) shot into five branches, that is, Cashawa, Catfish, Capefear, Linches Creek, and Mar's Bluff or Cliff. Mr. Joshua Edwards is one of the ministers who served those churches lately.

Mr. (now Dr.) J. Jones, in a letter of June 1784, said that he assisted at the constitution of a branch of Welshtract church, in Nov. 1780. That new church is called London tract; the minister Mr. Thomas Fleeson. He mentions another church formed out of it, but does not give the name. So the daughter church in America proved similar to the mother church in Wales both happily prolific. But more still from America.

Pastors of the American Churches

Mr. Jenkin Jones was born in the parish of Llandudoch, Pembrokeshire about 1686, and went to Pennsylvania about 1710 and was called to the ministry at Welshtract in 1724, but was chosen to the pastoral care at Pennepec in 1725, where he continued to 1746, when the Baptist church properly formed at Philadelphia, which was before a kind of a branch of Pennepec. But upon this formation, Mr. Jenkin Jones resigned at the latter place, and became the first proper pastor of the new formed church; which he continued till he died 1760. His character in the *Materials* is that he "was a good man and has done real services to the church, and to the Baptist interest."

Of Mr. James Davis, a member of Rhydwilim, see what is said above, and how useful he was. By the *Materials* he was one of the eight men who originally formed the church which settled at Welshtract, however the name is there; and he seems to be the same person. Mr. Hugh Davis, also mentioned there, belonged probably to Rhydwilim and those parts. His successor at great valley, Mr. John Davis, say the *Materials,* was born in the parish of Llanfornach and county of Pembroke, in 1702, went to America in 1713. Was called to the ministry in 1722. Ordained in 1732, assisted Mr. Hugh Davis till he died in 1753. Then succeeded in the pastoral care. He died in 1778, his funeral sermon was preached Nov. 1st, by the present Dr. J. Jones, as he informed in a letter. His brother was Mr. Thomas Davis, the first minister of the church at Oyster Bay, in the province of New York, formed in 1748. He died a few years before his brother John Davis (Dr. J). But a letter from Mr. Morgan Edwards says, Mr. Thomas Davis was born in Llanfornach 1708, went to America in 1713, was baptized 1727, ordained 1740, died a bachelor in 1777.

Mr. Joshua Jones was born in 1724, in the parish of Newcastle and county of Pembroke, went to America in 1726, was ordained at New Britian in 1761. He was there lately.

According to Mr. M. Edwards, Welshtract meeting is situated in the county of Newcastle, forty-five miles from Philadelphia. S.W.B.W. And Great Valley, where Mr. Hugh Davis was, in the township of Tredyssryn (a British word denoting a town in a valley) Chester county, eighteen miles from Philadelphia NNW. Thus for the American Digression. It is full time to return to Rhydwilim and proceed.

Progress of the Church at Wales

It is observed that Mr. Morgan Griffiths had his dismission to Hengoed about 1702. The death of Mr. G. Howells is not yet given, nor can it be given exactly. Information says that he died in 1705 or 6. He was buried in the place he had prepared for the purpose. As there was no stone put on his grave, his age is not known. It is remarkable, that of twelve ministers in this church about 1689 (as is supposed Mr. Morgan Griffiths had begun to preach about that time or soon after) that by 1702, there were left but Messrs. John Jenkins and Samuel Jones (then called S. John) and Mr. G. H. who soon finished.

That was a considerable reduction in 12 or 13 years of peace, and so many raised in a time of so much persecution, of the other nine it is supposed that four or five of them were dead, and four or five alive in other places serving honorably in the ministry.

In 1704 another distant branch formed a new church now Cilfowyr. Mr. Samuel Jones was one of the constituents and was then or soon after settled in the pastoral care.

Upon this the care of the Mother Church necessarily fell upon Mr. John Jenkins, though he soon had assistants, of whom more beyond by and by. Mr. John Jenkins, was baptized in 1677, as noted above. In the ms. Mr. John Richards saith of him, that before his conversion, he was a wild and willful youth, playing football, wrestling, and any robust diversion, profaning the Lord's day; stripping to fight, in an instant, if offended or provoked; but that divine grace wrought so great a change in his disposition, that he became a very solid prudent man, much respected by neighbors and acquaintance in general, who knew well his conduct and profane life.

When he entered upon the ministry, he exerted himself with indefatigable diligence at home, and often abroad. His great spirit still continued, but happily turned into a better channel. According to information he attended the Association at Bristol and in the West of England: but was highly pleased when the Association was set up in Wales in 1700. He was of a strong constitution and made good use of his strength. Ms.,p.76 above informs how he strove to assist Hengoed, in their straits. Information says that he did sometimes take that long journey afoot, quite from the border of Pembrokeshire. He bore his part of the persecution, as he bore the yoke in his youth, and was immune to hardships, he took pleasure in labor.

The Association in the Principality was kept alternately at Llanwenarth and Swansea, till 1708. That year it was held at the new place, Rhydwilim. For some years nothing remarkable occurs regarding this church; it appeared gloomy enough the latter part of Queen Ann's reign, here and through the land, but that cloud in mercy did blow over.

Ministers of Welsh and English Churches

There is a hint above, that Mr. Jenkins had helps in the ministry: those assistants were Mr. David James, Thomas Matthias and Philip Jones (then called John). By report these began to preach about the same time, which was about 1700, not much sooner or later.

Mr. Neal, in his ms. says of these parts, that the ministers of Rhydwilim, in 1715, were John Jenkins, David Matthias, and Samuel

John. Whoever sent this information, it was very deficient and wrong. Cilfowyr was a separate church, ten or eleven years before 1715, and Mr. Samuel Jones pastor there. Thomas (not David) Matthias has an assistant and John Jenkins pastor at Rhydwilim. But that ms. says that Deujland and Cilfowyr were destitute. Yet Deujland was a branch of Rhydwilim church and properly supplied.

In a list of our country ministers in London, 1718 those of this place are thus named, John Jenkins, Thomas Matthias, David James and Philip John. This is a proper time and list.

About this time or soon after, another new meeting house was erected, in the parish of Llanddewi, above named, not far from Rush-acre. That place in common is called Tfynnon. Soon after the house was finished, some frivolous wranglings took place among some of the members about a mere trifle. But the consequence proved very bitter indeed. Had they then well considered Prov. XVII:14 it had been well for them and many more. Tempers and some strong passions were much inflamed. Probably it was about 1755 that I happened to find some loose papers in Brecknockshire, giving a very particular account of the rise and progress of the debate. It would have been well, perhaps, if those particulars had never been written. But now I hope they are all buried for ever. What is recorded here is forwarn-ing, caution; and thanksgiving.

In the letter to the association in 1724, it is observed, that Mr. John Jenkins was the only pastor when Mr. John Evans, above named, died; that sometime after Mr. Thomas Matthias was ordained; but that not long after that the latter had given up preaching; that was on account of some dejection in his own mind, says report. But upon that Mr. David James and Philip Jones were ordained. Soon after that, says the letter, Mr. Philip Jones died. But no date given when any of these things happened.

Mr. Thomas Matthias, saith in the records, he was baptized in 1701. Other informations says that he was educated with a design to be in the established ministry, was about nine and twenty when he joined this church, so it may be supposed it was not long after before he began to preach.

It is recorded that Mr. Philip Jones was baptized in 1706. The above letter of 1724, gives him a worthy character. It is supposed he died about 1720. The writer of this often thought that the late worthy Mr. Philip Jones, many years minister of the Baptist church at Myton upon Severn, was a brother's son to this Philip Jones of Rhydwilim; but he never happened to ask Mr. Jones of Upton whence his father came else very probably he would have given the true information, but he used to call the Welsh his brethren.

In the life of the Rev. Thomas Hiller in the Baptist Register, he is said to have been a sister's son to Mr. Jones of Upton, and a grandson to "Mr. Samuel Jones of Kingstanley, a pious, persecuted, and imprisoned nonconformist." This Samuel Jones is supposed to have been from Rhydwilim, and probably a brother then to the above Philip Jones. If any further light may be cast upon this, best of all. Here now it must lie.

It is supposed the Tfynnon meeting house was finished about 1720. Soon after that the contention began to work; as a small quantity of leaven, which yet spread soon through the whole lump. The whole church split in two, one part headed by Mr. John Jenkins, the other unhappily by Mr. David James. The trouble originated chiefly betwixt the two ministers, but soon ran through the whole, and they were numerous. It distressed the Association greatly in 1724. They could there, by no means, reconcile the two parts. In the circular letter of that year there are hints of that sorrow. There it was desired and directed, that all the churches would keep the first Wednesday in the month, a day of fasting and prayer, on divers accounts and this contention in particular, for six months successively. But this society continued in two parties, and acted even as two separate churches, though bitter enough toward each other. They administered ordinances and received members to both parties. If the papers were rightly understood, Mr. John Jenkins' party was about fourscore; and the other about seven score. The churches in the connection were much grieved; there were public and private prayers, that at the approaching Association at Llanelli, 1725, a reconciliation might be brought about. In order to that several had written letters to promote the design. Both parties did write their separate letters to that meeting. The expected time came and after much debate, the two ministers and their respective parties, were prevailed upon to make concessions on each side. This laid a happy foundation for a future reconciliation. The churches were desired to observe days of thanksgiving in the same order as they had kept days of fasting and prayer the preceding year.

In 1726 the Association was at Cilfowyr. The Rhydwilim wound was not quite healed, it was there further handled, in order to finish and establish what had been so happily set on foot at Llanelli. That meeting being so near, many of the Rhydwilim members attended. In order to conciliate matters, it was agreed to have the Association at Rhydwilim in 1728 and at Llangloffan, the other part in 1729. Thus a tolerable end was made to a very disagreeable debate. There were godly and very worthy men on each side; provoking and irritating expressions were the chief crimes through the whole. These caused some unbecoming actions at times. But let these never be raised out of the grave of oblivion. How happy for church members to keep a due guard over their spirits and speeches!

No certainty appears when Mr. D. James ended his days. Information only says, that he died before the contention ended. By several circumstances, it is concluded that he finished his course between that convention of 1725, and that of 1726. The character given to him is very good. His ministerial talent very acceptable, and his conversation becoming the gospel. But his troubles in the passage through this wilderness were many. His distresses in that afflictive contention were neither small nor few. In parting with a dear friend, who long survived him, he said feelingly, "remember David and all his afflictions." Psalm 132:1. His name is among those who signed the circular letters in 1721 and 1722. He was appointed to preach at the association in 1723, but whether the contention prevented that is not uncertain. Thus it seems Mr. P. Jones died about the beginning of that trouble and Mr. David James before it wholly ended. Mr. John Jenkins still the pastor and probably Mr. Thomas Matthias persuaded again to return to the ministry and assist.

Mr. John Philips was baptized here in 1720. He was a sprightly young man, very ready of utterance, and promising for the ministry if not too forward, which is not always the best sign. He was the second pupil that Mr. Foskett had at Bristol under his tuition for the ministry. Having finished there he was some time at Usk in Monmouthshire. There was a wish to revive the interest there after the death of Mr. N. Morgan. Mr. Philips could preach in Welsh and in English. He was at Usk several years. See more of him below. But he left Usk, and went to Wrexham, then to London, he never settled long with any people, was a kind of itinerant, mostly in England, and was reckoned a good speaker, and an acceptable judicious preacher; but there was a roughness in his natural temper, which prevented his usefulness, he lived to advanced years; and died in 1761. He did not turn out so useful as at first expected. May young and aged ministers be ever well clothed with humility, that garment will warm and adorn.

About 1731, another branch formed a new church at Moleston in the parish of Narberth, near Rushacre, which had been of such note in the last century. Of that see below.

Now the account of the truly reverend and famous Mr. John Jenkins must be closed. He had been uncommonly active and useful in all the Baptist churches in South Wales. His penetration into persons and things, was very piercing and quick. He was warm in his natural temper and, though much molified by grace, by age and experience; he continued to be of a heroic undaunted spirit to the last. His discerning faculty was remarkable, and his talent to manage church affairs and discipline was excellent. He preached according to appointment at Penysai, the Association, 1733, though the journey to the place was so far, and he so advanced in years.

There was a Welsh Elegy composed upon his death, where his peculiar excellencies, are respectfully expressed: but I do not find that it was ever printed. There is now in the writer's possession in Welsh Manuscript an old bound book in Mr. J. Jenkins' handwriting. It was the property of Mr. Wm. Herbert, of whom see below. He wrote a title page to it thus, "A Golden Grove in a Stormy Day; or Saints Cordials in Persecuting Times." He further, on a blank page wrote thus, "Wm. Herbert's book had in exchange for another printed book, of John Jenkins' daughter, Jannet Prichard 1733, I received the book of John Jenkins before his decease. It contains notes of 40 sermons, chiefly calculated for times of persecution, mostly penned and preached for those times." Thus Mr. William Herbert. It was composed in younger days. In the close of it there is a serious address to the reader, by the author himself. He finished July 3rd, 1733, aged seventy-seven. He was buried at Rhydwilim, and a stone set upon his grave. His brother David was a ruling Elder in the church. Probably Mr. Evan Jenkins was also his brother. These two are named with him in the list of 1689. Of his son Mr. E. Jenkins and his grandson Dr. J. Jenkins, see above.

In the letter to the Association in 1734, they very affectionately lament their loss, observing, that their late aged minister was to them a very dear pastor and friend, much respected by them, and that the loss of him was like the fall of a great pillar, or as if a bright candle had gone out.

Now the pastoral care of this church devolved upon Mr. Thomas Matthias, who had been for many years an assistant and colleague with the deceased.

In the account sent to London of the Welsh ministers in 1734, it is said, that Mr. Thomas Matthias was a lively preacher and very useful, and that he had three in the church to assist in the ministry, who were named Messrs. David Richard, John James, and John Folk. Of these more below. Mr. Thomas Matthias was full of vivacity which he used to good purpose in the ministry. He was advanced in years when his predecessor died: so could not be many years the leading pastor here. He was a man of letters, as already noted: of good natural parts, and a quick ready disposition. His memory remarkable. By information, he had an uncommon talent to repeat an English sermon in Welsh, when the preacher happened to be an English man. Mr. Matthias was so ready both ways. He would remember it so well, and render it with such propriety in the other language, that it was amazing. He finished in May, 1745, aged seventy-three.

Mr. John Folk, according to the book, was baptized in 1702. He was a useful active member, a messenger to the Association often. He had ministerial gifts, which he used occasionally, when needful, to prevent more vacancies. He was deservedly esteemed among the ministering helpers. He thus assisted for many years, it does not appear exactly how many, nor what year he died, nor what his age. It is supposed that he died about 1740.

The Rhydwilim Church Divides

A numerous branch of Rhydwilim Church met to worship at Llangloffan, Densland, already mentioned, otherwise called the Hundred of Cibidiog. The church had for years consisted of two parts; one met at Rhydwilim, the other at Llangloffan; but they continued one church, during the life of Mr. Thomas Matthias out of respect to him in his old age. Upon his decease, the church was without a proper pastor, though there were two ordained assistants in the church, and other acceptable preachers. This juncture was prudently considered as a proper opportunity to divide, in love for mutual conveniency. In their letter to the Association that year this affair was mentioned, and the reasons for Llangloffan to be formed given thus, 1. Because members and hearers were more than one house could contain. 2. Because they were so far from each other. 3. Because they found it difficult to keep up proper discipline especially among those who lived about mid–way between the two parts. These reasons were approved by all. Ministers as well as members divided, all in love and harmony.

The two ordained assistants were Mr. David Richard, who had been ordained about 1726, after the death of Mr. David James; and Mr. John James, who had been ordained about 1734, after the death of Mr. John Jenkins. The latter was chosen to the pastoral care at Rhydwilim, and the former to that of the new church at Llangloffan. The major part of the assistants resided nearer the new church, so continued there.

Progress at Rhydwilim

Now let us follow the mother church still. We see who the pastor was, the assistant was Mr. John Griffiths. The pastor was esteemed a godly, solid, experimental preacher, yet not popular in those days. His method was not so taking with young people as some others were. The book mentions but few, if any, added there before 1748: several were baptized then, and for four or five years after; but not above one or two from 1752 to 1756. Some, though not many, were baptized afterward for a few years. In April 1757, Mr. Benjamin Morgan was baptized. Mr. James entertained some hope that he would be useful in the ministry. He behaved towards him with great tenderness and fondness encouraging him to exercise in prayer in a private way, and then more public at proper seasons. But the good man hastened to the end of his race. He appeared aged and feeble, though but sixty-two when he died in Feb. 1760.

At the death of that pastor the church was left more destitute of ministers than it had been in ever since it was constituted, then 92 years back. But they were assisted by others, particularly by Llangloffan and Cilfowyr, where they had plenty. At the former of these places, Mr. David Thomas was one of three ordained there lately. His lot was to take a farm not far from Rhydwilim. This was considered a kind providence in favor of the destitute church. That naturally led him to assist them more than others could do, he being so near. He being a popular preacher, the cause revived many were baptized, by one and another, before they fixed upon a pastor.

About 1762, they agreed in Mr. David Thomas to be their pastor. They had then had mutual trial on both sides. One book records, that he baptized at twelve different times there that year; but no account that he baptized any the preceeding year. Mr. Joshua Thomas was baptized there in 1762.

Mr. Benjamin Morgan, already named, began to preach in 1761. With the approbation and recommendation of the church, he went to Bristol, under the tuition of Messrs. H. and C. Evans, for further improvement, in 1762. There continued preaching occasionally, till 1765; then he went in a probationary way to King Stanley, Glocestershire. There they had about twenty baptized in the first year he went to them. Being chosen there to settle, he was ordained in 1767. But so unhappy it was, that they were not long after comfortable. Mr. Morgan left them in 1770, and was somewhat more than a year at or near Falmouth in Cornwall. Being not like to settle there, he removed to Gamlingay, which had been a branch of the famous Mr. Bunyan's church when he lived at Bedford. He was not very comfortable there. In 1776 he removed to Ashford, in Kent. From thence he removed to Swansea in 1784. And from there to Bridgewater, Somerset in 1791. Mr. Joshua Thomas went to Bristol, with the same view in 1766. He was a judicious promising young man. His time at Bristol was not long, for he was invited by the destitute church at Lymington, Hampshire, to supply in a probationary way before the end of 1767. There had been no addition to that church six or seven years, so they were in a dejected state; yet soon after he came, the auditory increased, and at a proper time some were baptized. They wanted a new meeting house, and resolved to build one, which they did, and exerted themselves honorably to defray the expense. They could not well bear it all, which was about 400£ of which they did about one half. He was sent to

London with their case, in hope of further help. He was well received and respected in the city. While there in May 1769, I had a letter from him,informing that he had met with great encouragement and success, and almost collected what was necessary. He expressed his thankfulness to God, and the grateful sense he had of the kindness of friends. Then observes that he designed to return that week, as some at Lymington were then to be baptized, and others expected soon. Thus he left the capital in hope of a speedy and comfortable interview with his friends at home. But alas! how great, how sudden the disappointment! Information says, that on the road he was put into a damp bed, fell ill, and died at or near Portsmouth, on his way to Lymington. This young minister was thus removed in the bloom of his youth and usefulness. How precarious all things here! Yet happy those who die in the Lord and in his work. All is well with them.

For some years Mr. D. Thomas went on very happy and prosperous at Rhydwilim. In about eight years the book records, that he baptized about 127. The last account of that ordinance administered by him is in August 1769. He had then been in the ministry about twenty years, was a popular preacher, and had been invited to the pastoral care of one church and another in the course of that time, yet he declined all but this.Very probably the applause of men did him an injury, nor did he sufficiently consider the solemn caution, "Be not highminded, but fear." It would be well for all, but especially ministers of the gospel, often to ponder upon another caution given by divine inspiration, "Let him that thinketh he standeth, take heed lest he fall." This popular preacher fell and brought much reproach upon his profession and the ministry. He was, not only silenced from preaching, "but excluded from all church fellowship and connection." They never would admit him after into this church. In a course of years he began to preach again, and appeared very penitent yet other churches refused communion to him, though he humbly applied. But at last he was admitted to a certain church. He finished his course in 1784. It is hoped all was pardoned through precious blood.

This sorrowful affair happened at Rhydwilim in 1769. They were reduced to the necessity of looking out for a pastor. They applied to Mr. George Rees, a collegue to the last at Llangloffan, they had been both ordained there the same time. He came occasionally to supply and administer ordinances. Others also assisted while in that situation. Mr. Rees was invited to the pastoral care; but his own church was not quite willing to spare him, though they had others. In 1771 he engaged to preach and administer ordinances to them as an occasional necessary supply, for some time, with the consent of Llangloffan church: but without a dismission. Thus it continued until 1775, when a dismission was at last granted; and he took their pastoral care; in which he continues to this day, (1793) with honor and reputation, as a worthy minister of the gospel of Christ. In 1782 the members were about three hundred, of late they had large additions. In the association this year the number stood thus: baptized– 36, restored– 2, dead– 11, excluded– 2.

In 1773 Salem church was constituted, and the major part of those constitutents were members of Rhydwilim.

It was observed that Rhydwilim meeting house was built in 1701. It was enlarged in 1763. The addition is near as large as the original house. It is now a double house, with a double roof. When Moleston was incorporated, it was agreed that both churches should have right to the Ffynnon meeting house. The ministers of the two churches continue to preach there still in their proper turns, as best suits, and as they agree among themselves.

There was a small meeting house erected in 1756, in the parish of Ciffyg, Carmarthen Shire. It is called Bwlch–gwynt. That place is also for the use of Rhydwilim and Moleston, from the beginning, as it may best suit.

They have another meeting house pertaining to Rhydwilim called Clynback, and the same county: and another built in 1776 in the parish of Llanboydy, called Ty–gwyn.

Rhydwilim meeting house is about eight miles from the town of Narberth, about Northwest. Clynback is about five miles from Rhydwilim Northeast; and Ty-gwyn about nine miles from Narberth, Northeast. The bearing of Ffynnon about 3 miles Northeast, and of Bwlch, about eight miles east of Narberth.

In 1779 Mr. John Griffiths, the aged assistant died.

Gradually Mr. Gabriel Rees was raised up in the church, and after proper trial of his ministerial gifts, he was ordained in July 1789, to assist Mr. George Rees, who had served this large church without any ordained help for near twenty years, and advancing in years too. They are both there now, 1794.

There are several other useful and acceptable promising assistants as Misters Morris Evans, Thomas Williams, William Williams, John Llewelyn, Morris Morris, and Daniel Evans. They are thus given in the order of their seniority, some of them have exercised for several years. There is another of a good character who exercises his talent, his name is not given. They are not only at peace among themselves, but indulged with happy success, and many added to them of late. The minutes of the Association in 1793, informs, that 36 were baptized as above that year, those of 1794, inform that 80 that year were added.

Of the new church formed at Bwlch-gwynt, mentioned in the last page, on the 29th October, 1794. There were only two of the members of Rhydwilim among the constituents there, but the ministers of this church assisted there, and probably still.

Below Mr. Benjamin Evans is named as one of the nephews of the aged pastor at Cilfowyr; and he is named among the ministers of that church. Though his relation to the pastor appears to be right; yet further information proves thus, that he was three years under the tuition of Mr. Griffiths of Glandwr, an independant minister, justly celebrated for learning abilities. There Mr. Benjamin Evans had his grammar and classical learning. While in that place he was baptized at Rhydwilim, being then nearer to him than Cilfowyr. Thus he became a member where he was baptized, in May, 1789. There was soon called to the ministry, and recommended to the Bristol seminary in August that very year. He was there till 1793, and in the summer, that year, he went to Sutton in the Elms, Leicester Shire. There he was ordained in July 1794. See the Register, Vol. 2, page 345. There he is comfortably and usefully situated at that time. May 1797.

Rhydwilim Ministers

1. Mr. William Jones, the origin of them all, it is supposed that he died rather before 1700.
2. Mr. Griffith Howells a very worthy useful minister, he finished about 1705.
3. Mr. Thomas David Rees separated with Glandwr about 1696.
4. Mr. George Jones the first raised up in the young church, died about 1700.
5. Mr. James James, was one of the constituents at Glandwr about 1696.
6. Mr. Evan David supposed to have been the same 1696.
7. Mr. John Jenkins served long and honorably in the ministry here 1733.
8. Mr. Richard Williams removed to Trosgoed about 1700.
9. Mr. John David, a worthy assistant died about 1700.
10. Mr. Thomas Griffith, went to America, where he was very honorable 1701.
11. Mr. Morgan Griffiths was chosen pastor at Hengoed about 1701.
12. Mr. Hugh David, as member here, went to America from Swansea 1710.
13. Mr. Samuel Jones, chosen pastor to Cilcam and Cilfowyr 1704.
14. Mr. Philip Jones, and useful minister, died rather young 1720.
15. Mr. David James who went through many troubles and died about 1725.
16. Mr. Thomas Matthias long in the ministry, though sole pastor but

about 12 years 1745.
17. Mr. John Philips he did not long settle in any place 1761.
18. Mr. Griffith Williams settled pastor at Moleston in 1731.
19. Mr. John Folk a useful help for many years, died about 1740.
20. Mr. David Richard a chosen pastor at Llangloffan 1745.
21. Mr. Evan Jenkinschosen pastor at Wrexham, where he died in 1752.
22. Mr. Daniel Garmon one of the Llangloffan constituents in 1745.
23. Mr. Evan Davis the same died 1745.
24. Mr. David Lewis the same died 1745.
25. Mr. Henry Morgan also the same died 1745.
26. Mr. John James who succeeded Mr. Thomas Matthias in the pastoral care and died 1760.
27. Mr. Benjamin Morgan, now pastor at Bridgewater, Bevon.
28. Mr. Joshua Thomas promising for usefulness at Lymington, but died 1769. (Not the Author)
29. Mr. David Thomas, succeeded Mr. J. James as pastor, but was excluded about 1769.
30. Mr. George Rees succeeded, and is the worthy aged pastor there now. (He died in 1795.)
31. Mr. Gabriel Rees worthy ordained assistant 1607.
32. Mr. John Griffiths, an assistant many years, but not ordained, he died 1779.
33. Mr. Daniel Thomas another acceptable and younger assistant, died 1781.
34. Mr. Morris Evans
35. Mr. Thomas Williams
36. Mr. William Williams
37. Mr. John Llewlyn
38. Mr. Morris Morris
39. Mr. Daniel Evans

These six acceptable candidates and helpers.

These are not all the ministers raised at Rhydwilim. Several from these parts were eminent elsewhere, as Mr.Jenkin Jones, Owen Thomas, David Davis, John Davis, Joshua Jones, already named, and probably other noted ministers in America drew their first breath in these parts, though they did not begin to preach here; and sons of some of them etc. (1794 J. Thomas.)

Of Mr. George Rees above, see the Baptist Register, Vol. 2, p. 336. Besides what is said there of him, I have heard the following anecdote of him;

Of Mr. B. Evans, see below.

The very first time he exercised in public his friends published him in a certain place unknown to him. When he heard of it he was much dejected, but his friends encouraged him all they could to prepare and go. He was very reluctant to comply, but when the time came, he set out, it seems by himself but on the road he so sunk in his mind that he lay down and slept, then he thought some voice said to him, "Be strong and show thyself a man." He soon got up, but could not recollect whether it were a passage of scripture or not. He went to the place and found many people come, and from among them a good old woman came to meet him, and addressed him with the very same words: Being rather surprised; he asked her where she had the words. Having her Bible under her arm she said. "It is David's advice to his son Solomon, I Kings 2:2."

PART TWO

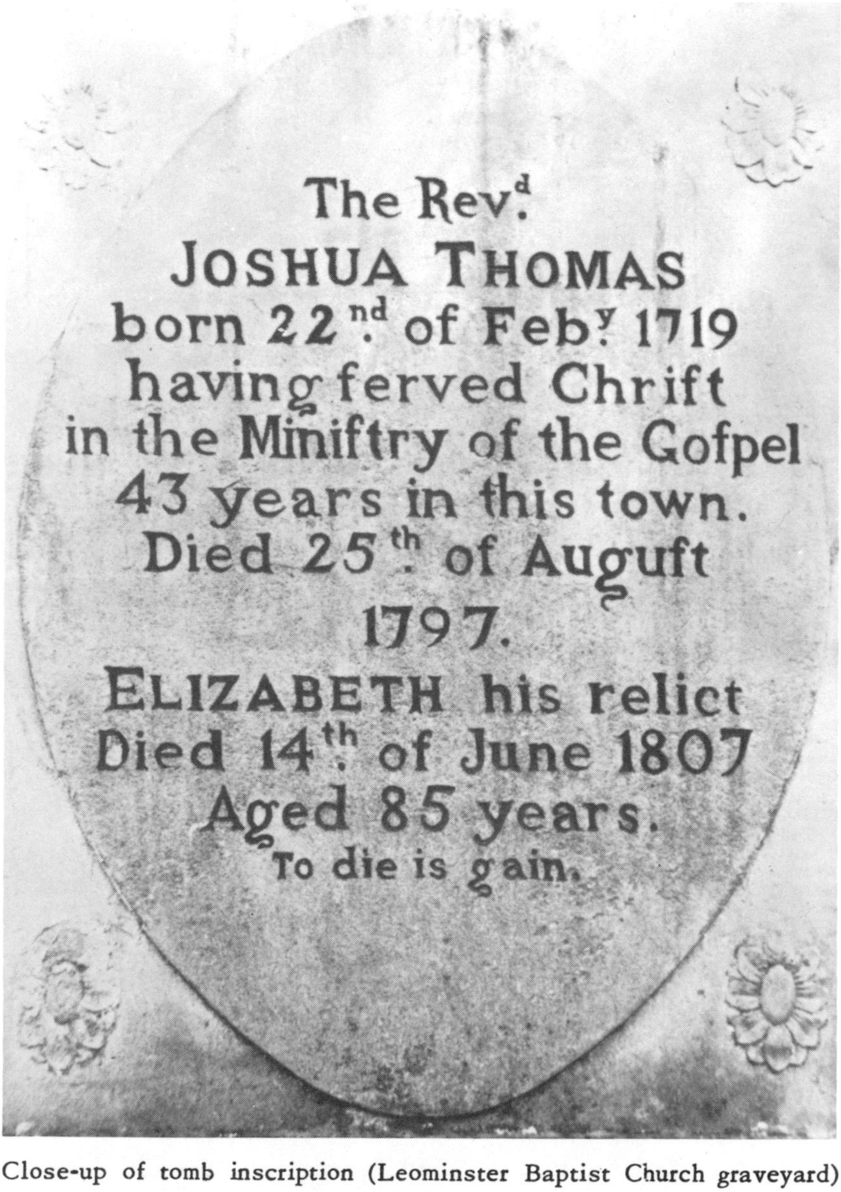
The Revd.
JOSHUA THOMAS
born 22nd. of Feby. 1719
having ferved Chrift
in the Miniftry of the Gofpel
43 years in this town.
Died 25th. of Auguft
1797.
ELIZABETH his relict
Died 14th. of June 1807
Aged 85 years.
To die is gain.

Close-up of tomb inscription (Leominster Baptist Church graveyard)

JOSHUA THOMAS

a biography
by

ERIC W. HAYDEN

ABOUT THE AUTHOR

After two years' architectural training and then six years' wartime service during the Second World War, Eric W. Hayden felt called of God to the Christian ministry. He received his theological and ministerial training at Spurgeon's College, London, England, and is also a graduate of the University of Durham. He obtained his Master of Arts degree by submitting a thesis on "The Pauline Conception of Baptism with special reference to the doctrine of Christ–mysticism."

Mr. Hayden's first church was Whitley Bay Baptist Church, Northumberland, and his second Claremont Baptist Church, Shrewsbury. He then became Pastor of Spurgeon's Metropolitan Tabernacle, London for almost six years. In 1962 he became Pastor of Leominster Baptist Church in Herefordshire, where Joshua Thomas was Minister for 43 years. During his years in Leominster Mr. Hayden did much research into Joshua Thomas's life and ministry, travelling to Aberystwyth in Wales, Oxford and Bristol, to study at first hand documents in Joshua Thomas's own handwriting.

Eleven books have been published by Mr. Hayden, several of them in America. One has been translated into German. He also wrote the "capsule histories" of C. H. Spurgeon for the jackets of the *Metropolitan Tabernacle Pulpit* being published in America by Pilgrim Publications of Pasadena, Texas. Pilgrim Publications are also re–issuing his *Centennial History of Spurgeon's Tabernacle,* published in England in 1962.

Mr. Hayden has preached on several occasions on British radio and television. He is married with two children.

AUTHOR'S PREFACE

How strange that no full biography has ever been written about a man whose career occupies two columns in the *Dictionary of Welsh Biography*! Since he was a Welshman, and has placed so many nonconformist church historians in his debt through his historical writings, one would have expected a fellow–countryman to have attempted a biography and assessment of the widely–renowned and greatly–used Joshua Thomas.

As a man he was obviously a dominating personality; as a preacher he was powerful and successful, although probably possessing little of the characteristic Welsh "fire" or *hwyl*; as a man of prayer he was devout and fervent; as a Pastor he was diligent and sympathetic; and as a "revivalist" he travelled far and wide, stirring up the churches, reviving flagging or dying causes. As a writer he both translated the works of other men and composed his own. His output was tremendous. But it is as an historian that he has left his true mark upon the religious scene.

The only traceable "likeness" of Joshua Thomas is an engraving in the *Evangelical Magazine* for 1798. There is no oil painting to grace the vestry walls of any church he served. He wrote little about himself in a descriptive way so it is difficult to build an identikit picture of Thomas the man. We must imagine him as we read about him and his wide ministry through tongue and pen.

For forty–three years Joshua Thomas was Minister of Leominster Baptist Church, Herefordshire. My only qualifications for writing this biography are that I was for eleven years the Minister of that Church and so had access to many manuscripts and books. Previously I was Pastor of Claremont Baptist Church, Shrewsbury, a cause which nearly died an untimely death, and would have done so but for the S.O.S. sent to Joshua Thomas of Leominster—which he was quick to answer. I do have some Welsh blood in me, which naturally draws me to this great man of Wales.

Being situated mid–way between Aberystwyth and Bristol I am indebted to Mr. B.G. Owens, Keeper of Manuscripts and Records of the National Library of Wales for allowing me free access to records, and providing other facilities for the preparation of this biography. The Rev. N.S. Moon, B.A., Librarian of Bristol Baptist College, kindly provided the same facilities, as did the Rev. Dr. B.R. White, M.A. of

Regent's Park College, Oxford. The Rev. J. Mansel John, B.A. of the South Wales Baptist College, Cardiff, has also supplied me with valuable information from time to time. Mrs. Olive Davies, B.A. of Leominster Grammar School, has kindly assisted with some translation into English of Joshua Thomas's Welsh. Professor Glanmor Williams of the University College of Swansea kindly read my original manuscript and offered valuable suggestions.

My deacons at Leominster Baptist Church thought it worth while spending money on having photostat or xerox copies of some of Joshua Thomas' manuscripts, housing them at the Church for the use of future historians. Writing a biography, however, entails more than sitting at a study desk consulting source material. It means visits to various places connected with the subject of the biography. This is what has turned laborious research into sheer delight. Joshua Thomas' country is deep in the hills of Carmarthenshire, and there, on mountain paths, in farmhouse, ruined cottage, and country chapel, the spirit of the man is caught. I can only hope that this "spirit" shines through the resultant printed page.

Ruined walls of Ty-hen, farmhouse in Caio, Carmarthenshire, where Joshua Thomas was born.

Bethel Chapel, Caio, Carmarthenshire, where the Thomas family worshipped. "Bethel" is a Baptist Chapel, erected in 1711, seating 200 people.

Interior of Bethel Chapel, Caio. Photograph taken from gallery – showing pulpit and pews with doors. Services are still conducted in the Welsh language to-day.

JOSHUA THOMAS

I

THE MAN

Joshua Thomas was born on 22 February 1719 at Ty–hen, a small farm in the parish of Caio, Carmarthenshire. Ty–hen, or rather the ruins, can be seen today by anyone willing to journey into remote Welsh hill country. Before reaching Ty–hen there is, in a state of good preservation, Nant–y–llyn farm, where Thomas Morgan Thomas, the father of Joshua, previously lived and worked.

Three boys and two girls were born to Thomas Morgan Thomas and his wife. All became Christians and the three boys all became preachers of the gospel: Joshua, Timothy and Zechariah. The father was at first a Presbyterian. After twenty years of this persuasion he became convinced of the truth of believer's baptism and became a Baptist. Through his influence Baptists were introduced to that part of the country.[1] Moving to Esgair–Ithri, Cwm–pedol, still in the parish of Caio, he and his family settled down in a farmhouse for thirty–eight years, worshipping at Bethel Chapel. He died in 1760, aged 70, when Joshua Thomas was forty–one.

The prevailing social and religious conditions at the time of Joshua's birth are adequately described by Welsh historians. G.N. Evans in *Social Life in Mid–eighteenth Century Anglesey* divides the people of Wales at that time into landowners, middle class, and the poor. Among the middle class were the professional men, including the clergy. Farmers were mainly included among the middle class, although small farmers were classified with artisans among the poor.[2] Of small farmers it is recorded: "They were very much at the mercy of their landlords... (some) threatened to evict from their farms tenants who disagreed with their political or religious views".[3]

Artisans and farmers often formed part of the same family, one son working the farm while another taking up some local craft. In spite of the poverty and hardship this kind of life had much to commend it, especially in the less exposed and more fertile areas.

L.T. Davies and A. Edwards in *Welsh Life in the Eighteenth Century* record that the majority of farms at that time were small, there being few from 600 to 800 acres. More numerous were those of 300 to

[1]*The Baptist Magazine,* 1816– Memoir of Rev. Zechariah Thomas
[2]Op. Cit., (Cardiff 1936) p.86
[3]Ibid.

500 acres, and there were still more of 100 to 200 acres. The general run of farms were from 30 to 100 acres, with the average size being 50 to 60 acres.[4]

The farmers themselves often lived almost as poorly as their labourers; barley, bread, bacon, salt beef, potatoes, cabbages and leeks being their limited menu. In the humbler abode a pocket–knife, with a long blade and a two–pronged fork at the opposite end, took the place of more elaborate cutlery.

This primitive kind of life, however, "in the earlier years of the eighteenth century, produced a fine type of character. Flocks of children were reared to healthy manhood; honest thrift, skill in handicraft, pride in bestowing comely forms upon the simple implements of household life, a full day's work and a sound night's sleep, were some of the rewards".[5]

In such circumstances and amidst such surroundings the young Joshua Thomas was brought up until the age of twenty. Cottages were generally made of mud walls with thatched roofs, although we are told that "the farmers were not averse to pilfering stones from the ruins of neighbouring castles".[6] The general run of Welsh cottage had only two rooms, and many only one. The larger houses, farms, or small houses, were generally colour–washed a warm yellow or pink, but the taste varied in different districts.

In such a cottage or small farmhouse the Thomas children were given a religious upbringing. Spiritual life in Wales at that time was at a low ebb. In some churches the Communion Service was celebrated only once a year. The need for a religious revival was made apparent by the publication in 1721, two years after Joshua Thomas was born, of Erasmus Saunders's *A View of the State of Religion in the Diocese of St. David's*. Saunders described the lamentable condition of the church both materially and spiritually. Men ordained to the church were in some cases practically illiterate, and were only in the ministry "because they were not likely to succeed in any other profession".[7]

It was soon realized that the spiritual regeneration of the country must be brought about through the children. Thus in Ty-hen Joshua and his brothers were taught the Cathechism; at twelve years of age Zechariah (and probably Joshua also) had read through the Old and New Testaments; they took notes of the sermons they heard and copied

---

[4] Op. cit., (London 1939) pp 3,4
[5] Ibid., p. 19
[6] J.E. Lloyd: *A History of Carmarthenshire* (Cardiff 1939), p. 297
[7] L.T. Davies & A. Edwards: *Welsh Life in the Eighteenth Century*, p. 119

out the hymns they sung. Zechariah tells us that he prayed aloud often with his small sister at that time.[8]

In *Seren Gomer,* 1821, we are told something of Thomas Morgan Thomas's Christian character. On moving from Ty-hen to Esgair-Ithri he received rather a cool reception from his new neighbours. Soon, however, his Christian life and witness won them over, his many acts of kindness commending his faith to them. He became like a "lantern" in the vicinity, showing sinners the way to the Saviour. He was gentle, humble, Godly, and like Gaius – a lover of hospitality. Thus his influence at home bore fruit in the life of his sons (Timothy became a useful preacher in and around Bethel Chapel while he lived at home), and his influence in the neighbourhood resulted in the Kingdom of God being extended and the Church of God enlarged. The poem beginning "Boed coffa da am T.M.T." at the end of his obituary notice (page 98, *Seren Gomer,* 1821) concludes:

"Thomas mewn eitha' tymor, – deg enw,
I ganol ei drysor,
Iach hwylgainc bur uchelgor,
Aeth at waith ei berffaith Bor."

Societies for the Reformation of Manners began to come into being at the start of the century and some success attended their efforts. Drunkeness, swearing, profanation of the Lord's Day, and so on, became "generally supressed, and the state of religion very much mended."[9] Independents, Presbyterians and Baptists became eager for an educated ministry and often inserted a clause in their trust deeds to the effect that only Academy-trained men should officiate in their buildings.

The farm or cottage kitchen, however, was the "theological college" of most lay or local preachers. It was there that religious topics were discussed and visiting preachers entertained. The young Joshua Thomas must have had his first taste of such subjects as Predestination and Election, freely discussed, in the kitchen of Ty-hen.

Of his upbringing, however, we have but scanty source material. Not so regarding his spiritual birth and upbringing. In the *Evangelical Magazine* for 1798 we are told how at the age of twenty he went to live and work in Hereford. There he remembered his religious upbringing and attended a Presbyterian meeting. He found the preacher dull and his doctrine heavy! Before we discover what steps he took to remedy

---

[8] *The Baptist Magazine,* 1816 – Memoir of Rev. Zechariah Thomas
[9] *Welsh Life in the Eighteenth Century,* p. 127

such a deplorable state of affairs, it must be noted that it was to an uncle's home he went in Hereford. This relative was a mercer by trade and Joshua Thomas was apprenticed to him. The uncle was also an Independent minister according to Sir J.E. Lloyd in his *History of Carmarthenshire.*[10] Now Carmarthenshire had "certain natural advantages for the growth of a woollen industry"[11], so why did the young man, Joshua Thomas, leave a strategic area and go so many miles from home to Hereford? Every householder in Wales at that time was skilled in a variety of trades. He could be carpenter, wheelwright, shoemaker or tailor, "and the same applied to his family".[12] The knitters, if their homes were near a coaching road, sought customers from a wide area, for they waited at likely places along the route and advertised their wares to the passengers. Spinning-wheels and looms were in almost every farmhouse. Wool was bought at the wool fairs and taken home to be woven. Prosperous farmers often kept one or two looms which were used in the slack periods of agriculture and their men-servants were accustomed to turn from jobs about the farm to spinning and weaving. The resultant cloth or flannel was disposed of in neighbouring markets until later on in the century when "Welsh drapers", working for wholesale firms in Shrewsbury or Liverpool would visit the farmer at his own premises and buy his goods outright. Obviously then the only answer to the question, Why did Joshua Thomas leave Carmarthenshire for Herefordshire? is the sovereignty of God. God in His purposes chose to use the young Welshman from distant Caio rather than some Baptist preacher already in Herefordshire.

In Hereford Joshua Thomas met an elderly woman who had previously lived in Leominster, thirteen miles to the north of Hereford. In Leominster this woman had belonged to the Baptist meeting house and she enthralled Joshua with tales of the Baptist membership during her forty years among them. Before, however, she could influence him more he paid a visit home. There he found his brothers and sister, and several of their friends, speaking freely about spiritual matters and he felt out of it all. He became tongue-tied in their presence, and greatly ignorant about spiritual things. But he came under Holy Spirit conviction of sin and suddenly "God took possession of his soul". He was now able to read the Bible and pray and returned to Hereford knowing that God had worked in his soul. As yet, however, he said nothing to anybody.

[10] According to the Dictionary of Welsh Biography this uncle was a Presbyterian, a preacher and author of some consequence.

[11] Op. cit., p. 314 (Note: Sir John Lloyd was general editor of this work and not the author of individual chapters).

[12] *Welsh Life in the Eighteenth Century,* p. 87

Back in Hereford he sought out the old lady again and was soon listening to more anecdotes about the Leominster Baptists. He decided to visit Leominster and attend a service at the Baptist meeting house. In December 1739, although there was a great "freeze-up", which lasted well into 1740, he walked the thirteen miles to Leominster to worship, and this he continued to do almost every week, in spite of the freezing conditions.

He was not made very welcome on his first visit, but that did not deter him, for he was of a retiring nature and disposition. For another thing, his English was not very fluent and this embarrassed him. In spite of this he soon sought believer's baptism by immersion and a seat with the baptised at the Lord's Table. He resolved: "I will give up myself to God, and to His people, and will take the church as instruments in His hand to shew me what I ought to do. If they ask me to relate my experience, that thereby they may be able to form a judgment, whether I have been brought to the knowledge of the truth as it is in Jesus, though in a broken way, I will do it and be sincere. If they are willing to receive me into their community, I shall reckon it my duty to proceed; but if they refuse me, I shall conclude, that I ought to wait in the exercise of prayer, and self-examination".[13] He was, however, accepted, baptised, and received into membership and full communion in May 1740. Little did he know then that later he was to be the Pastor of that church for over forty years, and as a Welsh Baptist historian write its history in two volumes.

Towards the end of 1743 Joshua returned to Wales and resolved to live and die in his native country. Leominster, it may be said, nearly lost their mighty minister and man of God on two occasions. The first was when his father was tempted to emigrate to America soon after marriage. So strong was Thomas Morgan Thomas's desire to go to America that soon after the birth of Joshua he took hold of the child's hand and said: "Probably this little hand will be ridding ground in Pennsylvania".[14] In his *History of the Welsh Association* describing the association meeting in 1719 held at Rhydwilym, Joshua Thomas adds this comment to his description of the proceedings of the meetings: "On the 22nd February preceeding this Meeting, I was born; about this time my father and some neighbours were strongly bent for America".[15] He concluded: "But something prevented and Providence said, 'No' ".[16] Instead of crossing the Atlantic, however, we know

---

[13] *The Evangelical Magazine* 1798, pp 92,93

[14] Ibid., p. 89

[15] Op. cit., p. 53

[16] Ibid

that Thomas Morgan Thomas did a "gipsy move" from one farm to another, but half-a-mile or so along the mountain track. And instead of a boyish hand "ridding" ground it later felt the quality of cloth and handled it for his uncle's customers in Hereford. Thomas Morgan Thomas, in the providence of God, was destined to stay in the Principality as Joshua Thomas was destined to return to Herefordshire and not spend his life in his native Wales.

After having joined the Leominster Baptists, Joshua attended not only the services for public worship on Sundays, but their prayer meetings as well. Although still rather imperfect in spoken English he joined with them in audible prayer. Because of his difficulty in speaking English he engaged in prayer with much diffidence, more as a duty than as a delight. This may have been the reason why later (1755-56) he compiled a *Book of Devotions* in English during his Leominster ministry; he must have found it easier to read his "long" prayers than pray extempore ones.

When twelve months' membership had passed the members urged Joshua Thomas to "make trial of his ministerial gifts" and "with great reluctance he submitted".[17] They approved of him, but he had many doubts and fears as to his own ability and call.

In September 1746 he was married to "a pious young woman"[18] of Lampeter and the couple moved to Hay in Brecknockshire. The Leominster Baptist meeting house was now twenty miles away so he transferred his membership to one nearer at hand, Maesyberllan, founded in 1700. There he began preaching again, and so continued for six or seven years. The anonymous note in Volume 2 of the *History of Leominster Baptist Church,* states that he was ordained in 1749, three years after joining in membership. No details are given, however, as to who conducted the service or performed the ordination. For the next six or seven years he continued preaching in and around Hay-on-Wye.

During this time the Baptist cause in Leominster suffered something of a decline. There had been no settled minister for five years and the membership had dropped to thirteen people. In 1753 they invited Joshua Thomas to preach, and on the 7th October that year he did so, taking as his text Isaiah 8:17 – "And I will wait upon the Lord, that hideth his face from the house of Jacob, and I will look for him". Friendships were renewed and he was asked to come and preach again in the near future. During the winter he visited Leominster once every two or three weeks and in the spring he was invited to the pastorate.

---

[17] Ibid., p. 93

[18] Anonymous note in MS copy of *History of Leominster Baptist Church* by Joshua Thomas (Vol. 2, frontispiece).

In spite of being strongly biased towards the Welsh language, the Welsh people and his beloved land of Wales, and in spite of the fact that he now had a family to support and the Leominster Baptists were not in a flourishing condition numerically or financially, he accepted the call and moved to Leominster in November 1754.

As his income from the chapel was slender he opened a day school which had a remarkable period of success. This, combined with an effective pulpit and pastoral ministry, made for a happy and harmonious church fellowship. The membership steadily increased in spite of frequent deletions from the roll through death.

As a man he was extremely diligent and conscientious. For fifty years he was an early riser, usually before five o'clock, summer and winter. He spent some of each day in the study and was a regular visitor of his flock. He was naturally cheerful by disposition and had a fund of anecdotes, most of them illustrative of the goodness of God to him and on behalf of his people. At Baptist annual meetings and assemblies (held in rotation at Hook Norton, Cirencester and Dudley) he was a welcome visitor, as preacher and adviser. He attended public meetings arranged by ministerial brethren, sometimes riding many miles on horseback through the night.

Naturally he never lost his affection for his native Wales and was always gathering material for a religious history of the Welsh Baptist churches, and an ecclesiastical history of Wales (the former being published during his lifetime and the latter being left in manuscript form after his death).

His character may be summed up in his own words, when he stated that he considered "duty before inclination".[19] This was his attitude towards life right up to the time of his death. In 1797, for instance, although the end was not far off, he rode to Worcester for the opening of the New Baptist Meeting House. About a month later, after preaching three times on Sunday, he complained of feeling unwell, his pain and cough increased and continued until Wednesday. Medicine seemed of no avail. On the Friday he died, having borne severe pain with patience and fortitude, many "savory expressions"[20] fell from his lips until he finally said: "I am almost come to the end of my journey. You are still in the wilderness, but have a safe Guide. Trust in Him, and all will be well".[21] As in life, so in death, his confidence was in God. "I am upon the Rock," he said, "I know in whom I have believed,

[19] *The Evangelical Magazine* 1798, p. 97
[20] Ibid.
[21] Ibid., p. 98

and I know that He is able to keep that which I have committed to Him against that day''.[22] He died as he lived, a preacher. At 78 years of age he went to be with the One whose Name he loved to declare.

From the *Queries and Solutions,* a collection of letters that passed between Joshua Thomas and Benjamin Francis, we gain much insight into the character and life of Joshua Thomas. In April 1760 he wrote to his friend of a particularly sharp trial he and his wife had to endure. Mrs. Thomas had given birth to a daughter on 23 January that year and ''the child was a fine, healthy, fat girl... but in about nine days the child was seized with the hooping-cough (as others call it – the chin-cough) in a very violent manner''.[23] Several times during the next five or six weeks they thought they had lost the child as she became black in the face through coughing. Soon she became pale and old-looking, with skin deeply furrowed like an old woman and her bones visible through the skin. Between the seventh and eighth weeks the nurse was dismissed, as a change for the better seemed to have occurred. Both mother and child came down stairs. But between the 28th and 29th March, after only two months of life, the child died.

In another letter to Benjamin Francis, soon after this premature death of Sarah, Thomas asked the question: ''What would you say to a parent under great Distress on the account of a Dying Infant's eternal State''?[24] Francis's views were that Godly parents had only to''commit his Infant to God by Prayer, and have it in the Arms, and to the Disposal of its Creator, who alone can dispose of its Creation, who alone can dispose of its eternal state... God is righteous, its Misery will not be so great as that of a grown sinner''.[25] Like Joshua Thomas, Benjamin Francis had buried an infant, his son Enoch, and he wrote to Thomas: ''I don't think that either of us felt one moment's distress about his eternal state''.[26] Finally he wrote: ''Those who live upon God, shall never be disappointed in their Expectation''.[27] This has always been the Baptist position, and one of their reasons for holding a Dedication or Presentation of Infant Service rather than a Christening ceremony, believing that the Judge of all the earth does right, and that children who have not reached the age of accountability or discretion will not be condemned for unbelief when they have had no

---

[22] Ibid., p. 99
[23] Op. cit., pp 57,58
[24] Ibid., 51
[25] Ibid.
[26] Ibid., p. 52
[27] Ibid., p. 54

chance of making any personal response to the gospel.

One interesting self-opinion that Joshua Thomas held was this: When writing to Francis in October, 1762, he signed himself for the first time "Jonathan", having called Francis "David". Adding a postscript to the letter, Thomas wrote: "You'll perhaps wonder at this new name. See I Sam. 18:3. I am sure you resemble David more than I do; he was so exceeding affectionate".[28] Does this imply that Thomas was more severe and less emotional than Benjamin Francis?

A hint of Thomas's humility is found in the second volume of the *Queries and Solutions*, Benjamin Francis's question was: "Wherein consists Christian humility?" Thomas replies: "Johnathan knows not what to answer". His answer then proceeded to occupy three-and-a-half pages! He emphasised that humility was closely connected with Mortification and Self-denial. But before these could be practised there must be a correct view of the Greatness and Glory of God and the littleness and sinfulness of man. Thus the true Christian "will be humble as a poor, naked, unworthy, hungry, thirsty, wretched, etc. Creature".[29] The Christian thus endeavours to mortify the "old man", dying to sin and self. Joshua Thomas appealed to the Letter to the Philippians 2:2 as "an excellent description" of true humility, that is, that Christ Himself must be the Christian's Pattern and Example.

His chief difficulty was that he found it easier to "describe an humble Person than to Describe Humility".[30] The humble person must not be mistaken for the Stoic. The Stoic's attitude to life was "bear it", but by contrast Joshua Thomas affirmed the Christian was a cheerful person. True humility is more than passive resignation, it was active rejoicing whatever the circumstances of life might be. It had nothing to do with his "station" or "education". Masters as well as servants must exhibit the grace of humility. Indeed, he wrote to Francis: "Humility makes us all servants" and "all Kings".[31]

In one letter Thomas told Francis of an interesting childhood incident. When eight years old he remembered his mother taking him to a neighbour's house to see their children who had small pox, "some with the scabbs on, others down in it". He commented to Francis that it was quite a common disease in Wales and "not dreaded as in this country (England)".[32] He also gave Francis his impressions of

---

[28] Ibid., p. 161
[29] Ibid., pp 38,39 – Vol. 2
[30] Ibid.
[31] Ibid., p. 41
[32] Ibid., p. 224

death as a young man, stating that he greatly feared it then, but later, when a Christian and in the Christian ministry, "I can look into the bottom of a grave with a pleasant look, and think of the heart of the earth with satisfaction"![33] Some remarks about Infant Baptism in 1760 give us an insight into the mortality rate of his time: "Those who are born into the World, scarce *a third part* attain to the age of even *one year*".[34]

Shortly after the death of Joshua Thomas on 25 August 1797, his friend Benjamin Francis wrote a poem for the benefit of his generation. It was entitled: *The Lamentation of Friendship,* and its sub-title was: An Elegy on the Death of The Reverend Joshua Thomas. While acknowledging the rather flowery language of the time, and the sentimentality of both writer and readers in that century, some phrases give us a clue to the character of Joshua Thomas and sum up his personality for us. Benjamin Francis described him in such terms as "glorious saint", "constant and sincere", "thy love was cordial", "thy judgment sound", "thy whole deportment amiable, discreet", "lovely saint", "heaven-born humility", "thy mind was placid, lowly mild and meek", "thy temper even" and "thy brow serene". The following lines are surely a portrait-in-miniature:

"How dead to earth was thy ascending mind!
In all thy traits, how tranquil and resign'd!
What sweet contentment and perpetual peace
Rul'd in thy breast, and dignified thy face!
Whilst age adorn'd with silver locks thy head,
Grace o'er thy soul her growing beauties spread.
Thy faith, thy hope, thy charity and zeal,
Thy deep concern for man's eternal weal,
Thy savoury speech, thy holy walk with God
In the straight path thy meek Redeemer trode,
Thy frequent flights on swift seraphic wings,
Far, far beyond time's transitory things,
Shew'd thee a Christian of no common size,
A guest on earth, a native of the skies".

The only other indication of Joshua Thomas the man is upon his tomb in Leominster Baptist graveyard. One inscription tells something of the trials he and his wife endured, by implication that is, for it reads: "Ebenezer, John, Mary and Sarah, sons and daughters of

---

[33] Ibid., p. 255
[34] Ibid., p. 90 – Vol. 1

the Revd Joshua Thomas by Elizabeth his wife. All died young''. On the other side is the inscription: ''The Revd Joshua Thomas, born 22nd February 1719, having served Christ in the Ministry of the Gospel 43 years in this town, died 25th August 1797''. Neither inscription, however, indicates the true greatness and the many gifts of Joshua Thomas the man. He was preacher, pastor, writer, historian, man of prayer, and theologian. Some of these are indicated in Benjamin Francis's Elegy; two or three can be inferred from his tombstone Each, however, deserves a separate study and chapter to itself.

II

THE PREACHER

Phillips Brooks, who delivered a series of lectures on preaching before the Divinity School of Yale College in 1877, is usually looked upon as an authority on the art of preaching. His definition was that "preaching is the communication of truth by man to men" and "it has in it two essential elements, truth and personality".[1] If either truth or personality is missing then there is no preaching. R.W. Dale in addressing the same theological faculty stressed that preaching was declaring "Divine truth" with "every faculty and resource which the preacher may happen to possess".[2] Dale was stating in different words the same truth as Brooks. Modern preachers who have delivered similar lectures or who have written books on preaching are in complete agreement. Preaching is the proclamation of Divine truth through human personality, that is, by a man wholly dedicated to God. Such a preacher was Joshua Thomas, who, during a pastorate of forty-three years at Leominster Baptist Church must have preached over four thousand sermons on Sundays alone. This figure does not take into account those delivered mid-week, nor his wider ministry, his preaching engagements further afield. He was greatly in demand as a preacher and calls for help came from near and far. He became something of a "revivalist" and travelled the neighbouring counties in England and the Principality preaching the gospel. A *History of the Baptists in Radnorshire*, published in 1895, with much of the material taken from Joshua Thomas's *History of the Welsh Baptists,* reveals the ministry he exercised in that county alone. The *Dictionary of Welsh Biography* in its summary of the life of Joshua Thomas states that he was an "influential figure in the Midland Association (Baptist)" and "a frequent visitor to Welsh Associations", and that he was behind the North Wales Baptist Crusade of 1776. These statements give some idea of the area covered by Thomas on his itinerant preaching tours.

L.T. Davies and A. Edwards in *Welsh Life in the Eighteenth Century,* describe the farm kitchen in Wales at that time as a kind of community centre to which came all degrees of society, from the squire to the pedlar. "There religious meetings were held, and much of the education obtainable by the eighteenth century peasant was acquir-

---

[1] P. Brooks: *Lectures on Preaching* (London, 1881), p. 5
[2] R.W. Dale: *Nine Lectures on Preaching* (London, 1878) p. 25

ed''.[3] There was friendly rivalry between Church and Chapel and the visiting Dissenting preachers would be compared with the local Vicar, ''generally to the latter's disadvantage''![4] Apart from ''the merely trivial, such doctrines as the Apostolic Succession, Predestination and Election, were freely discussed''.[5] Doubtless the young Joshua Thomas listened to such sermon criticism in the kitchen of Nant-y-llyn and Ty-hen.

There is, however, no example of Joshua Thomas's homiletic style left for us to consider. Of the written word we have several manuscripts and printed works, but of the spoken word there is no record. His nephew, David Thomas, a farmer of Llwyn, in the neighbouring parish to Caio, Llanhyhcrwys, invented a form of shorthand to record the sermons he listened to in Bethel Chapel. Many of these he transcribed later into longhand. The National Library of Wales has some of these manuscripts but it does not seem that he ever took down in shorthand any of his uncle's sermons when he returned to his native heath and preached in Bethel. However, from a variety of sources we can gauge something of Thomas's style of preaching, the content of his sermons, how he composed them, what he expected them to accomplish, and what they did, in fact, accomplish.

The *Evangelical Magazine* for 1798 informs us that when the young Joshua Thomas first attempted to preach at the suggestion of the fellow-members of Leominster Baptist Church he was ''harrassed with doubts and fears'', and since preaching in those days was in private houses he ''made choice of the most obscure places'' and ''where the smallest number of hearers was expected''![6] After some time his doubts and fears increased until he suffered great dejection and he gave up preaching altogether. Not for a considerable time could he be prevailed upon to preach again.

After removal to Hay-on-Wye, however, his preaching gifts were ''strongly solicited'',[7] and he felt it his duty to overcome his fears, his natural shyness, and his inadequacy of expression in the English tongue, and so for six or seven years he became a popular preacher in Brecknockshire.

Early in his Leominster ministry his congregation discovered that

---

[3] Op. cit. (London, 1939), p. 4
[4] Ibid., p. 5
[5] Ibid.
[6] Op. cit., pp 93,94
[7] Ibid., p. 94

he was a man "of natural elocution", having "knowledge of the Scriptures" and "acquaintance with the deep things of God".[8] He studied much and preached sermons that "came with warmth from the heart" and which were "delivered with an unction".[9] Wherever he preached he did so with a Holy Spirit authority that gave him a good hearing.

In the *Queries and Solutions,* a choice little volume of correspondence between Joshua Thomas and Benjamin Francis of Horsley, Gloucestershire (they soon began to call one another and sign themselves "David" and "Jonathan"), we discover how his sermons were composed. Francis described his method of sermon preparation as inadequate because his day school took up so much of his time. Thomas, too, had a day school at Leominster! Usually Francis studied when "in the best frame for it", that is, "sometimes in the morning, at other times the evening".[10] He studied discourses several months before delivering them. He wrote quite a deal but only carried "Heads" and "Proofs" (presumably sermon points, divisions and proof texts) into the pulpit. He did not think that "the most correct sermons were always the most useful". He was, however, fond of proper language, natural, clear, distinguished, and spoken with fervent delivery.

Thomas's reply to this was that "Ministers should aim at the Edification of Saints, and the Conversion of Sinners; that there are some Scriptures and Subjects only suitable to Saints and some to Sinners".[11] Enlarging upon this answer in a later section of the book Joshua Thomas then divided saints into "weak and strong", "old and young", and "zealous and lukewarm".[12] These various classes of believers had to be kept in mind when preaching. In the same way he divided up the sinners into "profane and moral" and "ignorant and knowing". Thus, when using Scripture in a sermon or as a sermon basis, it was important to "observe to whom the words are spoken; what their circumstances are".[13] In other words, Thomas was advocating the expository treatment of a text within its righful context, not the taking of a text as pretext!

He was convinced that "the Law and the Gospel should be preached to all" for "strong Believers are still to be stirred up to follow after greater Spiritual Maturity" and "to be minded of the Duties in-

---

[8] Ibid., p. 95
[9] Ibid.
[10] Op. cit., p. 2
[11] Ibid., p. 6
[12] Ibid., p. 9
[13] Ibid.

cumbant upon them as Heirs of Grace and Glory".[14] The weak, doubting, tempted, hypocrites and backsliders were to be dealt with in a spirit of helpfulness.

As regards preaching the gospel to unbelievers, then faith and repentance were to be stressed. His Calvinistic emphasis comes out at this point. Faith and repentance were not natural to a sinful man; they were spiritual gifts of a Sovereign God. He thus insisted in his sermons on "man's Inability and God's Sovereignty".[15]

Between 1758 and 1759 some correspondence between them took place as to whether a minister of the Gospel may "conclude he is influenced and assisted by the Spirit of God in Studying or Ministering the Word".[16] Thomas's feelings about the matter were that he himself needed a "Steady Heart" for "Application to the matter in hand".[17] He declared that he followed Dr. Owen's methods for choosing a subject, that is, he desired "to impart those Truths of whose Power I hope I have had, in some measure, a real experience" and also to "press those Duties which present occasions, Temptations, and other Circumstances".[18] He was, of course, alluding to Owen's *Treatise of Spiritual Mindedness.*

Regarding the preparation of a sermon he tried to divide his subject with "aptitude" and prove his contentions with "a Multitude of Scriptures and Strong Reasons".[19] As patterns for pulpit elocution he looked to Lawyers and Orators. In other words the preacher must speak to create "a lasting impression",[20] and to do this he must preach for the Glory of God, the Honour and Interest of Christ, and the Welfare of immortal souls. "Weight and Warmth upon the heart" he believed was the only way of accomplishing all this. First the Word must speak to the preacher, bearing fruit in his own soul before he can distribute it to others.

Side by side with diligent study, application to logic, taking appropriate examples such as lawyers and orators, there must be "the wise and gracious management of the Holy Spirit".[21] Our inborn pride and vanity necessitate this. Then as a footnote he added: "one may study and preach for the good of others, and neglect his own Soul,

---

[14] Ibid., pp 9,10
[15] Ibid., p. 11
[16] Ibid., p. 13
[17] Ibid
[18] Ibid
[19] Ibid., p. 14
[20] Ibid
[21] Ibid., p. 15

much easier than the contrary".[22] This he called "a Shocking thing".

In Volume II of *Queries and Solutions* the matter of sermon preparation and preaching is again taken up by Francis and answered by Thomas. The question asked was: "What is the most likely way of preaching: 1. For the conviction and conversion of sinners; 2. For the edification of saints?" Thomas replied: "Did I know, I hope it would be pursued so that not many in these parts would be unconverted, or Saints uncomfortable".[23] Attempting to answer Francis's question, however, Thomas stated that there must be a preaching of the whole Law and the whole Gospel to sinners. The glad tidings of the Gospel were insufficient in themselves. The Law, with its emphasis on holiness, justice and penalty, must be laid before the sinner. Man must be shown that he has fallen, that he is depraved, and that he is unable of himself to save himself. The diabolical nature of sin must be brought out and so "the preacher is to be a Boanerges."[24] Then the Gospel following after the law, is "free, bountiful, rich, wonderful".[25] Christ must be preached as Prophet, Priest and King, the "exalted and adorable Redeemer". This kind of preaching, said Joshua Thomas, would lead "to the gracious and efficacious Influence of the Holy Spirit, quickening, enlightening, sanctifying, strengthening, comforting, sealing".[26] It will result in pardon and peace. The preacher has turned from being a Boanerges to a Barnabas.

The whole Gospel must also be preached to the saints in the congregation. "What begets Faith is also adapted for its growth and nourishment".[27] He referred Francis to the Acts of the Apostles for examples of apostolic preaching—"they preached Christ: that being the sum of the whole"; but they did not "keep stiffly to Method".[28] Sometimes, he pointed out, the apostles began with the Person of Christ, then expounded the Law. The Letter to the Romans he considered a "very complete Plan for Preaching",[29] for the first three chapters set forth the law and man's depravity; the subsequent chapters explained the way of salvation through faith.

Finally, having dealt with these matters of homiletics he closed his correspondence to Francis with the following note: "What Minister

---

[22] Ibid., p. 16
[23] Op. cit., Vol. II p. 10
[24] Ibid
[25] Ibid
[26] Ibid., p. 11
[27] Ibid
[28] Ibid., p. 12
[29] Ibid

ever will be successful unless he is much in prayer, in studying the Scriptures''.[30]

He returned to the subject of preaching several pages later in *Queries and Solutions* Volume II by drawing a parallel between a doctor administering medicine to a patient and a preacher giving God's Gospel to his congregation, so stated that the preacher must watch ''the Manner of Administering'', he must take care of the spirit, temper, voice, gestures. Since patients and physicians differ widely in constitution and education, for instance, what is right for one preacher might be preposterous in another.

Regarding himself, he has discovered that his own weak point is ''speaking as to a third person''. He prays for more wisdom in order to know how to win souls, maintaining that in all successful preaching, however, ''there is something *natural* rather than *acquired*'' and if it is acquired then it is from God and not man.

The final query by Benjamin Francis in the Second Volume is: ''What is your method of fixing upon subjects for the Pulpit?'' Joshua Thomas immediately asked: ''Is it right to give my Sentiments or my Practice''?[31] Answering his own query he decides to give both! His sentiments are: to pray on Monday for a subject unless one has already been given. By thinking on this word throughout the week it will profit the preacher's own soul and become suitable for persons and cases when preached. This he calls ''digesting'' the subject. The following Saturday morning the chief ''branches'' should be written down on paper and committed to memory. Then by prayer and waiting upon God the influence of the Holy Spirit will come so that the sermon will be delivered with ''Light, Ease, Plainness, Savour, Affection, and Authority''.[32] His practice and experience, however, were as follows: sometimes ''as above'', but sometimes the word given on Monday he has to ''drop'' before Saturday comes. Often then he is left ''destitute''. At other times ''a Veil remains upon it'' (upon the word given on Monday). Usually, however, by Friday or Saturday God has given him another subject and light upon it. On the Saturday he would rise between five and six in the morning and write the ''Heads'' of his sermon. Then he filled in, and ''my Notes of one sermon is generally upon one Page of an Octavo of the size of this sheet (i.e. 4 x 6½ inches).[33] He usually wrote sixteen sermons to one book of paper, keeping an index of texts ''because I am apt to forget very soon

[30] Ibid
[31] Ibid., p. 76
[32] Ibid., p. 77
[33] Ibid., p. 78

that I have preached from a Word''.[34] He added: ''I very seldom at home preach over old sermons...but when I go abroad I always preach out of my *late* Notes, not *old* ones, lest I should preach from the same Texts in the same place''.[35] He kept no record of sermons preached during his wider ministry, which was strange for so methodical and fastidious a man as Joshua Thomas. He also liked to get a text on his mind from conversation with people he was visiting, for as he confessed, ''I am very barren when from home''.

We have already seen how in *Queries and Solutions* he likens sin to a disease and the Gospel preacher to a doctor. The doctor must know his diseases and his patients, and be able to show them the serious nature of their disease and the efficacy of the remedy. This leads to a difficulty, however, for the preacher must ''not appear to the Audience to have *some one Particular Person in View.*[36] For this reason, not wanting to be accused of 'preaching at' someone in his congregation he has ''sometimes deferred to preach some Discourses till a more favourable opportunity''.[37] Obviously in his pastoral work he came across some particular situation that could well be answered from the Scriptures in the pulpit, but he had to bide his time until the person visited could not accuse him of preaching with his particular case in mind!

Continuing this picture of the preacher as physician Joshua Thomas went on to instruct the preacher in his preaching so that he could be an effective Pastor of souls. As ''vomit first is necessary'' for the many physical cures, so the sinner must be shewn how ''bitter Draughts of Godly Repentance'' must first work in his soul. ''Divine Indignation'' must be preached as well as the sweetness of ''Free Grace''. The latter will be made more effective and ''palatable'' if mixed with ''Sovereignty, Grace and Mercy''. Then should be added ''some Drops of the Tincture of God's everlasting Love''.[38] This medicine must be taken daily and regularly by the patient himself: ''Draughts of the Peace and Love of God, Heavenly Delight in the Lord''. The preacher must also put before his patients the need for ''wholesome nutrition'' and ''rules respecting their exercise''—watchfulness, self-denial, fervent prayer, diligence, reading, meditation, examination, with constant attendance on the means of Grace and the Ordinances of the Lord. Finally, the spiritual doctor, the Gospel

[34]Ibid., p. 79
[35]Ibid
[36]Ibid., p. 20
[37]Ibid
[38]Ibid., p. 21

preacher, must inform his patient of the importance of abstinence, warning him against things injurious to spiritual health – distance from Christ, clinging to the world, worldly cares and anxieties, sensual pleasures, pride and vanity.

The manner of administering this medicine will vary from time to time, and from person to person, congregation to congregation. Sometimes the medicine will be given with a sharp rebuke, and at other times affectionately, with longsuffering on the part of the preacher.

It is said that the Victorian pulpit "giant", C. H. Spurgeon, brought humour and naturalness into the staid nineteenth century pulpit. What he accomplished in the nineteenth Joshua Thomas advocated for the eighteenth: "A plain, easy, familiar, not grave and solemn way of speaking in public, I think, is much to be desired, and most likely to be useful".[39] The usual Baptist preacher's manner of his day he condemned in the following words: "I have often thought that the Baptist Ministers in general do not address their hearers in so familiar, and affable a manner and speak *to* them in so convincing and affecting a way as could be wished; but confine themselves too much to the subject and the *third* Person".[40]

All the preparation in the world does not make a sermon effective, nor minute attention to such details as eloquence and gestures in delivery. Painstaking corrections and alterations to the manuscript; the insertion of telling illustrations and anecdotes; quotations from Christian classics or the Scriptures; the use of verses of hymns – these are of little use without a Holy Spirit unction, and that comes only in answer to prayer. The preparation of self is as important as the preparation of the sermon, and preparation of the preacher must precede preparation of his message. Joshua Thomas knew the value and the power of prayer in self and sermon preparation. In his *Book of Devotions* he compiled several prayers for "before Sermon". Again and again he prays for Divine illumination for himself and his hearers that they might give "serious attention to the great truths of Religion"[41]. Obviously then his sermons were doctrinal in content and not like some of the twentieth century superficial variety. He preached on the Goodness and Severity of God, life and death, the Christian's spiritual warfare, the holy, separated life for believers, and above all, the nature of God's Kingdom and the means of entry into it. These are all referred to in the prayers of his *Book of Devotions*, as is "the glad

[39] Ibid., p. 23
[40] Ibid., p. 28
[41] Op. cit., p. 9

tidings of salvation".

Knowing that we are meant to be "doers" as well as "hearers"[42] of the Word, he frequently prayed a "concluding prayer", asking that the word preached might "be as seed sown in good ground",[43] that advance might have been made in the understanding of the Christian faith so that in practical daily living there might be fruit borne to the glory of God. So, too, he prayed before preaching for Divine strength that he and his congregation might "discharge the Duties of religion" as well as accept the benefits. He believed in relating religion to life and expected lives to tally with lips and character with conduct on the part of his congregation.

In all probability his sermons frequently had an eschatological content. Again this can be gauged by his prayers before the sermon was delivered. Frequently he reminded his congregation of the "Day when the elements shall melt with fervent heat and the Heavens being on fire... when Thou shalt by Jesus Christ render to every man according to his Deeds".[44]

Before men and women can respond to such preaching, to the gospel invitation given so freely, they must be made aware of their sinful condition and their need of a Saviour. We have already seen from *Queries and Solutions* that law must precede grace in the evangelical sermon in order to rouse the unbelieving hearer to a sense of sin and the need of repentance. For this reason Joshua Thomas frequently prayed before preaching: "May we be fully convinced how odious our sins are in thy sight... Give us a right understanding of our need of a Saviour. Give us a true sense of our sins and affect our hearts with great Godly sorrow which is required to work a genuine evangelical repentance".[45]

While remembering his own responsible task of preaching the Gospel he was always mindful of preachers everywhere. He prayed from the pulpit: "Bless the Ministers of Thy Word. Lord, make them faithful and successful. Clothe them with salvation that thy saints may shout for joy. Enable them always to speak the things that become sound doctrine, and help thy people to profit by their labours".[46] Obviously what he prayed for others he would seek for himself, and in that brief prayer we have a summary in five words of Joshua Thomas as preacher: *faithful, successful,* proclaiming *salvation* and preaching *sound doctrine.*

---

[42] James 1:22

[43] *Book of Devotions,* p. 19

[44] Ibid., p. 27

[45] Ibid., p. 73

[46] Ibid., p. 116

Of his voice we know nothing for the day of microphones and tape recorders had not arrived. Obviously as a Welshman, more at home in his native tongue than in English, he would possess all the characteristic "fire" of the old Welsh preacher. Doubtless he would go into the *hwyl* when "carried away" or "carried aloft" by his theme. Neither have we any record of his pulpit mannerisms, his gestures and gesticulations. Of the length of his sermons we know nothing, except that the custom during the latter part of his ministry at Leominster was to have the clock bell ring at each hour! In all probability he took an hour and not "half an hour in which to raise the dead"! But these are incidentals. To dwell on them by conjecture would be to miss the grandeur of his pulpit ministry, his preaching of the doctrines of grace with the sole purpose of converting sinners and edifying saints.

No study of the past should be merely academic. We should always learn from the past, either to copy that which was good, so correcting present evil tendencies, or else that we might avoid to-day what was obviously bad then. To-day we are living in what has been called "an anti-preaching" campaign. The "foolishness of preaching" whereby men's lives are transformed is being replaced by brief talks, addresses or sermonettes. Sermonettes, it is said, only produce Christianettes! Sometimes the sermon is replaced by film or filmstrip or some other visual or audio aid. The sermons that are still delivered are hardly of the doctrinal variety of our forefathers in the faith, sermons that produced stirling and stalwart men of faith. We need a return to the expository, doctrinal sermons of which Joshua Thomas was a master. In our present time of short pastorates, in spite of the modern aids at the preacher's disposal, and in spite of the academic training and educational advantages he has had, a modern congregation soon tires of its preacher. A pastorate of forty-three years can only be sustained by delving into the "unsearchable riches" of Scripture, bringing "treasures new and old" out of the treasure chest for the benefit of the congregation week by week.

Let Benjamin Francis sum up Joshua Thomas the preacher as he referred to him in *An Elegy* written upon his death in 1797:

"How did thy heart with love to Jesus burn!
How did thy soul o'er dying sinners mourn!
How didst thou labour from thy blooming youth
To hoary age, in the dear cause of truth!"

III

THE MAN OF PRAYER

In Benjamin Francis's *Elegy on the death of Joshua Thomas*, published in 1797 in Rippon's *Baptist Register*, volume III, occur these two lines:

"How didst thou feel for all thy friends around,
And for the world in fervent prayer abound!"

Joshua Thomas was a great man of prayer. While some preachers have affirmed that their success is because their people pray for them, his was largely because he knew how to pray himself.

We have already seen how he connected prayer with preaching, both in preparation and in delivery of the sermon. If preaching is speaking to man on behalf of God, then public prayer is speaking to God on behalf of men. Both are solemn responsibilities and both need ample preparation. Thomas was an adept in both spheres.

Nonconformists in the past have been rather chary of writing out their prayers or of using set prayers in a prayer book. Some feel guilty at so doing; others are afraid of what their congregations might think. In this twentieth century there is a liturgical movement in the free church denominations and some younger ministers are again using the well-known "prayers of the church universal". The *Sursum Corda*, General Thanksgiving and General Confession are again being used in nonconformist services. Books of Orders and Prayers for Free Church worship have been printed and published. In this sense Joshua Thomas was long before his time, for his recently-discovered (1965) Book of Devotions was obviously for pulpit use rather than private devotions in the Manse. The proof of this is in certain marginal notes, and in the inclusion of the Lord's Prayer and Benedictions written out in full. For private use in his study he would not have needed to have these copied out in full. Then occasionally we find he has inserted in the margin: "Gen- Tha."—obviously his abbreviation for General Thanksgiving, the well-known:

"Almighty God, Father of all mercies, we Thine unworthy servants do give Thee most humble and hearty thanks for all Thy goodness and loving-kindness..."

Books of prayer usually divide their contents into prayers of Adoration, Invocation, Confession, Thanksgiving, Intercession, and so on. Joshua Thomas's *Book of Devotions* has prayers headed in the same way, as well as prayers for before and after the sermon. He also includes a variety of benedictions.

Before studying these prayers it is important to see something of his attitude towards prayer. In *Queries and Solutions* he answers questions put to him about prayer by Benjamin Francis. Francis once asked: "How often should a Christian pray?[1] and it is illuminating and revealing to study Thomas's answer. First, every head of the family should conduct public, audible, family worship. If he is a minister of the Gospel then he must pray often in his study and regularly with his church members when he visited them, especially if they were sick. But it is what he calls "ejaculatory prayer" that he treats in more detail, that is, prayers offered up as the need arises: dangers, difficulties and snares. These prayers "should be like the very breath of the new man" for this is "real prayer".[2] There should also be periods of "solemn and holy contemplation", the prayer that truly ascended to God like sweet perfume. This Thomas called "closet prayer".[3] Neither "social prayer" nor "ejaculatory prayer" should ever replace or displace these periods of regular prayer-time in secret. "Nature itself does almost tell us, we should pray morning and evening"[4] in this way. It was the apostle Paul's pattern, and that of the Psalmist, for the latter prayed three times a day. Joshua Thomas instanced how the "Turks pray five times daily",[5] the Papists even more frequently. For the Christian, however, he has no inexhaustible rule, although he believes "twice a day" during the "twenty-four hours" should be the minimum time spent in prayer.

Next he instanced exceptional seasons of prayer when circumstances dictated – severe times of sorrow or affliction. While the Lord's Day, by its very nature, should be an occasion of more prayer by the Christian than any other day of the week.

He ends his advice to Francis on a very practical note, suggesting fifteen minutes for prayer, followed by five or six minutes reading "something suitable".[6] But it is the "spirit of prayer" that matters more than the number of times we pray or the duration of our prayers.

In March 1769 Benjamin Francis took up the subject once again, this time asking: "What is the best method of praying in private for a variety of Persons at a Distance, and of recollecting the various Order we should in prayer"?[7] The answer was very full on this occa-

---

[1] Op. cit., p. 199
[2] Ibid
[3] Ibid., p. 200
[4] Ibid
[5] Ibid., p. 201
[6] Ibid., p. 202
[7] Op. cit. Vol. 2. p. 55

sion, occupying almost seven pages. It was a subject which Thomas felt many Christians, even ministers of the gospel, did not fully understand. He proposed to divide his answer into Practice and Thoughts on the question. Of the former, the practice of prayer, he was "stricken with shame and confusion". He also admitted that his practice was often contrary to his beliefs. In prayer and in preaching, he said, "I do nothing exactly corresponding with my Sentiments, and what I believe to be my Duty and Privilege. Poor depraved creature"![8] He said that "he laboured under guilt a long while before (he) steadily followed private Prayer".[9] Conscience pricked him occasionally and he felt obliged to pray, but he was about twenty years of age before he really knew what it was to pray. Since that time his practice was to pray twice each day. He paid tribute to "a little printed" work that "came out about fifteen years ago" that advised setting apart Wednesday morning one hour for prayer. This he began to do, setting aside between seven and eight in the morning for this purpose. Then he discovered *An Ernestt Invitation* which argued that an hour on the Lord's Day morning was preferable. The "little printed piece" was *The Call from the City to the Country,* printed in London; the *Ernest Invitation* was a Methodist booklet.

For a time he sought benefit from both books and set aside Wednesday morning and Sunday morning an hour for prayer. The Sunday session he found most preferable for during the week he was often away on Wednesday, engaged on wider ministry. He soon changed his time to between six and seven "before the family is up" and "often earlier than later"![10] He divided his time for prayer into three or four parts, each part sub-divided into two – "Thinking and Praying".[11] His "thinking period" was about his ministry, at home and further afield, and those with whom he came into contact. His "Praying time" was about spiritual thoughts, turned into petitions. Often he would "walk round the Table" while thinking, and then kneel down at it for his time of prayer. Not least in his "thinking period" would be personal petitions – the state of his own soul, his bodily wants, his trials and temptations. He would engage in prayer for about eight minutes and then "resume my Walking and Thinking".

His next subject would be the Church, going through one particular family at a time and praying for their needs. He states that

[8] Ibid., pp 55,56
[9] Ibid., p. 57
[10] Ibid
[11] Ibid., p. 58

there were always "extraordinary Cases" to think about and pray over and his petitions covered their temporal and spiritual needs.

Next he would turn his thoughts to a distance, people and churches, saints and sinners, the Kingdom of God and its extension. He mentioned to Benjamin Francis Wesley's people and their method of prayer, that is, the issuing of prayer cards, with names, circumstances, prayer requests and so on printed on them. He did not advocate such a method as it was praying "by Rotation" and had "too much formal strictness in it and too little Heart work".[12]

As we draw near, in imagination, and hear Joshua Thomas praying in public and in private, in his study and in his pulpit, we note first of all that as John Bunyan could be "pricked anywhere and he bled the Bible", so Thomas's prayers were full of Scripture, his petitions frequently couched in Scriptural language. However, he also had great felicity of phrase himself. These examples, taken at random from various prayers in his *Book of Devotions,* reveal his delicacy of expression, his lucidity of language. Whether the prayers in this book were first thought out in his native Welsh and then translated into English (as with some of his written works), we shall never know. If the prayers were originally in English then they are even more remarkable. For instance, he prayed:

"May God convert the unconverted, quicken the lukewarm, and strengthen the weak in Faith".[13]

Also:

"With all these petitions we resign ourselves to Thy will, intreating Thee to grant us those things which are good for us, and to deny us those things which would be hurtful to us".[14]

Then there is this example:

"Teach us contentedly to submit to all the Dispensation of Thy Providence. Thy omniscience and omnipotence, to govern all our thoughts, words and actions".[15]

Or this:

"We rejoice that Thy bright and glorious footsteps, the evidence of Thy Being, may be easily traced through all the works of nature".[16]

Finally:

"Let Thy good Spirit assist us in our Devotions that we may

---

[12] Ibid., p. 66
[13] Op. cit. p. 16
[14] Ibid., p. 38
[15] Ibid., p. 43
[16] Ibid., p. 55

worship God who is a Spirit in spirit and in truth''.[17]

On the flyleaf of the *Devotions* Joshua Thomas has written as a preamble:

''In our worship of God we should have in view:

1. To be humble for all our sins;
2. To apply to a Merciful God for pardon of them through Jesus Christ;
3. To intercede for new supplies of grace to carry us on in the Christian life;
4. To praise God for all our mercies:
5. To hear His most holy Word; and to recommend ourselves and others to the Blessing and protection of Heaven''.

On the title page – *A Book of Publick Devotions,* Leominster, July 24th, 1755, Thomas has also written:

> ''Devotion is the soul's converse with God. 'Tis particularly a work of the Sabbath, a special branch of worship, and 'tis the most difficult part of the Minister's work to lead on the Devotions of the Congregation with just propriety and becoming fervency''.

Within the next 128 pages there are eight prayers for Before Worship, eight for Before Sermon, eight for After Sermon or Conclusion of Worship, seven prayers of Intercession, nine of Thanksgiving, two of Confession, one of Adoration and one of Pardon. They are grouped under ''1st Sunday, 2nd Sunday'', etc., so obviously he went through his ''Prayer Book'' many times during his long stay in Leominster.

An example of his prayer to introduce worship is:

> ''We bless Thee, O God for the Encouragement we have to join together in Thy Worship. Graciously regard us through Jesus Christ the great Mediator. Accompany the Means of Grace with Thy Blessing that they may quicken us in Religion and prepare us for the more perfect Service of Heaven''.[18]

The following extract comes from a prayer Before Sermon:

> ''Comfort and edify all Thy people. Let sinners be convinced of the Danger of a sinful course. God dispose them Seriously to enquire what they shall do to be saved.
>
> Lord lead them to Repentance, to believe and obey the Gospel that they may obtain Life Everlasting through Jesus Christ.

---

[17] Ibid., p. 81
[18] Ibid., p. 3

Let all true and sincere Christians be greatly improved and refreshed and all the Parts of our worship be conducted to Thine honour and Glory to the advancement of Religion and the Salvation of our own souls.

Let our prayers and praises prove effectual means to purify our hearts and reform our Lives and to Sanctify us wholly through Jesus Christ to whom be Glory in the Churches, world without end''.[19]

From a Prayer After Sermon we extract this example:

''We humbly pray that Thy Word which is now gone forth may prosper in the thing whereto it is sent and accomplish the good end of righteous and godly Instruction. May it be as seed sown in good ground, nor let the Deceitfulness of Riches or the Cares of this Life choke it and render it unfruitful, but grant that Thy servants having heard the Word, may in honest and good Heart receive it and keep the same and bring forth fruit with Patience to Thy glory and their own Comfort, through Jesus Christ our Lord''.[20]

And in a Prayer to Conclude Worship he prayed:

''O God, we give Thee thanks for the Happiness we have had of Meeting in Thy House this holy Day to render unto Thee the Service which is Thy due, and to hear Thy Word.

We acknowledge Thy great Goodness that we enjoy these precious Advantages of which so many others are deprived.

Hear O Lord the prayers which have been offered... for the Salvation of Mankind... for the Ministers of Thy Word, the Establishment of Thy Kingdom, for the Conversion of Sinners and the preservation of the Just.

Accept the Worship which we have paid Thee and hear all that call upon Thee with their whole hearts''.[21]

Obeying the apostolic injunction to pray for ''all sorts and conditions of men'' – ''for kings, and for all that are in authority'' (I Timothy 2:1,2), Joshua Thomas included in his *Book of Devotions* prayers for the Kind of England, the Government, the Nations of the World, the Jews, educational establishments, and a variety of other worthy objects. For the King he prayed:

---

[19] Ibid., p. 4
[20] Ibid., p. 19
[21] Ibid., p. 118

"In a particular manner bless his Majesty K.G. and all the Branches of the Royal Family. Enrich them with heavenly Grace, prosper them with all Happiness, and bring them to Thine everlasting Kingdom".[22]

And again for the King:

"Look favourably upon our Most gracious Sovereign King George. Bless him with Health and long life, with peace and prosperity. May he rule with Justice and Equity, endeavouring faithfully to discharge the Duties of that High Station in which Thy Providence has placed him. Be his Defender and Preserver, giving him the victory over all his unjust enemies".[23]

For the world at that time he prayed:

"Pity those nations who know not the true God and are lost in idolatry and superstition".[24]

The Jews he singled out and remembered before God in this fashion:

"Have compassion on Thine ancient people the Jews, bringing Jew and Gentile to the knowledge of the truth as revealed by Jesus Christ".[25]

Regarding education, he referred to schools as "nurseries of learning" and prayed for both children and staff. The Christian training of children by parents was equally a matter for prayer, as were a host of other everyday matters. Like his contemporary John Newton, Joshua Thomas believed–

"Thou art coming to a King;
Large petitions with thee bring".

Prayer is not only petition, however; it is Thanksgiving and Confession. The spirit of Thanksgiving which Thomas endeavoured to impart to his congregation as he prayed is evident in this extract:

"May such a due sense of all Thy Mercies dwell upon our Minds that our hearts may be truly thankful, and that we may show forth Thy praise, not only with our Lips, but in our Lives, by giving up ourselves to Thy Service and by walking before Thee in Holiness and Righteousness all our days, through Jesus Christ our Lord".[26]

Finally, the spirit of Confession is seen in these words:

---

[22] Ibid., p. 14
[23] Ibid., p. 31
[24] Ibid., p. 87
[25] Ibid.
[26] Ibid., p. 34

"To us belong shame and Confusion of face, because we have sinned against Thee. How often have we offended Thy Divine Majesty! In how many instances neglected our Duty! Dispensed with Thy holy and righteous Laws. We have dishonoured the Gospel of Christ and Set Light by that Glory and Happiness which is there set before us".[27]

After Confession he prayed for Pardon of sin in such words as these:

"We humbly implore Thy Mercy in the pardon of all our sins through Jesus Christ. We desire to turn our feet to Thy Testimonies and we pray that God would enable us from the Heart to forgive one another".[28]

About the same subject of Death he prayed:

"Reconcile us to the thoughts of Death and prepare us for it whilst we live. May we live to Thy Glory and let Death at last be abundantly gainful to us".[29]

His ecumenical spirit is illustrated by these petitions:

"Be graciously present O Father in all religious Assemblies this day; hear their Prayers, receive their Praises, and let the great Truths of Religion Comfort and Edify all Thy people".[30]

And also:

"Succeed all the Ministers of Thy Word. Bless all Congregations of Christians of Every Denomination. May the Means of Grace be blessed to them and to us for our Salvation".[31]

A delightful Morning Prayer has these passages included:

"O Lord, we adore Thy Providence that has preserved us another week. We bless Thee for permitting us to assemble together for Thy Worship.

We bless Thee for this wise and gracious institution, that after the fatigues of six days, we are to devote the seventh to Celebrate Thy Perfections.

We would recollect with pleasure that God in the Beginning made the Heavens and the Earth, the Seas and all that in them is. We rejoice that He still upholds and

---

[27] Ibid., p. 7
[28] Ibid
[29] Ibid., p. 11
[30] Ibid., p. 3
[31] Ibid., p. 15

governs the whole Creation".[32]

Finally, mention must be made of two very choice prayers for special occasions – one for the New Year of 1756 and one for the Communion Service:

A PRAYER FOR THE NEW YEAR

"We thankfully, O Father, recall Thy goodness to us from the beginning of Life to this present moment.

Blessed be God in an especial Manner for the Mercies of the past year, for the Many Deliverances wrought for us. Thou hast been better to us than our deserts; than our reasonable expectations.

Thou hast permitted us to enter upon another year. We desire to renew the dedication of ourselves to Almighty God, the Giver and Preserver of our Lives and would proceed in our course in a due dependence upon Thy Grace and Holy Spirit.

O Lord guide us by Thy Counsel through the remaining Days, Months and years of our Life and then graciously receive us to Thy Glory through Jesus Christ.

May we always entertain such thoughts of Thee, our God, as may engage our esteem and attract our strongest affections, that we may love Thee with all our soul, with all our mind, and strength – yielding ourselves up to Thee as alive from the dead and presenting our bodies as living sacrifices, holy and acceptable unto God, through Jesus Christ".[33]

COMMUNION MEDITATIONS

"May the Name of Christ be ever dear and precious to us, He Who died for us and instituted a sacrament in commemoration of Dying Love for the comfort and edification of His church.

Let the Remembrance of our sins and of His bitter sufferings for them pierce our hearts and engage us for ever to love and serve Him who laid down His Life for us.

Cleanse us O Lord from Filthiness of the flesh and spirit that we may be meet guests for Thy holy Table and real partakers of those Blessings and Benefits which are

[32]Ibid., p. 2
[33]Ibid., pp 119-121

represented in the Sacrament of the Body and Blood of Christ.

Strengthen, O God, all good Resolutions in us and enable us by Thy Grace faithfully to perform the Conditions of our baptismal Covenant which we intend to renew in the Lord's Supper, by dedicating ourselves entirely and forever to the Service of our Blessed Redeemer who hath loved us."[34]

(A prayer for self before conducting the Communion Service):

"I lift up my soul to Thee, my God, humbly imploring Thy Blessing upon me and gracious assistance in the holy action I am now about. Forgive my want of due preparation and accept my sincere desire to perform an acceptable service unto Thee through Jesus Christ".[35]

(Before receiving the Bread):

"Lord, I am not worthy of the Crumbs which fall from Thy Table".[36]

Unfortunately Joshua Thomas did not finish composing his Communion prayers, for there is no similar prayer before receiving the wine. Unfortunately, too, on page 123 of the *Book of Devotions* there is a blank page except for the simple heading: A Prayer for Whitsunday. It is a great pity and a great loss that the prayer was never composed. The following sentences, however, give an indication as to how Joshua Thomas prayed upon the subject of the Holy Spirit:

"We ask a Constant Supply of the Spirit of Christ that we may shew forth all the fruits of the Spirit to the praise and Glory of God";[37]

"Fill us with all the Gifts and Graces of Thy Holy Spirit. Dispose us to yield to His blessed influences that we may be guided by Him in the paths of truth and peace and holiness towards Life Everlasting".[38]

---

[34] Ibid., p. 122
[35] Ibid
[36] Ibid
[37] Ibid., p. 126
[38] Ibid., p. 128

These brief extracts from the *Book of Devotions* are sufficient to reveal Joshua Thomas as a man of prayer, and to show us that prayer was the secret of his success: success as a preacher, a pastor, a writer and a historian. There was a simplicity, an orderliness, a fervency, a comprehensiveness about his praying that resulted in these same characteristics being used to the glory of God in every branch of Christian service that he undertook.

IV

THE PASTOR

It is certainly true to say that generally in Wales more importance has been placed upon a minister's preaching ability than upon his pastoral ministry. Any biography of a Welsh pulpit "giant" will emphasise first his preaching gifts. Vavasor Powell, Christmas Evans and a host of other "revivalists", are all known and remembered by the outstanding sermons they preached. Yet within forty years of the death of Joshua Thomas an *Essay on Dissent* by Arthur James Johnes of Garthmyl, Montgomeryshire (which was awarded the Royal Medal at the London Cambrian Institution's eisteddfod in May 1831) pointed out that lack of contact between clergy and congregation was one of the main reasons for the growth of Dissent. "The impulse to Dissent is not given by the noise and vociferation too often employed by Dissenting Ministers; but by ...the want of sympathy between clergy and their flocks".[1] A. J. Johnes pointed out later in his Essay that "an amiable sympathy with the feelings of the poor, are of the very essence of the Clerical profession".[2] Comparing clergy of the Established Church with Roman Catholic curates he said of the latter; "Visiting the sick... seemed to be the constant employment of their lives".[3] Johnes is too much of a Welshman to overlook preaching altogether. He draws a fine balance between preaching and pastoralia – admitting that the cause of dissent at the beginning of the nineteenth century was "for no other reason than for want of plain, practical, pressing, and zealous preaching... and freedom of friendly access to advise about their spiritual state".[4]

Joshua Thomas combined effective preaching with efficient visitation of the flock and so conducted a most successful ministry in Leominster for forty-three years. We have already seen something of his preaching gift, his powers of oratory, his conscientious preparation for the pulpit. Now it is time to study his pastoral concern for

---

[1] Op. cit., p. 50

[2] Ibid., p. 69 Johnes neglected to emphasise, however, that clergy of the Established Church were at that time largely drawn from, and regarded as, minor gentry. Thus the gap between clergy and congregation was sometimes one of social class.

[3] Ibid., p. 70

[4] Ibid., p. 159

his people.

The New Testament word translated "pastor" means literally "a helper or a feeder of sheep". Figuratively it came to be used for an office in the early church, a minister in charge of a congregation. From Ephesians 4:11 and 12 it is clear that the pastoral office was for "the perfecting of the saints" and "for the edifying of the body of Christ". Here we have the dual emphasis on a preaching and pastoral ministry.

Whereas a man may have education, knowledge, logic, rhetoric and oratory for the pulpit, he must be a man of integrity, sympathy, consistency and conscientiousness to exercise an equally fruitful ministry in the homes of his people. Of Joshua Thomas we are told that "in visiting his people, unless upon particular occasions, as illness, etc., most of them knew not only the day, but the hour when they might expect him, and how long he would remain".[5] Obviously he had a plan for pastoral visitation to which he adhered with great strictness. As he spent every morning in the study for devotion and sermon preparation, so he spent regular times in visiting his members, and they became familiar with his time-table. On the other hand, when cases of illness or trouble or other necessity occasioned it he would make such cases his primary concern. And when in the homes of his people on routine visits and they desired him to stay longer, they "knew that to solicit it would be in vain, when he had signified it was time for him to depart", and so all they could do was to "express their regret that he could stay no longer".[6] We need no further proof of the value of his pastoral work. He was welcome; his people liked his company; he was helpful to them in time of need.

Benjamin Francis sums up Joshua Thomas's pastoral concern and ministry in his *Elegy* written upon his death:

"How didst thou watch with tender, constant care,
Thy precious charge, and in its sorrows share".

Here is conscientiousness and sympathy, and in later lines there follows his motive and satisfaction:

"How didst thou seek prosperity and peace
To Zion's sons, and joy in their increase!"

But it is to the *Queries and Solutions* that we must turn to learn the real secrets of his pastoral ministry. For instance, some of his letters to Benjamin Francis give us an insight into the problems of his people with which he had to deal when visiting them. Attendance at Com-

---

[5] *The Evangelical Magazine* 1798, p. 96
[6] Ibid.

munion, the unequal yoke or mixed marriages between believers and unbelievers, growth in grace, the fear of death, and even the innoculation for small pox! No wonder it was said of him that in spite of his preaching ministry and his teaching in day school, he did not "neglect the various duties of his pastoral office, to which he applied with great seriousness, fidelity, and perseverance; nor were his labours wholly without success".[7] Without such diligent pastoral visitation Joshua Thomas would not have been able to write in such detail his well-known *History of Leominster Baptist Church* in two volumes, containing many illustrations and illuminating details about members of the church and the prevailing conditions of the time.

This faithful pastoral work had as much influence on building up the Leominster church as his preaching ability. When he came to the pastorate in 1754 there were but fourteen members. During his forty-three years ministry over one hundred new members were added. A fitting tribute to this great pastor was inscribed in the church minute book after his death:

"He was a laborious and judicious minister; possessed a very strong judgment, a very capacious memory and a clear understanding; firm in his belief of the distinguishing doctrines of grace which he continued to preach and under the benign influence of which he lived and died. He was a pious Christian, a sincere friend, kind and benevolent to all who requested his services and offensive to none. He presided over this church in the pastoral office near 43 years and discharged the duties incumbent on that station with great honour and reputation to himself".

Turning to his own written works we have several examples of his pastoral visitation. In the *History of Leominster Baptist Church*, volume 2, Thomas describes how while he was preaching at Leominster one Sunday a woman named Ann Nash fell ill. She was never able to attend the services again but "I visited her pretty often".[8]

His pastoral concern was great; he felt it keenly when his members did not avail themselves of "the means of grace" and absented themselves from the Communion Table. He records one such absentee for many years and adds this personal comment: "I would almost tremble whenever I hear of any one Declining and revolting from true religion. Lord, keep me by Thy mighty power and rich grace".[9]

He was very concerned as a pastor that all his members should grow in grace and he wrote about this subject in *Queries and Solutions*

---

[7] Ibid., p. 95
[8] *History of Leominster Baptist Church*, p. 15
[9] Ibid., p. 99

in March 1762. Benjamin Francis replied in a most unsatisfactory manner, however, which with all Christian charity Thomas described as "savory tho' short".[10] He agreed with Francis as far as he went, "without any mental reservation",[11] but later he himself has more to say about spiritual growth and how its hindrances must be dealt with. He was a firm believer in church discipline on the New Testament pattern, the church putting out of membership offenders or rather the church *withdrawing itself* from the offender. One of the chief drawbacks in his opinion to progress in the spiritual life was the "unequal yoke". He stated: "It would be well for Baptists to marry those of their own Persuasion: but sometimes it cannot be done without manifest inconvenience. Where that is the case, I don't think it unlawful to marry any pious protestant".[12] But he went on to state: "To marry one that hath no signs of Grace, if the pious person cannot remain single: this must be a very rare and uncommon case, if the pious person acts in the fear of God".[13] He did not forbid "unequally yoked" persons the Lord's Communion Table, however. And in 1765 he defended his opinion that a Christian may marry "out of the Lord" in these words: "All men do not agree in defining *a person out of the world*".

Discipline was exercised for other reasons than the unequal yoke. Members' names were "noted", and their place at the Communion Table denied, on Scriptural grounds. In reply to a question by Benjamin Francis in April 1759: "Do you think it right or wrong, according to the Gospel Rule to put any out of the Communion for a time, and not always by Excommunication?" Joshua Thomas replied: "I do think it right" and he instanced a member who might be charged with a civil crime and was awaiting trial to see if he was "clear or criminal".[14] Such a person ought to be out of communion until the the church was satisfied of his lack of guilt. Next, he believed people should be disciplined by the church who had been admonished about their profligate living and were continuing to live such lives, disregarding the church's warning. If, by contrast, a member of his own will absented himself from the Communion Table, then it was not a matter to be dealt with by the church but by the minister in his pastoral visitation, the wayward member having first been visited by deacons appointed for the task (or by two responsible church members). Only after this had been done three or four times would he then bring

[10] Ibid., p. 152
[11] Ibid.
[12] Ibid., p. 140
[13] Ibid.
[14] Ibid., p. 35

the matter to the church.

In his visitation of members he really entered into the personal and domestic lives of his flock. In the *Queries and Solutions* he deals with such subjects as Innoculation for Small Pox and the marrying of sisters-in-law. Of innoculation he said: "The design of it is good: to preserve life",[15] and then went on to say that it was the prerogative of God to send and take away disease, and to take such precautions as innoculation was at variance with the Christian's resignation to the will of the Almighty Preserver.

He visited his members whatever disease was prevalent, and he comforted those who had a fear of death. Of this fear he wrote to Benjamin Francis: "Nothing but the glorious prospect under the influence of the blessed Spirit, can take away the dread in a right way".[16] For Thomas death had been dealt with in the cross by Christ and so "Death will be unspeakable gain – Hanner y gair i gall".[17]

Of marrying sisters-in-law he said: "I believe the Marriage is unlawful. It seems to be very plain, that tho' a woman might marry two Brothers for a particular Reason, and perhaps seven Brothers for the very same Reason (Luke 20:28, etc.), yet that two sisters might not marry the same Man, the case widely differing". He believed that the "Consanguinity" of the Book of Leviticus to be still in force and quoted Dr. Gill as agreeing with him. Such a marriage was therefore unclean in the sight of God and also contravened the civil laws of the land. As clergymen could not marry the parties in such a case he thought that Dissenters should not countenance "that which was contrary to the Scriptures and the Law of the Land".[18]

In case these strongly-worded opinions, and the strictness of the discipline exercised, should present too harsh a picture of the pastoral concern and oversight of Joshua Thomas, we must quote a note written to Benjamin Francis in July 1768. The church meeting at Leominster had met and decided upon the exclusion of a young married couple for wrong-doing. The decision was arrived at only after a day of prayer. All agreed upon the fact of the wrong-doing and the decision to discipline was unanimous. Joshua Thomas added, however, these words: "I thought it best not to be too hasty, tho' I do not know whether that is right or no. Lord, direct!"[19]. In any case, Thomas had made it quite plain what was expected of church members for he had

---

[15]Ibid., p. 221
[16]Ibid., p. 256
[17]Ibid.
[18]Ibid., p. 54, Vol. 2
[19]Ibid.

drawn up a set of rules for them. These he listed for the sake of Benjamin Francis in June 1761. They were: "1. That the Holy Scriptures be the Standing Rule of Belief, Conduct and Practice; 2. That any case that could not be settled by Scripture, then the 'Minor Part shall submit to the Major'; 3. That all members should give up themselves to each other in the fear of God that they should watch over each other, exhort and instruct; 4. That a meeting for discipline should be kept monthly or quarterly – ten days before the Lord's Supper; 5. That a member suspected of any disorder, if the suspicion became known fact, and only then, should be reported to the church. Enquiry should then be made and an occasion for repentance given before any action be taken; 6. No matter should be brought before the church unless it was 'scandalous and public to the world and the Church'; 7. That only one person should speak at a time and to do so standing up, expressing himself audibly; 8. That women may speak as evidence or in their own defense, otherwise not to debate; 9. That cases decided upon should be minuted legibly and orderly in the church Book".[20]

This, then, was Joshua Thomas's pastoral concern for his members. Through the Church Meeting – the exercise of discipline, mutual exhortation and encouragement, under pastoral guidance, that church members might grow in grace, making progress in their spiritual life, becoming a conspicuous testimony to those in the world around. Through visitation – comfort for the bereaved, sympathy for the sick, sharing in personal, family and domestic problems – his first concern being those with special needs, and after that regular and systematic visitation. Such a pastoral ministry is all the more remarkable when the area influenced by the church is considered. Thomas's *History of Leominster Baptist Church* speaks of members coming from as far away as Ludlow in Shropshire (11 miles), Tenbury Wells in Worcestershire (10 miles), as well as local trades-people who lived in surrounding villages (Dilwyn, Hope-under-Dinmore, etc. – averaging five or six miles out of Leominster) and many scattered farms. Pastoral visits in such a rural area would take up plenty of time when they had to be done on horseback or on foot. Doubtless on the outgoing journey he would compose his sermons, for he was, first and foremost, a preacher; on the homeward journey, being a man of prayer, he would be praying for the people he had visited, knowing something of their trials and sufferings. If the apostle Paul had "the care of all the churches", then Joshua Thomas, as his writings convince us, had the care of all his congregation upon his large pastoral heart.

---

[20] Ibid., pp 122-124

V

THE WRITER

"The weal of man, each side the spacious main,
The growing spread of the Redeemer's reign,
Employed thy pen, engag'd thy active mind".

So wrote Benjamin Francis in his *Elegy* of 1797.[1] None knew Thomas better than Francis, for their correspondence was prolific during a forty-year period. Thus, besides knowing of the writings of Joshua Thomas, Francis was well able to assess his literary style.

"Style", said Sir Arthur Quiller-Couch, "is the power to touch with ease, grace, precision, any note in the gamut of human thought or emotion".[2] A close study of Thomas's writings reveals a man of great literary style; he was truly an author who wrote with ease, grace and precision. More than that, since "Literature is not a mere Science, to be studied; but an Art, to be practised",[3] Thomas was indeed a literary man of a high order when the number of works he wrote is catalogued, although multiplicity of works is far from being the only criterion by which to judge a man's literary quality. His historical works, which predominate, will be considered in a later chapter (*The Historian*), but without these copious volumes there is a formidable list of his translations of other authors into Welsh and from Welsh into English; then there are his several original compositions.

Brief mention must here be made of some of his historical writings, notably those he wrote for others, or those he helped others to write. He helped Rippon with his *Baptist Register* for instance. Dr. John Rippon, renowned London Baptist preacher of Carter Lane, Southwark in 1773, began his *Annual Register* in 1790. Until 1802 it played "an important part in making churches and Associations aware of one another and of their fellow-Baptists overseas".[4] In the dedication of the first number Gill said that it was published "with a desire of promoting an universal interchange of kind offices among them and in serious expectation that before many years elapse... a deputation from all these climes will meet probably in London to consult the

---

[1] Rippon: *The Baptist Register,* 1797, p. 112
[2] A. Quiller-Couch: *On the Art of Writing* (London 1946), p. 166
[3] Ibid., Preface
[4] E. A. Payne: *The Baptist Union — A Short History* (London 1959), p.38

ecclesiastical good of the whole".[5] Thus there were included letters from William Carey and his colleagues as well as from Baptists in America. It also contained obituary notices of ministers and missionaries, as well as news of the churches and associations. Joshua Thomas wrote obituaries for Caleb Harris, Thomas Adams and others, and helped Rippon with the history of the Welsh Association of Baptist churches and a history of the Particular Baptist Churches in the Principality of Wales. Proof sheets passed between Thomas at Leominster and the Rev. Dr. Rippon at Mr. Thos. Rippon, at the Drawing Office, Bank of England, London. Joshua Thomas's corrections in the margins of the printed proof sheets show the same care for correctness of detail as he exercised in all his written works.

On one proof sheet he adds this note: "Dear Sir, You may depend upon my doing all in my power towards the History of the Bristol Academy". He mentions "parcels No. 9 and No. 10" giving some indication of the colossal task that these two men were engaged in. His *History of the Welsh Associations* for the *Annual Baptist Register* he divided into three convenient parts: the South-West Association, the South-East Association, and the North Wales Association. Finally he appended some *Observations*. His *History of the Particular Baptist Churches in the Principality of Wales* for the *Register* he divides into sections corresponding with the Welsh counties, listing the number of churches, the year founded, the Association to which they belonged, their present minister, and the number of members on the roll. Notes are appended which turn what could be dull statistics into living history. Sentences such as "the three ministers now with them were raised up among themselves", give an insight into early Baptist (and perhaps New Testament!) practice. "The latter continued in these parts through all the persecutions", throws light upon the troublous times of those days. Of one church it was said: "For above twenty years a few serious persons formed a friendly society of a religious nature", thus emphasising the rather unorganised, irregular state of the early Baptists in Wales. Again he wrote: "Some churches are grown so numerous, that on ordinance days there is not room enough for the members to sit down, therefore part of them are obliged to sit without, and there receive the ordinance. In some places the people have come to be baptized by scores; many more are impatient to show that they esteem the reproach of Christ better than great treasures. Gifts increase in several churches. In some churches there are sever-

[5] A. C. Underwood: *A History of the English Baptists* (London 1956), p. 179

al labourers, but work plenty for all".[6]

In 1786 Joshua Thomas was requested to write a brief *History of the Baptist Church at Hook Norton.* It was dedicated to a Mr. Wilmot with the words: "I have taken all the pains I could to gather all the limits I could of your respectable family". Of this work Dr. Barrie White of Regents Park College, Oxford, says: "It is a fine example of the making of bricks without straw".[7] All writers have to be adept at this sort of thing on occasions and Joshua Thomas was as adept as any other. However, Thomas assures us that in these requested historical writings, "in framing them, care has been taken to preserve facts".[8] This fulfills one of the requirements later laid down by Sir Arthur Quiller-Couch in the *Art of Writing*: "I choose these four epithets—*accurate,* perspicuous, persuasive, appropriate".[9] As we shall later see, Joshua Thomas was renowned for his accuracy, so as Sir Arthur told his Cambridge hearers, "I will assume that we are agreed to desire *appropriateness*", so we may assume Thomas's accuracy.

Naturally *persuasion* was also a characteristic of Thomas the writer, for first and foremost he was a preacher, and the preacher in the New Testament style of the apostle Paul is one who seeks to "persuade men". But "the highest form of persuasion cannot be achieved without a sense of beauty".[10] Being born and brought up in Carmarthenshire, and preaching and ministering in Herefordshire, the natural style for Thomas the writer was likely to be one of beauty and persuasiveness. This we see most clearly in his original works in his own native language. Harmony, order, sublimity, beauty of diction, "charm" (as Sir Arthur would put it)—these are the characteristics of Thomas's prose. But first we must note his works of translating other men's writings.

In 1689 the London Baptist Association issued a Confession of Faith. It was approved by representatives of over a hundred churches and was more rigid in its Calvinism than the earlier Confessions of 1677 and 1644. In 1791 Joshua Thomas made a translation of the Confession into Welsh and it was published in Carmarthen.

Robert Hall, renowned Baptist and missionary advocate of the

---

6 All the above quotations are from a Joshua Thomas annotated proof sheet of the *Annual Baptist Register,* 1794 (original in the Angus Library, Regents Park College, Oxford; xerox copy at Leominster Baptist Church.

7 Personal letter to the author.

8 J. Rippon: *Annual Baptist Register,* 1791-3, p. 191

9 Op. cit., p. 27

10 Ibid., p. 31

eighteenth century, and a contemporary of Joshua Thomas, published a volume on *The Doctrine of the Trinity.* Hall had read Jonathan Edwards and Bishop Butler before he was nine years of age, having carried them in his pinafore to lie and read them in the long grass of a burial ground. His work on the Trinity was translated by Joshua Thomas in 1794 and published in Carmarthen under the title *Athrawiaeth y Drindod.* Once again, a work characterised by accuracy and felicity of phrase.

Describing the Association meetings held in 1757, Joshua Thomas inserted an interesting note: "That year I had translated a small tract entitled *The Believer's Evidence for Heaven,* and gave the copy to my son Timothy to print in Welsh". This Timothy did, printing it with a sermon of his own on 2 Peter 1:10. The volume was given the title *The White Stone* from Revelation 6:17, so Joshua tells us in his *History of the Welsh Association.*[11]

Thomas's original works, those not listed under historical writings or translations of works by other authors, were of a varying nature.

At the Welsh Association held at Llanelli in 1749 it was pointed out that an *Exposition of the Church Cathecism* published in Welsh by a Church of England clergyman, containing twenty reasons for infant baptism, should be answered by some Welsh Baptist ministers of the Association. Five were delegated to do this work, but only one or two put some thoughts on paper. Joshua Thomas, however, drew up some "hints" and was encouraged to go on by the Association.[12] The work was further commended at the next Association Meetings, held the following year, and a printer was suggested. Since Dr. Gill of London had also written a short *Reply* to the clergyman's *Exposition,* and since Joshua Thomas had also turned his original manuscript into English it was thought that the two replies could be printed together.

A *Reply* of a different character was written by Joshua Thomas in 1775. Abel Francis, an Arminian, had published a sermon propounding Arminian doctrine. Thomas replied with *Notes of a Calvinistic Baptist upon Abel Francis.* The work was published in Welsh and printed in Brecon, the title being: *Nodiadau ar bregeth Mr. Abel Francis.* It is in these notes, hints and replies upon controversial subjects that we see Thomas fulfilling Sir Arthur Quiller-Couch's criteria of good literature – persuasion and perspicuity. "The first aim of speech is to be understood",[13] and Joshua Thomas wrote with

[11] Op. cit., p. 76
[12] Ibid., p. 74
[13] *The Art of Writing,* p. 27

great clarity and simplicity of diction; and he wrote in a most persuasive manner, persuading his readers to listen to his views. He had the power of influencing others by his reasoning, his rhetoric, his simplicity and felicity of speech and language.

In 1788 there was published in London Joshua Thomas's *Remarks.* A Baptist Circular Letter had been composed by a Mr. Bradford in 1786. Thomas's *Remarks* contain his reflections upon this letter.

Unfortunately, all too few of Thomas's works are available to the research student today, either in the original manuscript form or in printed and published form. The historical works, which we shall study in detail later, are preserved in manuscript form in the library of the Baptist College, Bristol; others are in the National Library of Wales, Aberystwyth, and copies are held at the Baptist Church, Leominster. Few of his writings are listed in the space devoted to him in the *Dictionary of Welsh Biography.* No Welsh library seems to have copies of *Nodiadau ar bregeth, Athrawiaeth y Drindod,* or the *Remarks.* Also at Regents Park College, Oxford there is a transcription re Isaac Marlow (6 February 1795) which refers to a *History of the Midland Association* written by Joshua Thomas.

In spite of all this Joshua Thomas is listed among thirteen pages of brief biographies of literary men in J. E. Lloyd's *A History of Carmarthenshire* (Cardiff 1939), alongside such worthies as Stephen Hughes (who wrote his own version of *The Pilgrim's Progress*), Eliezer Williams (essayist and founder of Lampeter Grammar School), Peter Bayley Williams (translator of Richard Baxter's *Saints' Everlasting Rest* and *Call to the Unconverted*), and David Owen or "Brutus" (essayist, editor and satirist). J. E. Lloyd has confined his biographies to those whose "literary works have effectively borne his name beyond his district and after his day".[14] Joshua Thomas's works certainly accomplished this.

It is a man's correspondence that carries his name far and wide. Unfortunately most of Joshua Thomas's prolific correspondence has been lost. The Rev. J. R. Jones of Ramoth claimed in 1821 or early 1822 to possess no fewer than 42 of Joshua Thomas's letters (all written during period 1790-97), but their present whereabouts is not known.[15] The letters that are in existence are mostly to relatives in the ministry, and other ministerial colleagues, in which Thomas gives

[14] Op. cit., p. 431

[15] See *Seren Gomer,* 1822, p. 69; *Cofiant J. R. Jones, Ramoth* by D. Williams, p. 660 (referred to by B. G. Owens in *The National Library of Wales Journal,* Vol. 2 (1941-42), p. 17

the briefest of family news and discusses spiritual experiences and ministerial responsibilities, before going on to give, or ask for, statistics regarding baptisms, additions and deletions to membership – all needed for his historical writings.[16] All that can be said here is that as a letter writer Joshua Thomas was conscientious and consistent, although he does seem to have delayed answering unduly in many instances – understandably so considering his busy life of writing, preaching and pastoral work.

---

[16] *National Library of Wales Journal,* Vol. 2 (1941-42), p. 17 Note 2

VI

THE THEOLOGIAN

Baker's *Dictionary of Theology* defines theology as "that which is thought and said concerning God" or "the revelation of God in human terms".[1] A theologian, therefore, is one who is "learned in theology" or who "adheres to a certain theological position".[2] Theology is sometimes divided into four main groups: patristic or post-apostolic writers; scholastic or formative theology stimulated by the rediscovery of Greek thought; reformed or biblical theology; and modern or independent theories of East and West, Protestant and Roman Catholic.

The Reverend Joshua Thomas was a theologian in both senses: he was learned in theology, his preaching, prayers and writings being full of God; and he was an adherent of a certain theological position, namely, that of the Reformed School. As G. W. Bromiley has put it: "Its first business is to know and expound the Bible ... to talk of God it must be taught by God. Its positive theological work is preceded, accompanied, informed and corrected by biblical study".[3]

Thomas then was a great believer in theology, the Queen of the Sciences, and the content of all he wrote and said was biblical theology. And since the exponents of Reformed theology were Calvinists we shall see that plenty of Calvinism was included in his written and spoken ministry. The whole process of personal salvation was according to Calvin's "five points" – Divine Election, Human Depravity, Particular Redemption, Effectual Calling and Final Perseverance. Joshua Thomas outlined his beliefs in this respect in a lengthy period of correspondence throughout 1760 with Benjamin Francis. Beginning with the sinner's state of unbelief, which he affirmed was "different from the Questioning and Fears of the Christian",[4] he divided unbelievers into the following classes: Atheists, Deists, Jews, Socinians, down-right Arminians, the Openly Profane and Backsliders. The unbeliever's duty was to "come to Faith and Repentance".[5] These two he believed were one and the same thing. They were, however, God-given gifts, for man has no ability of his own to two essentially spiritual acts. With a tiny hand and pointing finger drawn in the margin

---

1 Op. cit. (London, 1960), p. 518

2 *Oxford Dictionary*

3 Baker's *Dictionary of Theology*, p. 519

4 *Queries and Solutions*, p. 74

5 Ibid., p. 10

of the manuscript, to impress upon his readers the importance of this point, Joshua Thomas stated with Calvinistic certainty the truth of "Man's inability and God's Sovereign Grace".[6] Thus a person cannot "repent and believe *evangelically*", but it is his duty to do so "according to his light". The Law says repent and believe and a man can and must do this as he receives the Light. All ungodly will be condemned who do not do so. But it is not the unbeliever's duty, rather it is an impossibility, for him to repent and believe in his own strength to be saved eternally – that must be the word of God upon the soul.

That raised the question of Election for Benjamin Francis, and Thomas had this to say: any person who feared he might not be one of the elect, that is, had a genuine concern about his spiritual state, was already receiving "Gospel Light",[7] and God would never send such light except upon His own elect. He recommended a booklet entitled *The Believer's Evidence for Heaven* as suitable for putting into the hands of any concerned unbeliever. He approved of it so much that he translated it into Welsh, Timothy publishing it for him. Election, like faith and repentance, was Divine – "free and sovereign".[8]

Expressing Christian conversion in the New Testament fashion as a New Birth, Thomas found difficulty in drawing an analogy between natural and spiritual birth, a man's first and second birth. Apart from both having "a Formation, Growth, Quickening",[9] he could not see any parallel. To press such an analogy was to impose a supernatural idea upon a purely natural principle. However, he proceeded to define the New Birth in the following way to Benjamin Francis: "It is an infusion of a Supernatural Principle of Life and Holiness, or, the Sowing of the incorruptible Seed, that abideth for ever, or it is a Breathing of Spiritual Life into the Soul".[10] He then thinks of a better definition of the New Birth by quoting in his native language Matthias Maurice: "Cen.....iad n... Greadigaeth newydd* yn yr Enaid yn yr tueddu oddiwrth Bechod, Hunan, a'r Byd; at Dduw yng

---

[6] Ibid., p. 11
[7] Ibid., p. 16
[8] Ibid., p. 83
[9] Ibid., p. 75
[10] Ibid., p. 76
* Thomas's handwriting is rather obscure at this point, or else his Welsh had become "rusty" through ministering so long in England!

Nghrist" (It is a begetting, on a new creation in the soul, inclining from sin, self, and the world, to God in Christ).[11]

With regard to the time of the New Birth he confessed that he was still in the dark. It could be "instantaneous" and not "progressive". There could be a lengthy condition of conviction of sin, the conviction wearing off and returning (maybe for ten or twenty years), this making the New Birth *seem* gradual, but the actual regeneration by the Holy Spirit still being instantaneous.

Remission or forgiveness of sin was entirely God's work and was again instantaneous, although the manifestation of it could be gradual. Such forgiveness was only possible because of a substitutionary atonement—"God's imputing unto, and laying upon Christ all the Sins of the Elect, and his accepting of His Obedience and Satisfaction in their Room".[12] True remission was "God speaking Peace and Pardon to the wounded Conscience of His People. Whenever, therefore, the Blood of Christ is applied to the Believer's Conscience, and the Love and Joy of the Holy Ghost shed abroad in his Heart so that he experiences peace with God, and a sweet, soul-satisfying Sense of Divine Love, through Jesus Christ, God may be said, in Scripture Language, to forgive his Sin".[13] This he calls the Discovery of Forgiveness.

Justification, yet another aspect of eternal salvation, Joshua Thomas defined as "a free, Sovereign Act of Divine Grace, wherein God looks upon a Person just and righteous in his sight. It stands opposed to Condemnation, and not to unrighteousness or sin. It includes in it Acceptance with God, and a Right to Glory. The Author of it is the Father; the Spring of it is free Love and goodwill in God; the Matter of it is the Complete Righteousness of Christ; the Form of it is the Imputation, or Acceptance of the Righteousness of Christ; the Subject of it is an elect Person that shall inherit Glory".[14] He linked Justification with the Calvinistic doctrine of eternal security or the Perseverance of the Saints. Justification was *eternal,* for Joshua Thomas, "an Act abiding in God, or rather finished in the eternal MIND, and not a Decree".[15] Such justification was manifested in various ways: "There is a Manifestation of it to the Angels in Heaven; to the Devils; in a general way in the gospel; particularly in Regeneration".[16] It was at this point that he differed from Benjamin Francis,

[11] Ibid., pp. 76-77
[12] Ibid., p. 71
[13] Ibid., pp 71-72
[14] Ibid., p. 88
[15] Ibid.
[16] Ibid.

who maintained justification was "a Divine Act that passed upon individuals at the very first Moment of Believing''.[17]

Sin he compared with a physical disease and sinners to a doctor's patients. Ministers of the gospel were thus physicians and needed to know how to administer "the physic''. Soul doctors must thus know their patients, their diseases, and be able to convince them that they are suffering from such-and-such disease and that the remedy is safe and sure. "Thus in preaching we should get as near the Conscience and particular sins of our Hearers as we can, and yet take heed we do not appear to the Audience to have some one particular Person in View''[18]

Thomas was able to impart assurance of eternal salvation to his congregation, for this was another aspect of the Bible's teaching about personal salvation. Assurance (much-neglected today) was considered a vital teaching for him for it gave the new convert peace of mind and a testimony to others. In 1759 he stated that believers "should look for Assurance much more than they do'' and that ministers should preach it more than they do. For him assurance of salvation depended upon the "Sovereign Pleasure of the Almighty'' but that in no way "discouraged Duty'' for God "meets His People in His appointed ways''.[19]

Joshua Thomas's eschatological theology was rather confused and not at all clearly defined. This he admitted himself to Benjamin Francis in 1760, after thinking about such subjects as the Millennium for twenty years or more! He had read several books on the subject, but with little profit. Dr. Gill was his favourite and most satisfying commentator on the Last Things. However, his "own confused thoughts'' he recorded in this way: "I believe there will be a very numerous part of the Gentile world converted, called The Fulness of the Gentiles: that the Body of the Jews shall be in some wonderful manner enlightened, and the Veil taken away: and that they are preserved a distinct Body (tho' dispersed thro' the Gentile world) for this very Purpose. ...But as to their returning to the land of Palestine, and building the City upon its own Heap; whether the Glory will be exactly a 1000 years according to our Notion of years: and the manner of that Glory: with the Form of worship during that Period: also the Employment of the People; whether they will till the ground; eat, drink, be clothed, and multiply: whether there will be the Beast, Fish and Fowls: Winter and Summer, with the annual volutions, etc., I am quite in the Dark. Since good Men have very diligently Searched into

[17] Ibid., p. 89
[18] Ibid., Vol. 2, p. 20
[19] Ibid., Vol. 1, p. 33

this Point, some of them have been very confident in their Sentiments; others more Modest: but most of them differed in Somethings: and perhaps it lies more dormant now than ever it did, since the Ascension of Christ. Now this does not weaken my Belief. This was the Case, even with inspired Men under the Mosaic Dispensation. They were much in the Dark about the Time and Manner of Gospel Glory; and wished they might see it''.[20]

The first volume of *Queries and Solutions* ends with a further note on the Millennium and attendant happenings during the Last Days. Once more Thomas confessed that ''it is a Point that I seldom think of. I justify myself not in that, but others appear to me far more important''.[21] Obviously he agreed with the man who said that he did not preach much about the *second* coming of Christ as people knew so little about the *first!* On the other hand he did not censure those who did diligently study prophetic events. Nor did he point the finger of scorn at those who believed in a literal thousand years' reign of Jesus Christ. He was content to hold an open mind about eschatological matters, looking upon the Last Days as but ''a Porch into those everlasting Mansions''.[22]

At the beginning of the second volume of *Queries and Solutions,* however, he does give an outline of the programme of the Last Things. It is his own programme since he disapproved of Dr. Gill's at this point, the learned doctor's being ''forced and foreign...and in many Particulars too singular''.[23] Thomas's time-table was as follows:

''The Saints shall rise first, shall be crowned and enthroned before the ungodly are raised. Then fallen Angels and impenitent sinners of mankind are brought in Chains to the awful Bar; Jesus Christ will appear as seated on a glorious Throne, clothed with all Majesty and invested with judicial Power. All His saints will be with Him, as so many Justices (if I may use the expression) sitting with the Judge (wonderful Dignity!). True, our exalted Lord with particularity will hear the causes, or rather open or read them, judge them, condemn and pronounce the dreadful Sentence: so all judgment is committed to the SON. But all Saints (and I believe all Holy Angels) shall, not barely sit and hear, but judge also in themselves and so be capable of seeing and understand how exactly wise and just the Judge proceeds; and when the whole closed they will, with united heart and voice close the solemn Process with their loud Amen! Alleluja, etc''.[24]

20 Ibid., pp 59-61
21 Ibid., p. 272
22 Ibid.
23 Ibid., Vol. 2, p. 14
24 Ibid., pp. 14-15

He then asked Benjamin Francis: "What say Hammond and Henry (two commentators he did not possess) on the subject? Don't pass it by, now it is started".[25] A note from Francis assured Thomas that both Hammond and Henry agreed with his interpretation.

The same subject is resumed some letters later when Jonathan answers David's query: "What will be the order of Christ's second coming, of the Resurrection of the Godly and unjust, and of the judgment of both?" Again Thomas expressed his uncertainty, saying that "no mere Man in Heaven or on Earth or Angel either, shall have a full and distinct View of these Things until they take place." This time, however, Thomas entered into more detail. He questioned whether "day" was a period of 12, 16 or 24 hours or whether, which he thought more likely, time in the eschatological sense "will not be measured by hours." Thus he cannot give any indication of the duration of the Day of Judgment, or of the Millennium. For himself he has come to the position when he can say: "I now take no notice of what is commonly called the Millennium." He also began to wonder if there would be any "Motion" at the Day of Judgment, concluding that probably there would be for there are angels "somewhere in the Air, ethereal Regions". He also questioned Dr. Gill's interpretation of the saints meeting the returning Christ in the air and ascending with Him to the third heaven, with an earthly conflagration and a thousand years' reign on a new heaven and a new earth.[26]

The origin of the soul occupied the minds of these two correspondents for some time in 1761. Joshua Thomas cannot be quoted, for he wrote to Benjamin Francis: "I can't find one Word in what you said, but I agree to it...being the very Sentiments of my Heart".[27] Francis had said that if Solomon knew not how the bone grew in the womb how could he expect to know how the individual soul was created by God? He concluded that it must have been "propagated by virtue of God's Word" as was man's animal life. Naturally this led to consideration of when original sin entered into the soul, and whether sin first is bestowed by man's parents or whether it is prior-implanted or inherited beforehand. Joshua Thomas thought that an infant had "no soul till quickened in the Womb" and that sin could not exist until "the exercise of Reason doth exist".[28]

Only in modern times have Baptists begun to develop a theology of children, or the place of children in the Kingdom of God and in the

---

[25] Ibid., p. 17
[26] Ibid., see p. 41ff
[27] Ibid., Vol. 1, p. 112
[28] Ibid., pp 113-114

Church visible. Because of their practice of baptising only *believer's,* which usually precludes small children and limits baptism to those of more mature years (not necessarily *adults,* but young people who have reached the age of discretion or accountability), Baptists have only just begun to work out their theology of children and the Church. From Thomas's theology of baptism it will be seen that he, too, had come to no definite conclusions about the position of unbelieving and unbaptised chidren, even of Christian parents.

In his Introduction to the History of *Leominster Baptist Church,* he states his theology of baptism in these words: "According to Scripture, primitive Baptism continued in the Church about 300 years after the Days of our Saviour Jesus Christ, without any material change But afterward, as errors and Superstition flowed in like a Torrent, so the ordinance of Baptism was corrupted and perverted; particularly regarding the Subject of it, and the manner of administration. Thus Infant Sprinkling was introduced, and it obtained by degrees; then Believer's Baptism, according to gospel Rule, was at length discountenanced by many". He went on to describe the growth of infant baptism until it was universally received by about the seventh or eighth century. Not till the Reformation, in about 1533, does he think that there "appeared witness for Believer's Baptism".

In *Queries and Solutions* he again expresses his theology of baptism. In September 1760, after reading Towgood's *The Baptism of Infants a Reasonable Service,* he penned his comments to Benjamin Francis. Already that year they had corresponded on the same subject. Towgood's fault, according to Thomas, was that he based his arguments on "the Covenant Privileges of Believers' Infants",[29] believing that Abraham's descendents received privileges solely on account of their father's piety.

Joshua Thomas thought English Baptists more neglectful and disparaging of credal statements than Welsh Baptists – hence, perhaps his readiness to translate the early Baptist *Confession* into Welsh. He could not agree with those who thought that the Scriptures alone were sufficient as a statement of creed. While he did not put credal statements in place of, or above the Bible, he did consider that such statements helped towards an understanding of God's Word. They helped God's people to a better understanding of the Trinity, the Divine nature, baptism, Calvinism, the deity of Christ, and so on.[30]

In theology, then, Joshua Thomas was Reformed, Calvinistic, evangelistic, Baptist, and Biblical. He was, like so many of his time,

29 Ibid., p. 90

30 For a fuller treatment of Thomas and creeds see: J. Gwili Jenkins *Hanfod Duw a Pherson Crist,* pp 248-9

defective in his theology of the Last Things, refusing to commit himself to any particular school of thought, either pre- or post-millennial. Thus Benjamin Francis, upon the death of his friend Jonathan, could have the last word on the Last Things and state in his *Elegy:*

> "Adieu, my friend! do thou with Jesus rest,
> Completely holy, and supremely blest:
> And when He shall descend to earth again,
> O, may I meet thee in this glorious train!"

VII

THE HISTORIAN

It is as a historian that Joshua Thomas is now best known. To his contemporaries he might have been that "glorious saint", that "lovely saint", that "Christian of no common size".[1] To the present members of Leominster Baptist he is, and always will be, the Pastor with a long record of ministerial charge in that particular church. To members of many other Baptist churches in the surrounding counties he is still known as a "revivalist", for many are the tales told of his journeys and preaching expeditions. But to the wider Baptist, and indeed nonconformist, constituency he is the pre-eminent historian. Today he is remembered as the renowned Baptist historian of the eighteenth century who has placed so many later historians greatly in his debt.

"Each generation must study its heritage afresh, and as the story of the past is retold, a new chapter is added and the older accounts are seen from a different standpoint, for the perspective has changed"[2] – so wrote Dr. E. A. Payne in the Preface to his *Free Church Tradition in the Life of England.* In this respect Joshua Thomas has been overlooked. True others have been indebted to his monumental historical works and have made use of them in their lesser way, but few have studied him closely and carefully, interpreting him for their own generation. David Davies referred to Joshua Thomas in his book *Vavasor Powell*[3] in connection with a biography of John Penry. He made lengthy quotations from Thomas's *History of the Baptist Churches in Wales.* We have already seen that Dr. Rippon, the renowned English Baptist historian, called on Joshua Thomas for help with his *Baptist Annual Register* and a *History of Bristol Academy.* From letters that Thomas wrote to Rippon it is clear that he was always searching out historical records. A letter dated 20 May 1795 refers to Worcester Baptist Church records, giving details of men and their movements; one dated 19 March of the same year has a postscript stating that Thomas was lending Rippon his manuscript of the *History of the Welsh Association;* in the same letter he refers to a

1 Benjamin Francis: *An Elegy.*
2 Op. cit., (London, 1944), p. 7
3 London, 1896

Life of English Students that he was engaged upon; on 6 February that year he gives details to Rippon of a book by Isaac Marlow (a former London jeweller who settled near Leominster) which he was transcribing; while in the previous year (13 October 1794) he referred to several histories of churches he had either written, or for which he was collecting material. When in 1895 John Jones of Llandrindod Wells wrote *The History of the Baptists in Radnorshire,* he drew largely from Joshua Thomas's historical works, as did E. L. Wallis in 1930 when writing *The Story of the Hereford Baptist Church,* and Messrs T. H. Price and J. P. Pugh in 1966 in *A Brief History of the Beginning and Growth of Nantgwyn and Beulah Baptist Churches.* So the list could be enlarged, but sufficient has been mentioned to show that from the mid-1700s to the mid-1900s, historians have gone straight to the fountain–head of Thomas's works for their material when compiling local church history.

Thomas's historical works are in the main a trilogy: the *Hanes,* as it is commonly called–*The History of the Baptist Churches in Wales,* then *The History of the Welsh Association* (1650-1790), and finally his *Ecclesiastical History of Wales.* He began gathering material for his *Hanes y Bedyddwyr* (History of the Baptists) as early as 1745, but it was not finished until 1778. The *History of the Welsh Association* was first published a sheet at a time as an extra to Rippon's *Register,* the first sheet in 1791, being finally completed in 1796.

Before studying in detail the trilogy, we must turn to the *History of Leominster and Olchon Baptist Churches.* Already this work has provided us with much excellent material for an assessment of Joshua Thomas as Pastor, but it will also help us to evaluate Thomas the historian for it reveals his genius as "a new kind of historian, courteous, impartial, dogmatic on fundamentals of belief, but slow and hesitant on details".[4] All his historical works are characterised by many cross-references and frequent repetition for the sake of accuracy. His standards have been described as "eminently judicial and scientific". He laboured assiduously to gather evidence from America regarding the beginning of Baptists in Wales. The debt was repaid when in 1857 an American, G. H. Orchard, visited England and paid a visit to Bristol Baptist College to look at the Joshua Thomas manuscripts deposited there by Timothy Thomas. A note dated 15 May 1857 in Orchard's handwriting reads: "With the kind permission of the Revd J. Crisp, President of the Baptist College, this MS of the Welsh Bap-

[4] *Welsh Dictionary of Biography:* article on Joshua Thomas by Dr. Thomas Richards

tist Churches, has been perused, and such extracts made as were deemed suitable, for a printed History to be published at Nashville, Tennessee, U. S. A., by Graves and Co." Unfortunately the present author who has friends on the other side of the Atlantic, cannot trace any surviving volume of this American history of the Baptists. It would be interesting to see what was extracted from Joshua Thomas's *History,* and how indebted the Americans were to this historian of Leominster.

As we study the historical works of Thomas it is plain that he believed with Shakespeare that "there is a history in all men's lives" for much of Thomas's history is brief biography. Carlyle and Emerson who came after him agreed with this treatment of history. In *Hero and Hero-Worship* Carlyle says: "The history of the world is but the biography of great men". Joshua Thomas also believed history was made by lesser men as well and no tiny incident in their lives was insignificant. Emerson, in his *Essay on History* stated: "There is properly no history; only biography". Thus biography looms large in all Joshua Thomas's historical volumes, and this method of historical writing, employed in primitive form by Thomas, is what is widely used and admired among contemporary historians. The title page of *The History of Leominster Baptist Church* states: "First, a general account of its Beginning and Progress, by way of Introduction. Secondly, more particular Hints of all the Members Deceased, as far as they could be obtained, authenticated, and judged useful to Posterity".

His purpose in writing such history he expressed in these words: "I considered the work as profitable to myself, (although) I expected no worldly profit, but much fatigue, labour, and expense of Paper... (but) perhaps some may be glad to persue it in order to obtain some account of their Predecessors and Godly Forefathers, and to see how they behaved here in former Days, as well as how the Lord was pleased to deal with them".[5]

He stated that his method was to list personalities "in an Alphabetical order on the top of the leaves in a waste blank Book. That being done I carried my Waste Book generally with me and went to one and another of the aged Members to read my Catalogue of Names".[6] Besides that he "wrote to several Distant Persons, Descendants or friends of former Members" and "accidentally obtained some of the Notes of Mr. Holder's (a former Pastor of Leominster Baptist Church) Sermons, writ with his own hand, wherein I found several Funeral Discourses, in which he gave some account of the Persons deceased:

---

[5] *History of Leominster Baptist Church,* Preface, p. viii
[6] Ibid., p. ix

and at the same time I had a MS begun by Mr. Holder in 1718''.[7] He admitted that such a plan was not perfect, and that his ''labour has not been small''.[8] When completed, however, he dedicated and devoted the work ''to your treasury of books, and desire your acceptance of it, as a Token of my indisputable Regard for you and your worthy Predecessors'',[9] that is, his fellow members of Leominster Baptist Church.

From reading this *History of Leominster Baptist Church* we glean much information about Baptist life and witness in troublous times. First, however, he describes the early days of Leominster Baptist Church in almost New Testament wording: Some few people ''agreed to meet on the Lord's Day morning in the little room behind the Pulpit, to spend an hour before the public worship began ... chiefly in prayer''. However, persecution in one form or another soon stopped this and ''in a few years Providence scattered all these young Men''.[10]

With a reference to baptism by John the Baptist and the baptism of Christ in Jordan, Thomas immediately stated his Baptist convictions by asserting: ''Nor have we any hint there (i.e. New Testament) that Infants were Members of the Gospel Church''.[11] Indeed, the Baptist cause in Leominster was started by an Anglican Vicar of the town, John Tombs, who in 1631 declared that ''he was in doubt concerning Infant Baptism''. This Mr. Tombs was ''a great scholar and a popular preacher, being more concerned for the Glory of God and the Souls of Men than the generality of the Clergy''.[12] In 1656, however, several people saw that they could not continue their Baptist witness in ''a mixt Communion'' and so separated from Mr. Tombs and formed themselves into a Baptist Church.

From 1660 to 1688 the Baptist Dissenters in the town and district of Leominster experienced twenty-eight years of severe ''Trouble and Persecution'' and yet ''many were added to them''.[13] Through the instrumentality of Leominster members two other Baptist churches were started in the surrounding districts, Ludlow and Broseley, both in Shropshire. By now King William had ''established Liberty of Conscience to the Dissenters through the land''.[14]

In presenting his brief biographies of members Thomas concen-

---

[7] Ibid., pp ix,x
[8] Ibid., p. xi
[9] Ibid., p. xii
[10] Ibid., p. iv
[11] Ibid., p. 1
[12] Ibid.
[13] Ibid., p. 9
[14] Ibid.

trated on three things: their spiritual experience, their Christian character, and the persecution they endured. Joan Abberley, for instance, bore a heavy trial of persecution for "near 30 years continuance"; Thomas Adams' daughter Mary was visited "with affliction of body, something like consumption"; Bridget Bullock was one of the few "rich in the world, rich in faith, and rich in good works" – she visited imprisoned Baptists in the county gaol at Hereford, although this brought her before the Mayor for questioning.

Burial was difficult for dissenters in those early days. They often took place at night, with much secrecy, the bodies frequently being buried in their own gardens as the common burying places were denied them. Sometimes, Thomas tells us, enemies of the Baptists raided the graves and disfigured the dead. Mary Bowles was buried in her own garden at Pembridge, some eight miles from Leominster.

A lighter touch is given when Joshua Thomas comments on the virtue of punctuality in Daniel Bott – "He was not one of those who habitually come late to Divine worship, as if they came against their will and left their heart at home"!

Ministers and members had their differences in those days as today. There was a conflict of personality between Pastor Oulton and Deacon Joseph Bache. A reconciliation took place after thirteen years! Ann Brown's husband was imprisoned for his faith and soon died. His widow walked the eleven miles from Ludlow to Leominster to worship. Joshua Thomas describes her as "a neat, aged woman, and a worthy Christian". Richard Butcher also travelled from Ludlow every Sunday. One day he met Dr. Buckley, a Canon of Hereford, who was to preach in Ludlow. "Why will you go so many miles to hear a calf bleat?" asked the good doctor of Baptist Butcher. The answer given was: "I'd rather go eight miles to hear a calf bleat than go one mile to hear a canon rore"!

The membership was depleted often from various causes. In 1758 the small pox took its toll. Occasionally discipline was exercised, a person's misdemeanour being "noted" in the church book. When repentance was satisfactory to the church meeting then restoration was made. Gross forms of misbehaviour resulted in "excommunication", absence from the Communion Service for several months.[15] Discipline was even exercised when a person sought civic office. James Caswell, one of Tombs's original flock, was chosen in 1698 to be "Baily of the Borough". A church meeting was called and the following noted in the minutes: "We signified our dislike thereof, and diverse of us sought faithfully to convince him of his mistake therein".

---

[15] Ibid., p. 44

The wider influence of Leominster Baptist Church has always been notable, not only through the exertions of some of the ministers like Joshua Thomas, but also some of the members. Thomas takes pains to record that John Edwards in the early 1700s had eleven children. All became Christians and seven of them undertook important Christian service. The eldest son became a Dissenting Pastor in Dublin, another brother succeeding him when he died. The father, John Edwards, Snr., was the first "ruling Elder"of Leominster Baptist Church, revealing that early Baptists believed in the plurality of Elders as well as Deacons.

A terrible death was experienced by John Eddins or Edwins. A chandler by trade he one day fell into his boiling furnace of fat. Taken out alive he was nevertheless demented and died in a short while. The Christian's minister's attitude to such tragedies at that time was: "Little do we know what a Day may bring forth" and "the Judgments of God are a great Deep"!

Besides tradesmen and labourers, the membership of dissenting chapels at that time included soldiers of Cromwell's army from time to time. Another person who applied for membership was an ejected minister from the Established Church. He caused much trouble, however, in the church and surrounding churches, and his case was referred to the notable William Kiffin and Joseph Crosby. He was put out of the church and once again conformed to the Church of England.

As others later drew upon Joshua Thomas's history when writing the history of American Baptists, so Thomas went to American sources when writing his *History of Leominster Baptist Church.* He refers to *The History of the American Baptists* by Morgan Edwards and in it discovers that a Leominster member, William Kinnersley, became Baptist Minister of the first Baptist church in Pennsylvania.

When in his alphabetical list of members Thomas comes to Marlow he gives lengthy and intimate details about the famous family. Living in London at the time of the plague in 1665 they removed to relations in Herefordshire. There they associated with the Baptists at Leominster. Owing to persecution (they were meeting for worship at night) they fled to Holland. Mrs. Marlow was a member of Benjamin Keach's church at Horsleydown, Southwark, London. Returning from Holland to London they joined Mile End Green Baptist Church. Some years later they again moved to Herefordshire, living first in Leominster itself, then at Dilwyn a few miles out. Mr. Marlow never joined Leominster Baptist Church, but kept his membership in London. He wrote several books, some of which were published and others left in manuscript form. His daughter, Mary, was baptised by Mr. Holder in 1729 at the age of thirty-seven. She was extremely generous to good causes and all denominations. Being left a generous legacy by a cousin she was able to build the new church in 1771, also Manse and almshouses. She gave the ground and graveyard. According to the custom of the time, although she remained single, in latter life she was given the courtesy title of "Mrs." which is inscribed on her tombstone in Leominster Baptist graveyard.

Another influential member in the early1700s was William Prichard. Living a long way from Leominster, between Ross and Abergavenny, he had his own house licensed for services and they were held there once a month.

One prevalent cause for church discipline was when the custom started of prospective Members of Parliament giving money to people to persuade them to vote for them. John Nash was "noted" in the minute book for this "very sinful" custom, as were several other members. They were barred from the Communion Table for one month, "happily he (John Nash) did not live to see another election"!

One member, John Owen, lived on the road to Bromyard. To his house the Baptists of Leominster in 1694 would go to worship by candlelight, after dark, returning home before daylight, "that their enemies would not suspect them".

Mrs. Jane Owen went into service with Sir William Hopton in London and until that time had never seen any eating forks! She then moved into service with the Marlows and experienced both the Plague and the Fire of London. From the latter she saved many precious jewels. Under Mr. Marlow's influence she became a Christian and returned to Leominster where she married and kept a day school, having scholars from London "and other distant places".

Some members had literary learnings. Joseph Price composed verses in defence of believer's baptism which Thomas says were "very smart". He became, in 1695, the Baptist Pastor at Tewkesbury.

John Price, in 1690, was in great concern of soul and went to speak about spiritual things with a Doctor of Divinity, the Church of England minister at Kingsland. The good doctor told him he was "disordered in the head and that he wanted to be bleeded"! He subsequently found relief of soul in Leominster Baptist Church, being converted and baptised.

Rowland Stead was a Cromwellian soldier who had been wounded and left for dead. Discharged from the army he came to live in Leominster. His trade was weaving and he set up a Baptist cause in his mill house and was looked upon as the Elder or Pastor. In 1680 he was imprisoned for four years. Once when preaching in Stafford he was imprisoned and fined £20.

One peculiar custom mentioned by Joshua Thomas was that of

removing the lid of a coffin in the grave that "the Mould might be cast more immediately upon the corpse".[16]

Joseph Stennett was baptised when fifteen years of age. He was the son of a well-known London minister. The boy later began to preach himself and ultimately was awarded a Doctorate in Divinity by St. Andrews University on the recommendation of the Duke of Cumberland. His funeral service was conducted by Dr. Gill.

Francis Shuter must have been a delight to any minister. Although not a member he was a regular attender and Thomas tells us that when he observed anything about the Meeting House that wanted to be done, he gave order to do it, and he would pay for it himself "quietly".

Joshua Thomas follows the same biographical procedure in *The History of Olchon Baptist Church,* which he wrote in 1790. On the title page he informs his readers that Olchon "purports to have been the first Baptist Church in Wales since the Reformation". After a brief introduction, giving the historical background of the times, he gives an account of "six eminent men" from the vicinity. These twenty-four pages on Olchon are vitally important to any church historian for they reveal how the first Puritans and Dissenters appeared in the Principality.

Thomas's source material was the historical manuscripts of the Bradwardine family, gentry of Herefordshire, in that part of the county that Thomas claims to have been always Cambro-Briton. Olchon he thinks was originally Golchon, situated in a small valley along a line between Hay-on-Wye and Abergavenny.

The Bradwardine family moved to Sussex but Dr. Bradwardine, an "eminent man of Letters, Doctrine, and Piety",[17] was kindly disposed to the Baptists of Olchon and recorded something of their history and that of the Principality as a whole.

Using this ready-made historical material Joshua Thomas rewrites it, highlighting such persons as Walter Brute, a graduate of Oxford and "a gentleman of rank, learning, and parts, though regarded as a Layman by the popish clergy".[18]

Other Thomas sources are: *The Memoirs of Monmouthshire* and *The History of England,* always quoting volume and page numbers for the sake of future historians. He also refers to Neale's *History of the Puritans.* From such sources he is able to write of William Tyndale as a native of those parts, "on the borders of Wales" though he does

---

[16] Ibid., p. 89
[17] *The History of Olchon Baptist Church,* p. 2
[18] Ibid., p. 3

not know "in which county he drew his first breath".[19] He is certain, however, that Llewelyn Tyndal and his son Hezekiah were members of the Llanwenarth Baptist Church, near Abergavenny at the close of the seventeenth century. John Penry was also born in Brecknockshire, in the vicinity of Olchon. Both an Oxford and a Cambridge man Penry was a "notorious Anabaptist".[20]

Finally he names Sir William Cecil, Earl of Burghley. He describes him as "a great friend to the Reformation".[21]

After offering his readers these "names of no small renown",[22] he states most emphatically that Olchon was "the mother church in Wales" and not Llanfaches in Monmouth as other historians had asserted. Llanfaches, he maintained, was a mixture of Baptists and Independents, whereas Olchon was strictly Baptist.

One large piece of history is missing, however. John Rees Howel, "an occasional aspirant to the ministry" at Olchon, went to America for some years. Upon his return to Wales he collected much historical material about Olchon until his death in 1692. In 1770 Joshua Thomas heard that Howel had left a large chestful of papers in a certain house in Olchon. He went there in 1775 but by then the papers had been disposed of in various ways. Such is frequently the misfortune of historians when papers fall into the hands of disinterested or uninformed people.

Besides having men of influence to help the church in its early days, Olchon later sent out men who influenced others. Dr. Caleb Evans, first of all Pastor of Broadmead Baptist Church, Bristol, then tutor at the Baptist College there, was in membership at Olchon.

From the biographical history of Leominster and Olchon we turn next to one of the great trilogy of historical works by Joshua Thomas – his *History of the Welsh Baptist Association,* written in 1790. This we might refer to as statistical history. He covered the period 1650 to 1790 and his intention was to "shew the Times, and the Places where they met in Association in Wales, London, Bristol, etc., with the names of many Ministers who preached at those annual Meetings; and several other incidental, but interesting Articles".[23] His sources are Baptist historians Crosby, Weatley and Neale. He also consulted Vavasor Powell's brief narrative *Bird in the Cage* in which there was a description of the low state of religion in Wales in 1641

[19] Ibid., p. 6

[20] Ibid., p. 8

[21] Ibid., p. 9

[22] Ibid., p. 10

[23] *History of the Welsh Baptist Association*

(Thomas fixes the date of formation of the Welsh Association between 1644 and 1650). Bacchus's *History of New England* (1777), Walker's *Attempt on the Sufferings of the Clergy*, and the Minutes of the General Meeting held at Abergavenny (a meeting of five churches) in 1652, were also consulted. The reason for the American source was that a Pastor of Ilston Baptist Church took the church minutes with him to America and Thomas had to write for extracts to be made. The said Pastor was one John Myles.

A holograph letter of Joshua Thomas, described by B. G. Owens in *The National Library of Wales Journal* (Vol. 2, 1941-42), shows that while others thought Thomas careful to the *n*th degree in compiling his statistics, he himself was not always sure of his facts. The letter was written to his nephew, the Rev. Benjamin Thomas of Prescott, Devon, and consists of details of the Baptist churches of the Welsh Association during the year preceding the annual meeting held at Maesyberllan in June 1789. In the letter Joshua Thomas uses such phrases as "I think they are right, tho am not quite certain" and "I think... but am not certain". Obviously, as a historian, Thomas was not entirely above suspicion as some of his later admirers would have us think!

The first Baptist Church in Wales after the Reformation he stated was Ilston, for Olchon was rightly in Herefordshire. Ilston was near Swansea and was founded in 1649, "less than twenty years after the Bible came among the common people in their own language":[24] an edition intended for householders and not merely churches.

A new church was formed at Abergavenny in 1652 with 60 members. Seven weeks after the Association meetings a public dispute was held between the Baptists and Anglicans, in St. Mary's Church, the chief speaker for the Baptists being the Rev. John Tombs, a former Vicar of Leominster Priory who had turned Baptist. This was the first public profession of Baptist principles in Wales and Joshua Thomas studied all the relevant letters and reports of Messengers.

Other matters discussed at the Abergavenny Association meetings were: the singing of Psalms, the keeping of appointed feast days by Baptists, the duties of church officers, and the nature of church oversight. The offices listed were Pastors, Teachers, Helps (those that rule), Elders (those who would take care of controversies, advise in matters of doubt, visit the sick if sent for, etc.) – but only one Pastor. Scriptural references or proof texts are listed by Thomas against each of these. The qualifications for holding any of these offices were also given. Widows, following the New Testament pattern, were a special

---

[24] Ibid., p. 6

class and given a special place by the Association: they assisted the deacons in the oversight of the poor. For the edifying of the church there were Prophets as well as Pastors. There were then five churches in the Association and between them they had 21 Elders and several Helps.

Three such meetings were held at Abergavenny, but when the Association then met at Hay, Joshua Thomas was unable to find any record of the business conducted. These records may have gone to America with the Ilston minute book.

Only one more meeting was held during that "time of liberty",[25] and Thomas considered it the chief of them all between the years 1650 and 1660. Held at Brecknock in 1656, it was agreed to publish a tract, the contents of which were to be: An Antidote against the times, a Watchword from Mount Sion (to prevent the ruin of souls),Admonitions to saints, and an Invitation to Backsliders. There were eventually 55 pages, and the contributing churches were Ilston, Abergavenny, Tredynog, Carmarthen, Hereford, Bredwardine, Cludock and Llangors. The tract was printed in London in 1656 by T. Brewster at the Three Bibbs, St Pauls: reprinted by the Welsh Baptist Historical Society in 1904.

In 1690 a General Meeting of Baptists in London was held, but with only one representative of Wales present. It was proposed to divide the churches into convenient Associations: London, Bristol, English and Welsh churches into "proper convenient Associations".[26] The Welsh Association consisted of North and South and Dr. Christopher Price, "a gentleman of property",[27] a physician and surgeon, brought out a list of the various churches for presentation to the London Assembly. With his love of detail and correctness Joshua Thomas comments: "I have before me the original Letters from the churches or congregations at Blaenau, Llanwennarth, Olchon, and Craig-yr-Allt to the Assembly in London in 1690."[28]

Within thirty-five years the two Welsh Associations had greatly changed, some churches being dissolved and others being formed. In 1696 a query was sent to the General Assembly at Bristol: "Whether it was lawful for an ordinary Gospel church to redivide, by general consent, into two or more churches, for the sake of edification, because the members live far asunder, and are perhaps numerous".[29]

---

[25] Ibid., p. 20
[26] Ibid., p. 28
[27] Ibid.
[28] Ibid., p. 30
[29] Ibid., p. 34

The answer was in the affirmative.

In 1700 at Llanwenarth thirty-six such queries were answered "judicially and Scripturally",[30] and twenty-four the following year—all these latter were upon the subject of church discipline! This was also a memorable meeting of the Associations for sixteen families had emigrated to Pennsylvania, forming in America a regular Baptist church.

From 1708 onwards the affairs of the churches were conducted at Association meetings in Welsh but letters were written in English. But that same year was marked by much "lukewarmness, lack of love, zeal, etc."[31]

A scarcity of source material now hinders Thomas from writing consecutive history for a few years. Until 1712 he can only list more emigrations to America. But after 1713 he is once again able to become statistical regarding the state of the churches in the Associations. An encouraging year was 1721 when at the Association meetings at Coomb it was reported that "peace and prosperity" was in the churches and "sinners had been converted".[32] That was also the year when Joshua Thomas was commissioned by the Association to translate into Welsh the Baptist Confession of Faith, "put forth in London in 1689".[33]

1723 was another encouraging year for the Welsh churches, and also the occasion for encouraging John Harris to proceed with a translation into Welsh of the *New Heavens and a New Earth.*

Discussion gradually moved from the lower levels of church discipline to a higher theological level. In 1727 at Swansea "debates were started about the eternal filiation or generation of the Son of God". But Ministers were advised to preach the "plain clear Gospel, and not puzzle the people with inexplicable mysteries"![34] The following year some younger ministers who were unorthodox in their beliefs and teachings were urged to be silenced. Thomas states that he knows of one who became orthodox again as a result of the Association meetings. Further unorthodoxy was reported the next year, however, and Arminian doctrines were also said to be preached by some, and so it was suggested that a Cathecism be printed and Cole's *God's Sovereignty* be reprinted in English and Welsh. A few years later Benjamin Francis published *A Word in Season,* but his cousin Abel Francis sought to counteract this by preaching openly against

---

[30]Ibid., p. 36
[31]Ibid., p. 43
[32]Ibid., p. 54
[33]Ibid., p. 55
[34]Ibid., p. 58

him.

Until that time the laying on of hands had been practised at a service of believer's baptism. Some young ministers now queried the propriety of the practice. Feelings waxed "warm". The older men decided to continue the practice during their lifetime. Thomas does not tell us what decision was reached by the younger element!

In 1749 some ministers were given the task of replying to a Church of England clergyman's cathecism which had been translated into Welsh. A few "wrote a few thoughts on the subject" and then dropped the idea, but "Joshua Thomas drew up a few hints and was encouraged to go on when the others dropped it".[35] So in 1750, when the doctrine of the Trinity was perplexing many, "Brother Joshua Thomas had written in answer" in Welsh and it had been "turned into English",[36] Dr. Gill of London writing upon the same subject. In 1757 it was reported that Thomas had translated a small tract entitled *The Believer's Evidence for Heaven,* which was given to his son Timothy to print in Welsh.

The Imposition of Hands at baptismal services was raised again in 1764. Again it was discussed in a half-hearted manner, "some more zealous for it, and others more moderate".[37] Timothy Thomas was in favour of it and "drew up a few thoughts upon it" which he was urged to print. He received an anonymous reply to it.

"Singing, the method of it",[38] was discussed in 1775, and certainly they had something to sing about! Thomas's statistics listed 333 baptised during the past year. With deaths and disciplined members there was a total increase of 268. The following year the baptisms were 278 and a net increase of 217. The next year also an increase of 193 was recorded. It was also reported that the Managers of the Particular Baptist Fund in London had allotted a sum of money for a Mission to be held in North Wales, especially in the counties of Merioneth, Caernarvon and Anglesey, for here the Baptists were "unknown for their Principles and Practices".[39] Joshua Thomas was suggested as one of the missioners but declined the invitation as he said he was living outside the Principality.

In 1777 the Association urged Joshua Thomas to print *The History of the Baptists in Wales* in Welsh. He said he would not do so

35 Ibid., p. 74
36 Ibid., p. 75
37 Ibid., p. 80
38 Ibid., p. 87
39 Ibid., p. 88

"without their approbation".[40] Every church gave their whole-hearted assent and most contributed financially towards it.

The mission to North Wales bore fruit. In 1779 the meetings were held in Denbighshire, near Wrexham. Thus the Association grew and flourished. Yearly baptisms remained around the 200 to 400 level, being 410 in 1786 and 402 in 1789. In 1790, 544 were baptised and at that Assembly Joshua Thomas offered to see to the re-printing of the Baptist Confession of Faith into Welsh, revising the first edition.

Having begun his history with five churches, Thomas ends it with 48. He then adds lists of places of meeting, and preachers who delivered association sermons. Finally a Ministerial List completes the book, and page numbers are given beside the names so that the reader can turn up their brief biographies. There are 219 ministers so listed.

Statistic history can be dull and dry, a mere collection of facts and figures. Not so with Joshua Thomas. His insight into human nature, his interest in theology, his passion for the slightest detail that will throw some light upon the day and age of which he was writing, all make for living history. For instance, he closes this *History of the Welsh Association* with a graphic description of an association meeting: "Nine to ten thousand people could be gathered for an Association and the method of accommodation was as follows: A large piece of ground in the close vicinity of the meeting house is kept during the year with good grass. The horses are turned into that. One or two take care of them. The inhabitants for five miles round provide lodgings. All denominations open their doors cordially. Delegates were allocated four to six a place. They had breakfast before they left the house, about seven or eight o'clock. Plenty of bread was baked and table beer brewed and put in the vestry or some convenient place, with butter and cheese. This made the dinner which was eaten in the Meeting House. Should it turn to rain or be very hot then it is disagreeable to the hearers – many of whom were outside the building! The expense was borne by the church in which the meetings were held".[41]

We have already seen that Joshua Thomas supplied details of the Welsh Associations for Rippon's *Baptist Annual Register* of 1794. It is thus assumed that *The History of the Welsh Association* listed by biographers among his historical writings is the printed work of 1794. In fact the real *History of the Baptist Association in Wales* was compiled four years earlier (1790), and in manuscript form is housed in the National Library of Wales. The later work supplied to Dr. Rippon is vastly different in character. It is even more statistical and

[40] Ibid., p. 89
[41] Ibid., pp 112-113

factual, the Welsh Baptist Churches now being divided into three Associations: South-East, South-West, and North. Each county is taken separately and details of every church given: when founded, number of members, minister, Helpers or Candidates not ordained. One can only wonder at the thoroughness of the work, the duplication of the original manuscript, the observations that bring dead statistics to life.

Another of the great trilogy seems to be similarly duplicated. In 1784 Joshua Thomas wrote his *Materials for a History of the Baptist Churches in the Principality* (1630-1782). It contains 560 pages. But the library of Bristol Baptist College also contains a manuscript composed of far larger page size, of 540 pages. In the early pages of the book, which is entitled in Thomas's own hand *The History of the Baptist Churches in Wales,* he refers to *The History of the Welsh Association* printed in the *Baptist Register* in 1794. This monumental work, therefore, *The History of the Baptist Churches in Wales,* must have been written *after* 1794. The *Materials* was written in 1784, ten years earlier. Since there is no preface or introduction in the larger work we have no means of discovering why it was written when ten years previously the same ground was covered by the *Materials.* The *Materials* (1784) are, of course, something of a duplication of the first *History* (1778) in Welsh, much of it being freely translated from Welsh into English. But, as Thomas explains in the Preface to the *Materials:* "This is now as much an original as the Welsh book is" and was "far from being a plain translation of the original". It also extended the scope of the original *History,* carrying the latter to 1782 where the first printed edition ended at 1777. The *Materials* in manuscript form (with printed frontispiece) he purposed "to commit to the care of my son Timothy. Should he at any time think it prudent, it may be deposited in the Museum at Bristol".[42]

The two works, although possessing almost identical titles, are not in the least identical in substance. The *Materials* begins with the history of Olchon and Capel-y-ffin, while the *History of the Baptist Churches in Wales* begins with Swansea. Both are characterised, however, with the same Joshua Thomas accuracy, love for detail, brief biographical sketches, and observations upon Baptist life and customs. If generalizations may continue to be made, then *The History of Leominster Baptist Church* is largely biographical, *The History of the Welsh Associations* is largely statistical, and the *History of The Baptist Churches in Wales* largely ecclesiastical.

In the *Materials for a History of the Baptist Churches in the*

[42] *Materials for a History of the Baptist Churches in the Principality,* Preface, p. xi

Principality (which we will refer to as *The Materials,* for short, and the larger work as *The History*), Thomas describes Baptist Churches, their geographical location, their early formation, their ministers, and so on, drawing upon his usual sources as Vavasor Powel. Twenty-nine pages are devoted to Olchon in *The Materials,* yet there is little similarity of treatment between this history of Olchon and *The History of Olchon Baptist Church* (24 pages) written in 1790. He obviously did not slavishly copy the latter from the former.

In *The Materials* Joshua Thomas occasionally inserted poems of a rather doggerel quality. Joseph Price of Hay wrote a seven-verse poem upon being baptised by immersion. One verse will suffice:

> If I was baptised, I am not ashamed,
> Christ Jesus was dipped, God's only dear Son:
> We have his word for it; the Gospel doth prove it,
> No man can deny it with reason.[43]

He wrote another poem about a country clergyman who railed at Dissenting Ministers in his sermons. Eleven verses of the following calibre are quoted by Thomas:

> No gown or cassock do they wear,
> But living always in God's fear,
> His doctrine they adorn.
> They don't demand a new found pay
> For preaching more than once a day,
> Such actions they do scorn.[44]

After Olchon Joshua Thomas turned his attention to Maes-y-berllan in Brecknockshire, for he was in membership with this church for a number of years and had opportunities of gleaning its history from various sources, mainly personal for "there were no written Records, they could but relate what they had heard".[45] The only way of confirming what he heard by word of mouth was by consulting the Baptist historian Thomas Crosby. He was able to place on record a list of twelve ministers from 1724 to 1782.

Glasgwm in Radnorshire he dealt with next, appealing to such authorities as Vavasor Powel and Dr. Calamy for verification of his facts.

New Radnor, Dolau, Pentref and other Radnorshire chapels are

---

43 Ibid., p. 33
44 Ibid., p. 35
45 Ibid., p. 44

incorporated in *The Materials* and later became source material for John Jones when writing *The History of the Baptists in Radnorshire* (London, 1895). A quaint accrostic anagram is included in the history of Dolau, composed upon the name John Price. This Joshua Thomas culled from a gravestone, commenting: "Whatever inaccuracy may appear in the poetry of this,it cannot be attributed to the deceased"![46]

Under Llanbrynmair, Montgomeryshire Thomas takes pains to write as much about the great Welsh worthy Vavasor Powell, quoting from Neal's fourth volume of the *History of the Puritans*. Strange to relate, much of the opposition to Vavasor Powell's ministry came from the Quakers. His ministry at Llanbrynmair was from 1670 to 1685. Ten other ministries followed his up to the time of Thomas writing his history.

Wrexham in Denbighshire, Glyn in the same country, more chapels in Montgomeryshire, Usk and other churches in Monmouthshire – all are treated with the same care and exactitude, in spite of scarcity of written records in some places.

Hengoed in Glamorgan is dealt with at greater length, obviously because greater source material was available. And so he writes on, obviously writing about a particular church whenever sufficient historical material has been collected, for the churches are neither listed in alphabetical order, nor grouped within their various counties or associations. He follows no chronological order of foundation.

This same lack of order is seen when comparing *The Materials* with *The History*. The Baptist cause at Swansea appears on page 302 in *The Materials*; it is the first church to be dealt with in *The History*. Much of the individual histories of churches in *The Materials* is copied out in *The History*. Olchon appears first in *The Materials* but in *The History* it is Swansea first, for Olchon was not rightly in the Principality but in Herefordshire. Later in the book, on page 111 it is Llangwrn in Monmouthshire that is called "the Mother Church of Nonconformity in the Principality".

Both volumes are carefully and comprehensively indexed. One index covers personal names and the other an alphabetical list of the churches. At the end of *The Materials* there is an appendix of some twenty-four pages giving additions and corrections. No such appendix appears in the larger and later *History*, so we may safely assume that it was more correctly compiled, the mistakes of *The Materials* being corrected and the additions inserted.

A final monumental work, the third in the trilogy, is Thomas's *Ecclesiastical History of the Principality of Wales*, dated 1779 and

---

[46]Ibid., p. 76

in manuscript form comprising two volumes, the first having 121 pages the second 470.

Thomas's scheme in this work was to give an account of Christianity "from the apostolic age to our time" since in similar histories of England the Principality is only referred to in a "partial and imperfect way".[47] After a brief Biblical review of early religion he begins with Julius Caesar's invasion of Britain about fifty years before the birth of Christ. From there he proceeds to Claudius Caesar of Acts 11:28, and quoting from several authorities of his time Drs. Gill, Charles Owen, Curtis, Fuller, Godwin, and others, proceeds to establish the coming of Christianity to Wales. His appeal to authorities in the ecclesiastical history field is abundant evidence of his wide reading and desire for accuracy in his work.

After his setting of the scene in an introductory way, Thomas then deals with each century of history separately. In the first century of Christianity, however, he cannot trace "the names of any British Ministers or other Christians who resided in this country (Wales), nor much said about them in the former part of the second century".[48] Even so, he believes with several authorities that Paul preached in Britain, and probably Wales, and so concludes that early ecclesiastical life in the Principality knew "Scripture Elders, Bishops, or Pastors, and Ministers of the Gospel".[49] Towards the end of the second century he believes there was "a very happy revival, and the Gospel spread thro' the land, and the very king himself embraced it and helped much to further the good work".[50]

Of the third century he can find very little account of religion in Briton, many historians leaving this age blank in their records. He is able, however, to describe one or two "remarkable occurances" such as the death of King Lucius and the birth of Constantine the Great, who became the first Christian Emperor in the world.

The fourth century he describes as "a century of much variety in Church and State".[51] This was the period of Alban, the first Christian martyr in Britain, followed by others such as Aaron and Julius, who died at Usk.

"A most dismal age"[52] is how he describes the fifth century. It was a time of great persecution against Christians. Similarly the

---

[47] Op. cit., Preface, p. 1
[48] Ibid., p. 11
[49] Ibid., p. 12
[50] Ibid., p. 20
[51] Ibid., p. 25
[52] Ibid., p. 31

sixth century was "another age that proved very fatal to our progenitors".[53] It is here, however, at the close of the sixth century and the beginning of the seventh that he begins to find reasons for the terms Wales and Welsh being convenient terms. In a fairly long digression, which he admits to the reader, he explains the term Cymru and its variants.

The eighth century he finds is also scarcely written about by ecclesiastical historians, and he only devotes just over four pages to it. Centuries nine and ten are also acknowledged as a time when "our ancestors were forsaken more and more by Historians".[54] So with the eleventh century and the twelth century. But none compared with the thirteenth century which Thomas terms "the midnight century".[55] It was a time of ignorance and distress. The following century, the fourteenth, he describes as "a cock-crowing age".[56] The prevailing religious climate was one of "rank Popery", "Popery in great plenty", and the reader need only to turn to the works of Fox for confirmation of the persecution and martyrdom to which people were subjected. This was only exceeded in the following century, the fifteenth, of which Thomas comments: "We are now entering upon a shocking century to our dear country and the inhabitants thereof. The very report is enough to wound tender hearts, but what was it to live at that time!"[57]

Since the dark is always followed by the dawn he is able to describe the sixteenth century as one "of happy revolutions".[58] He can now write of Reformation, of Cromwell, of Protestant itinerant preachers who went all over Wales. Great names began to appear from among his own countrymen. Books and Bibles began to be printed in Wales, and by Act of Parliament it was decreed that the latter should be placed in every parish church in Wales by March 1567. His description of such Bibles is interesting and detailed:

"Printed in a handsome Quarto of 399 leaves – in Black Letter, as it is called, disposed and divided, as to Books and chapters, with arguments and contents to each Book and each chapter, with explanations of difficult words in the Margins; but no references to parallel passages".[59]

---

[53] Ibid., p. 46
[54] Ibid., p. 75
[55] Ibid., p. 98
[56] Ibid., p. 103
[57] Ibid., p. 110
[58] Vol. 2, p. 122
[59] Ibid., p. 198

The year of the defeat of the Spanish Armada, 1588, was also "a remarkable year to Wales on the account of religion".[60] Although there seemed to be a lack of preachers, especially in North Wales, several influential books were printed by John Penry of Brecknockshire. Altogether Thomas lists fourteen books that were published between 1546 and 1594 (including The Lord's Prayer and Ten Commandments, a Dictionary, a Defence of the Church of England) that greatly influenced the spiritual life of the Principality: "they were all very useful in their places at that time"![61]

The seventeenth century Thomas calls "a century of great light, yet of great confusion".[62] Queen Elizabeth died at the beginning of the century and she had been "a valiant Queen regarding State affairs", and "opposed to Popery".[63] But many Christians were urging still further reformations in matters of religion. There was much confusion concerning certain rites and ceremonies in worship, and in general the ordinary people in Wales still knew little or nothing of the Scriptures. Then in 1618 the *Book of Sports,* a declaration concerning recreation and sports on the Lord's Day, put a stop to the growth of Puritanism. Gradually, however, "our country wore a new face, having a new impression of the Bible".[64] In 1630 the Bible was printed in an octavo edition in Welsh for the families of the country of Wales and not merely for the churches. The people were now able to read it for themselves at their own convenience. "The knowledge of God did increase visibly among our countrymen".[65]

By mid-century the Bishops in Wales were powerless, having little authority, and the Clergy opposed to Parliament. Some of the Clergy, from their preaching, were more Independent, Baptist or Presbyterian than Established Church. The true non-conformists were worshipping and preaching in private houses rather than in church buildings. During the second half of the century, however, Dissenters grew rapidly, and in his description of the Baptists and their growth, Thomas draws largely upon his previous historical works. He traces their growth and development in every county of the Principality. Naturally it is this period that receives most attention from Joshua Thomas, and to which he devotes most pages. His source material is more prolific and the growth of nonconformity is more rapid. After

---

[60] Ibid., p. 222
[61] Ibid., p. 246
[62] Ibid., p. 250
[63] Ibid., p. 252
[64] Ibid., p. 272
[65] Ibid., p. 280

writing some 470 pages, however, Thomas concludes by saying that he will give "a few observations" on the state of the church, and religion, among all denominations, for the last eighty years. This he fails to do, and the work closes without his usual and careful index of names and places and subjects.

To the present writer this second volume of the *Ecclesiastical History of Wales* is most interesting for it is annotated by one who signed himself "W.R." He was obviously W. Richards of Lymm (1749 – 1818), a devout admirer of Joshua Thomas, and yet one of the few who seem to have been able to discover mistakes in Thomas's otherwise extremely accurate writing. One note by W.R. is especially interesting. In volume 2 of the *Ecclesiastical History* Thomas writes a footnote: "See more above pp 106, 140, 148". W. Richards adds: "This note proves the existence of another volume, i.e., the first". When W.R. was doing his research into Joshua Thomas's history it is quite obvious that the manuscript copy of volume 1 was lost or mislaid. Fortunately it must have been rediscovered, but unfortunately these two volumes never seem to have been published in printed form.

Such, then, were the monumental historical works of the Baptist historian of Wales. Compiled in the eighteenth they became the basis for later historians, right up to the present century. In 1839 David Jones of Carmarthen published his *Hanes y Bedyddwyr yn Neheudir Cymru.* According to J.E. Lloyd's *A History of Carmarthenshire* this was a book "which depends mainly on Joshua Thomas up to 1778".[66] J.E. Lloyd's *A History of Carmarthenshire* (Cardiff, 1939), makes many references to Joshua Thomas for confirmation of historical points, especially when drawing a distinction between the Baptists at Carmarthen in the early 1650's and those of West Carmarthenshire of the Restoration era. He does this because he is able to say of Joshua Thomas: "He hardly ever imposes upon his readers the task of discounting his prejudices, and (within the limits of his materials) his care for accuracy is scrupulous".[67]

As a man, a preacher, a man of prayer, a pastor, a writer and an historian –

"Long will Cambria thy great worth proclaim".[68]

---

66 Op. cit., p. 259
67 Ibid., p. 230
68 B. Francis: *An Elegy*

BIBLIOGRAPHY

WORKS BY JOSHUA THOMAS	Location of MSS
Histories:	
History of Leominster Baptist Church (1769)	National Library of Wales, Aberystwyth. Photo. copy at Leominster Baptist Church, Herefordshire
History of Hook Norton Baptist Church	Hook Norton Baptist Church, Oxfordshire
History of Olchon Baptist Church (1790)	National Library of Wales; Photo. copy at Leominster Baptist Church
History of the Midland Baptist Association	
History of the Welsh Association 1795	Bristol Baptist College Library; Xerox copies at Aberystwyth and Leominster
History of the Baptist Churches in Wales (Hanes y Bedyddwyr) (1778)	Bristol; Xerox copies at Aberystwyth and Leominster
Materials for a History of the Baptist Churches in the Principality (1784)	Bristol; Xerox copies at Aberystwyth and Leominster
Ecclesiastical History of Wales (1779)	Bristol; Xerox copies at Aberystwyth and Leominster
Devotional:	
Book of Public Devotions (1755–56)	Aberystwyth; Xerox copy at Leominster

The Believer's Evidence for Heaven (1757)	

Personal:

Various Letters to Dr. John Rippon	Angus Library, Regent's Park College, Oxford
Queries and Solutions (1770) .	Bristol; Xerox copies at Aberystwyth and Leominster

Theological:

Athrawiaeth y Drindod	Aberystwyth
(Carmarthen 1794) – translation of Robert Hall's work on the Trinity	Aberystwyth
Angherubedrwydd i Gredint Gwobrwyon	
Nodiadau ar Bregeth Mr. Abel Francis (Brecon 1775) – Notes of a Calvinistic Baptist upon Mr. Abel Francis	
Remarks (London 1788)	
Translation of the 1689 Baptist Confession of Faith (Carmarthen 1791)	Angus Library, Oxford

BOOKS REFERRED TO AND CITED IN THE TEXT
(Other than by Joshua Thomas)

The Baptist Magazine, 1816

The Baptist Register: J. Rippon, 1791–3, 1797

The Baptist Union – A Short History: E. A. Payne (London 1959)

Baker's Dictionary of Theology (London 1960)

Cymdeithas Hanes Bedyddwyr Cymru, 1901

Essay on Dissent: A. J. Johnes (London 1831)

Evangelical Magazine, 1798

Free Church Tradition in the Life of England: E. A. Payne (London 1944)

Hanfod Duw a Pherson Crist: J. Gwili Jenkins (Liverpool 1931)

History of the Baptists in Radnorshire: J. Jones (London 1895)

A History of Carmarthenshire: J. E. Lloyd (Cardiff 1939)

A History of the English Baptists: A. C. Underwood (London 1956)

Lectures on Preaching: P. Brooks (London 1881)

Nine Lectures on Preaching: R. W. Dale (London 1878)

On the Art of Writing: A. Quiller-Couch (London 1946)

Seren Gomer: 1820, 1821, 1822

Social Life in Mid–eighteenth Century Anglesey: G. N. Evans (Cardiff, 1936)

The National Library of Wales Journal 1941–43, Vol. 2

Vavasor Powell: David Davies (London 1896)

Welsh Dictionary of Biography

Welsh Life in the Eighteenth Century: L. T. Davies & A. Edwards (London 1939)